Birmingham University Field Archaeology Unit
Monograph Series 2

I0092087

Severn Valley Ware Production at Newland Hopfields

Excavation of a Romano-British kiln site at
North End Farm, Great Malvern, Worcestershire
in 1992 and 1994

C Jane Evans
Laurence Jones
Peter Ellis

BAR British Series 313
2000

Published in 2016 by
BAR Publishing, Oxford

BAR British Series 313

Birmingham University Field Archaeology Unit Monograph Series 2
Severn Valley Ware Production at Newland Hopfields

ISBN 978 1 84171 204 8

© BUFAU and the Publisher 2000

BAR Publishing is the trading name of British Archaeological Reports (Oxford) Ltd.
British Archaeological Reports was first incorporated in 1974 to publish the BAR
Series, International and British. In 1992 Hadrian Books Ltd became part of the BAR
group. This volume was originally published by Archaeopress in conjunction with
British Archaeological Reports (Oxford) Ltd / Hadrian Books Ltd, the Series principal
publisher, in 2000. This present volume is published by BAR Publishing, 2016.

Printed in England

BAR
PUBLISHING

BAR titles are available from:

BAR Publishing
122 Banbury Rd, Oxford, OX2 7BP, UK
EMAIL   info@barpublishing.com
PHONE   +44 (0)1865 310431
FAX   +44 (0)1865 316916
www.barpublishing.com

Severn Valley Ware production at Newland Hopfields: Excavation of a Romano-British kiln site at North End Farm, Great Malvern, Worcestershire in 1992 and 1994

by C Jane Evans, Laurence Jones and Peter Ellis

with contributions by Lynne Bevan, Simon Butler, Brenda Dickinson, Rowena Gale, Kay Hartley, Rob Ixer, Donald Mackreth, Joanna Mills, Kirsty Nichol, Stephanie Pinter-Bellows, Fiona Roe, Sarah Watt and David Williams

Severn Valley Ware production at Newland Hopfields: Excavation of a Romano-British kiln site at North End Farm, Great Malvern, Worcestershire in 1992 and 1994

CONTENTS

List of Figures

List of Tables

List of plates
(Plates follow Bibliography)

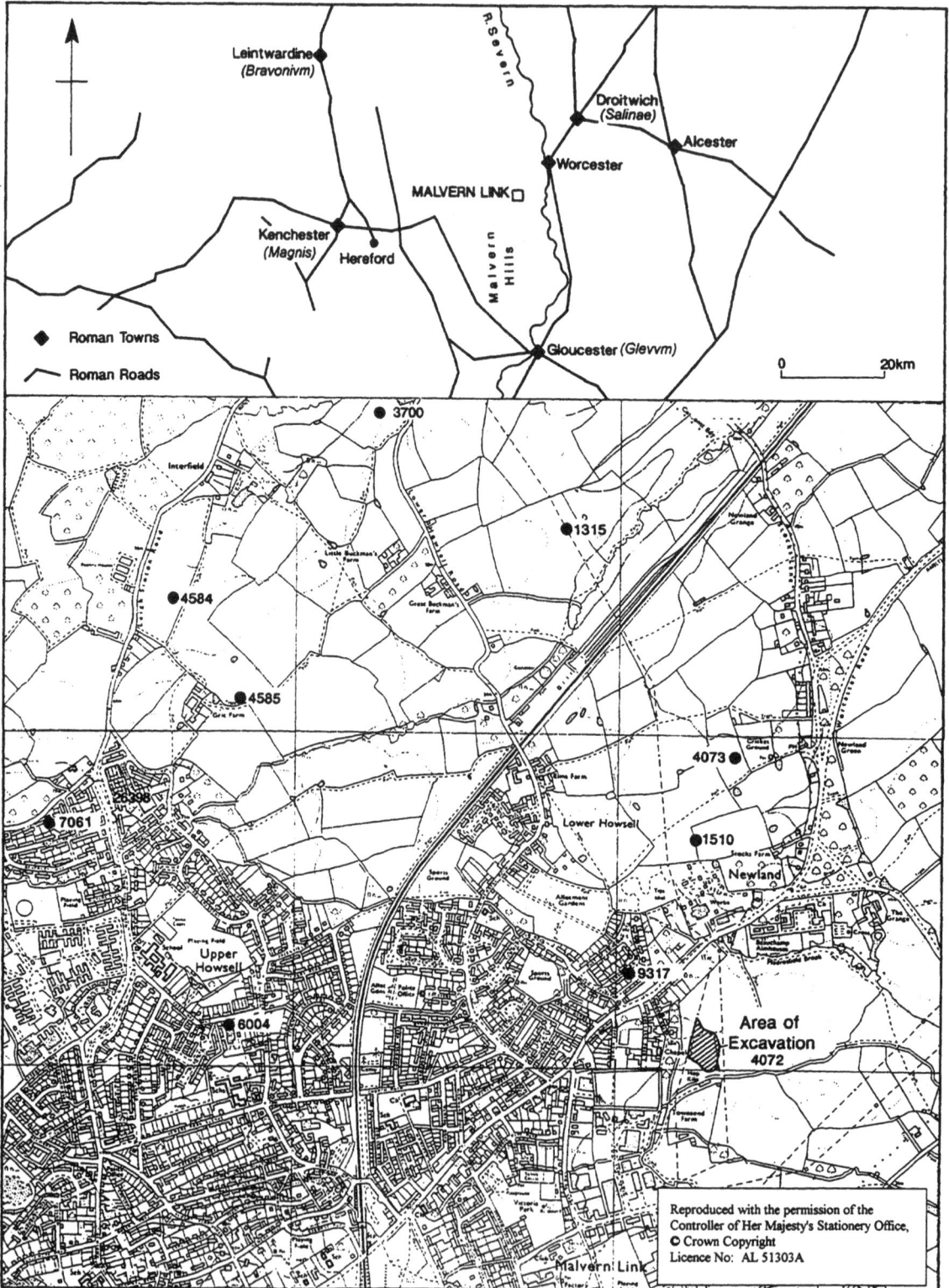

Figure 1: Location maps: top – regional, bottom – local, with Romano-British sites marked

Severn Valley Ware production at Newland Hopfields:
Excavation of a Romano-British kiln site at North End Farm, Great Malvern, Worcestershire in 1992 and 1994

by C Jane Evans, Laurence Jones and Peter Ellis

with contributions by Lynne Bevan, Simon Butler, Brenda Dickinson, Rowena Gale, Kay Hartley, Rob Ixer, Donald Mackreth, Joanna Mills, Kirsty Nichol, Stephanie Pinter-Bellows, Fiona Roe, Sarah Watt and David Williams

INTRODUCTION

This report presents the results of two campaigns of archaeological work at North End Farm, Newland, Great Malvern, Worcestershire. The first was undertaken by the Hereford and Worcester County Archaeological Service in June and July 1992, preceded by an evaluation in 1991, and the second by Birmingham University Field Archaeology Unit between March and June 1994. The excavations were commissioned by the Trustees of the Madresfield Estate and carried out as a condition of planning consent prior to the proposed development of land for retail, industrial and residential purposes.

The excavation site (NGR SO 7925 4810) is situated on a gentle south-facing slope at about 50m above OD, and lies in the modern civil parish of Great Malvern. To the south of the site is Sandy's Spring and to the north, Madresfield Brook, which joins the River Severn 5km to the east. The underlying drift geology is fine, reddish, silty clays overlying Mercian Mudstone (Keuper Marl). The major topographical feature is the Malvern Hills to the south-west (Fig. 1).

The fields proposed for development, Newland Hopfields in the archaeological literature, have been known to archaeologists for some years as the location of a suspected kiln site or sites. Two surface scatters of pottery, including waster sherds, were first recognised in the late 1950s (SMR WSM 4072). In addition to the Newland Hopfields site there is a number of suspected kiln sites nearby. Limited excavation at Great Buckmans Farm (WSM 1315) and Grit Farm, East (WSM 4585) yielded large amounts of local pottery, including wasters. The finds survive from a kiln reported in 1887 at the Hygienic Laundry (WSM 6004), but any site records have been lost and the existence of a kiln remains unproven. Dumps of wasters from Grit Farm, North (WSM 4584, WSM 11392) have been recorded, as well as large amounts of pottery and possible kiln structures (WSM 1510 and WSM 9317). Finally, surface scatters, including wasters, are known from Swan Inn, Newland (WSM 4073), Half Key Lane (WSM 7061), Lower Howsell Road (WSM 3700) and Leigh (WSM 26398).

These sites represent the largest group of Severn Valley ware kilns so far found (Webster 1976, 38). They lie toward the centre of the Severn Valley ware production area. This extends to Shropshire in the north and Somerset in the south, although Severn Valley ware is also found in northern Britain (Webster 1977; Carrington 1977), and in very small quantities in south-east Britain (Tomber 1980, 15). A number of studies of the industry have been made (Webster 1971;

1976; Tomber 1980; Rawes 1982). These have defined the range of forms produced and a broad Severn Valley ware fabric, but fabrics from known production sites are not petrologically distinctive (Tomber 1980). Discussion has also focused on the origins of the ware (Timby 1990) and its distribution (Hodder 1974, 346, fig. 6; Allen and Fulford 1996, 262, fig. 14a, b).

A programme of petrological analysis in the 1960s defined another significant pottery industry in the Malvern area (Peacock 1967; 1968). The highly distinctive inclusions in these Malvernian wares enabled them to be identified with certainty at many sites. This industry was well established by the middle Iron Age (*op. cit.* 1968), and may have originated as early as the late Bronze Age (Evans 1990, 28, fig. 16.11). No production sites have been identified, and the clay beds are not precisely known, but the potters probably worked on or very near to the hills (Peacock 1982, 82). Production of these hand-made, coarsely tempered wares continued into the Roman period (*op. cit.* 1967).

The development proposals therefore led to a campaign of archaeological prospection. The excavations themselves were preceded by an evaluation undertaken by the Hereford and Worcester County Archaeology Service using geophysical survey, fieldwalking and trial trenching (Jackson 1991). This defined two relatively well-preserved areas of archaeological features together with Romano-British pottery deposits (Fig. 2). In total, an area of archaeological potential of about 1.45ha was identified, located in two fields formerly used for hop cultivation and divided by a farm track, with the area of better preservation in the south field and in a small part of a field to the east. Site 1, excavated in 1992, lay to the north of the track, and Site 2, excavated in 1994, to the south, with some investigation of the field to the east. Prior to excavation, scatters of Romano-British pottery sherds, mainly Severn Valley Ware, were visible on the ground.

The strategy adopted for both phases of excavation was based on a research design intended to use initial trial trenching prior to area excavation (HWCAS 1992). A number of trenches, 4m wide, was stripped of topsoil by mechanical excavator within the area of archaeological significance defined by the evaluation (Fig. 2). The six trenches in Site 1 were numbered T1000–T6000 (Dalwood 1992). After manual cleaning, the archaeological features and deposits revealed were recorded and planned at a scale of 1:50. Contexts and features were not distinguished in the record, both being numbered consecutively from 1001. Features have, however,

1

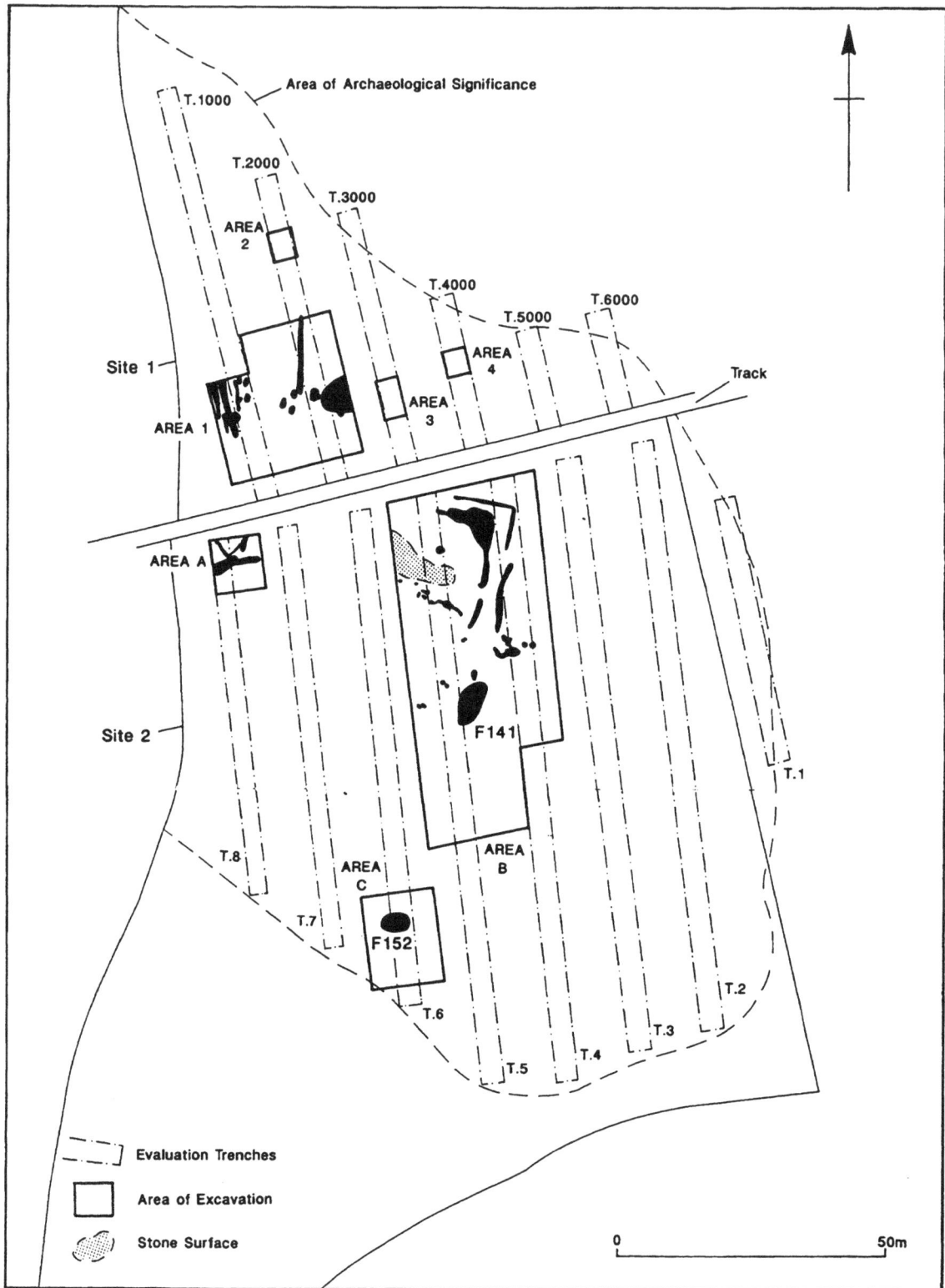

Figure 2: Location of evaluation trenches, 1992 and 1994 excavations, and main features; scale 1:1250

been identified in post-excavation for this report, and are preceded with the letter F. Thus 2290 recorded on site is F2290 in this report. Most of the deposits in T3000 and T4000 and all the deposits in T5000 and T6000 were modern in date. Romano-British features were concentrated in the southern part of T1000 and T2000 and the main excavation area, Area 1, was sited here, with three other smaller areas,

Areas 2–4, to the east and north. The area excavations were recorded in plan at a scale of 1:20, using a grid aligned on OS grid north, while sections were drawn at 1:10.

In Site 2, eight trenches, T1–T8, were excavated, cleaned and recorded in the same way as for Site 1. Contexts were numbered from 7000 and features from F100. Only modern features were recorded in T2 and T3, while T1 and T7 were

2

blank. Three area excavations, A–C, were sited where Romano-British features and deposits were concentrated. Following the excavation of Area B, four 1.5m-wide sondage trenches were excavated east–west across the site. Recording of the area excavations in Site 2 followed that used for Site 1, with some areas additionally recorded by vertical quadropod photography (Renow 1985). The spatial distribution of finds was recorded in detail on Site 2, with artefacts recovered during the initial cleaning recorded by 5m grid square. Finds recorded as surface spreads and from extensive contexts within features were recorded by 1m grid square.

On both sites a number of modern features was identified, in particular land drains and hop pole holes. These were sampled and recorded on all areas excavated, except Site 2, Areas A–C. The natural subsoil had been severely disturbed by deep ploughing and subsoiling; some features only became apparent after repeated cleaning.

The archaeology at Site 1 revealed no direct evidence of pottery production but sufficient features to indicate occupation, and the 1992 excavation evidence was therefore interpreted as representing a Romano-British settlement related to the Malvernian pottery industry (Dalwood 1992). This interpretation is reconsidered in this report in the light of the 1994 excavations.

Acknowledgements
The 1994 excavations were directed by Laurence Jones, with Richard Cuttler as site supervisor. The initial processing of the finds was supervised by Lucy Salmon and Kirsty Nichol. The bulk of the pottery cataloguing was undertaken by Kirsty Nichol, only the non-Severn Valley wares being recorded by Jane Evans. Thanks are due to Vivien Swan for her advice regarding the structure of the kiln and the layout of the site. Peter Webster provided valuable comments on an earlier version of the text, as did Hal Dalwood, on behalf of staff at the Worcestershire County Archaeology Service. The report was compiled and edited by Peter Ellis, with additional editing by Iain Ferris.

—◇—

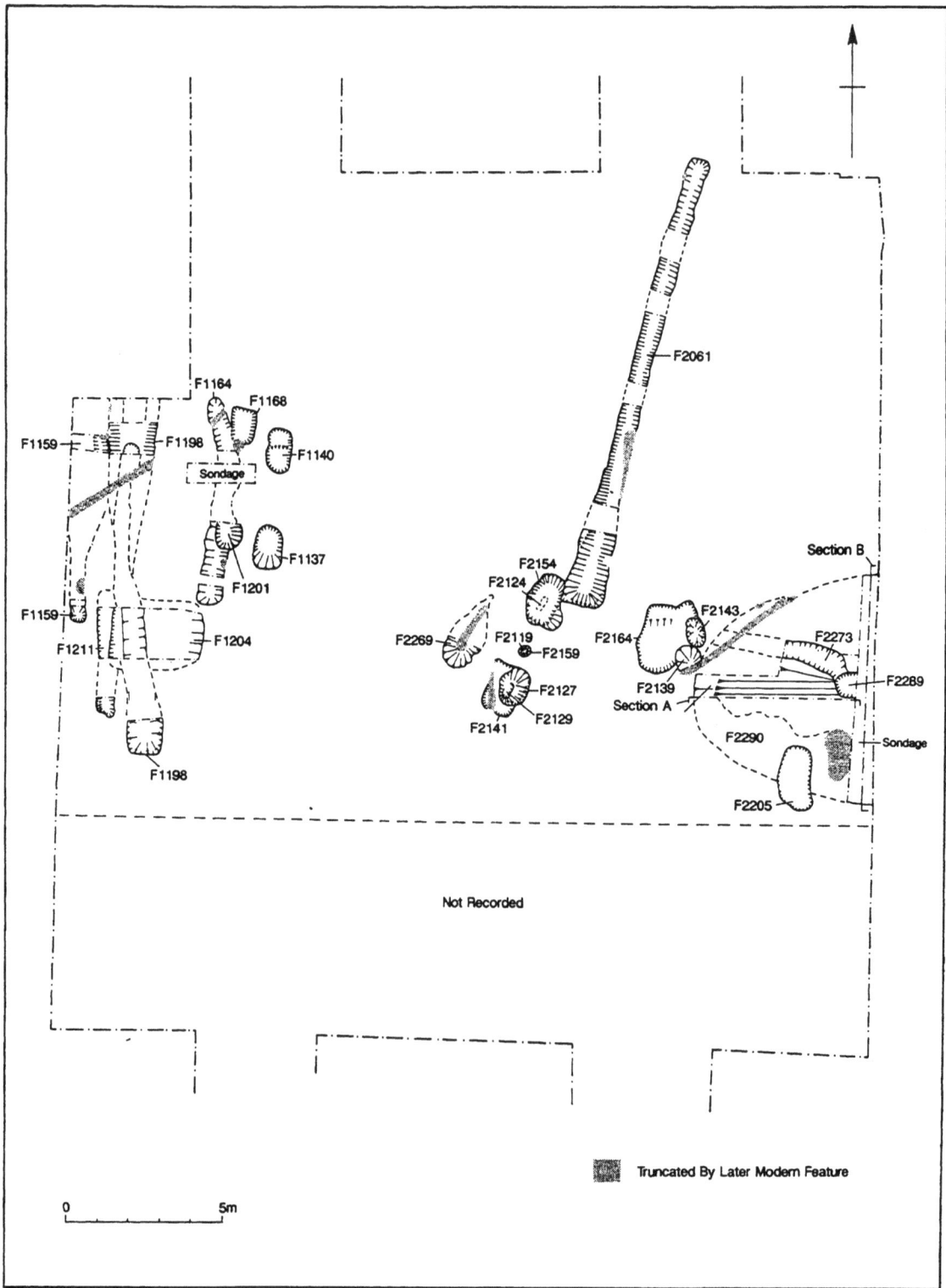

Figure 3: Site 1, Area 1, plan; scale 1:200

EXCAVATION RESULTS

by Laurence Jones and Peter Ellis

The archaeological contexts and features from the Romano-British period fall into groups comprising two-post structures, field boundaries and pottery production features together with a miscellaneous group (Table 1, p.13). These grouped features, which formed the basis of the finds analysis, are discussed following the site by site summary.

Site 1, Area 1

Only Site 1, Area 1 contained archaeological features of Roman date, Areas 2-4 containing evidence only of post-medieval activity. Site 1 in this text therefore refers henceforward to Site 1, Area 1. On the east side of the area was a large, shallow feature, F2290, 0.54m deep, with steep sides and a flat base (Figs. 3 and 4). A lower fill of reddish-brown silty clay, 2209, was sealed by a charcoal-rich layer of greyish-brown sandy clay loam, 2183, and a reddish-brown sandy loam, 2184 (Fig. 4). F2290 was cut by a linear feature, F2273, 0.34m deep, filled with a brown silty clay, 2258, and apparently terminating at the western edge of F2290. To the east F2290 was cut by F2289, filled with a greyish brown sandy clay-loam, 2288, and to the south by F2205. It was 0.17m deep, with vertical sides, a flat base, and a brown loamy clay fill, 2204.

To the west of F2290 was F2164. This was 0.3m deep with steep sides and an uneven base and was filled with reddish-brown silty clay, 2160 and 2163. F2164 was cut by F2143, which was 0.2m deep, with steep sides and a rounded base and was filled with a reddish brown silty clay, 2142. It was also cut by F2139, 0.1m deep, which, like F2143, had gently sloping sides and a rounded base, and a fill of reddish brown silty clay, 2138. To its west, beyond a group of post-pits, was F2269, oval in plan with a rounded profile, 0.35m deep, and filled with yellow grey silty loam, 2268.

On the west side of the area was a linear feature, F1159. This was 0.24m deep, with steep sides and a narrow slot set on the east side of its flat base, and was filled with a reddish-brown silty clay, 1158. To its east was another linear feature, F1211, 0.25m deep, with steeply sloping sides and a flat base and a fill of reddish-brown silty clay, 1210. F1211 was cut by F1204 and F1198. F1204, was 0.1m deep, with gently sloping sides and a flat base and a fill of dark greyish-brown sandy clay loam, 1203. F1198 also cut F1204 and had a U-shaped profile, with a lower fill of reddish-brown silty loam, 1197, beneath a dark greyish-brown silty clay, 1202.

Three pairs of post-pits were identified, F1168 and F1201, F1140 and F1137 nearby, and F2154 and F2141 to their east. The post-pits were sub-rectangular in plan, with steeply sloping sides and, in most cases, flat bases. Post-pit F1140 had a step in its northern side which was 0.25m deep and 0.50m wide. The pit depths varied from 0.18m–0.75m. Post-pit pair F1168 and F1201 and post pit F2141 were each filled with a single deposit of similar reddish brown silty clay, respectively 1167, 1200 and 2140. The fill of F2154, paired with F2141, was of a similar clay, 2125, but with a concentration of large angular stones, c.0.25m x 0.12m, at its southern end. Layer 2125 overlay a layer of charcoal-rich dark greyish brown silty clay, 2111, which in turn overlay a dark grey silty clay, 2122, cut by two possible post-pipes F2123 and F2124. Of these, F2123 was circular, 0.23m in diameter and 0.23m deep, and

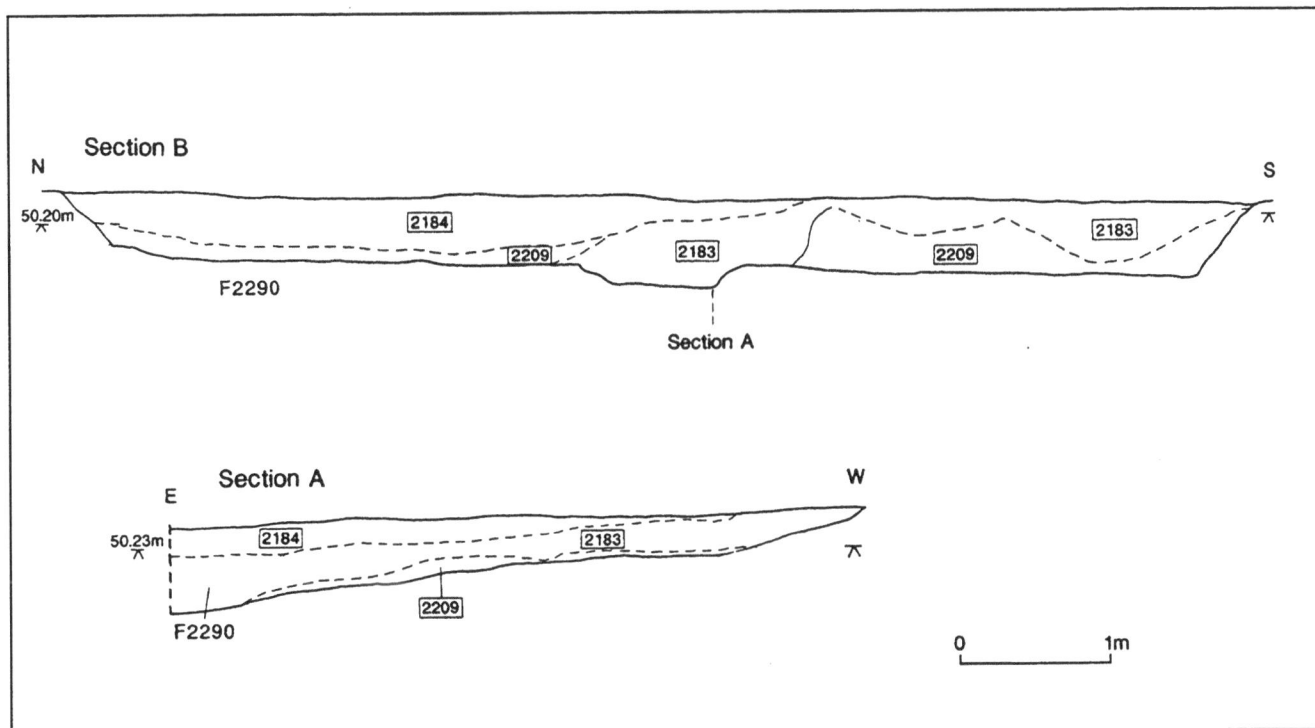

Figure 4: Site 1, Area 1, sections, scale 1:40

F2124 was sub-rectangular in plan, 0.3m x 0.16m, and 0.2m deep. The fills of post-pit pair F1137 and F1140 differed from the others. F1140 was filled with greyish brown clay, 1030, similar to the lowest fill of F1137, 1139, which lay beneath two further deposits of silt, 1138, 1024.

Pit F2141 was cut by a sloping-sided, concave-profiled pit, F2127, 0.22m deep, and with a fill of orange brown loamy clay, 2126. This was in turn cut by a post-pit, F2129, similar to F2141, 0.28m deep, with vertical sides, a flat base and a fill of greyish brown silty loam, 2128. To its north was a smaller posthole, F2159, 0.27m deep with a fill of orange-brown loamy clay, 2158, and angular stones, possibly used as packing. The posthole had been replaced by a smaller posthole, F2119, cut to a depth of 0.18m and filled with a charcoal-rich, loamy clay, 2118.

Post-pits F1168 and F1201 were cut by a shallow linear feature, F1164, 0.6m deep. F1164 had sloping sides and an irregular base and was filled with a yellowish brown silty clay, 1163. Post-pit F2154 was cut by a similar but much deeper linear feature, F2061. This was 0.5–0.8m deep, with steeply sloping sides and a flat base, and was filled with a greyish-brown sandy clay loam, 2059, with a deposit of charcoal-rich, dark grey silty clay, 2060, at its north end. These sealed a layer of orange brown silty clay, 2065.

Pit F2290 and its associated features and the group of shallow ditches on the west side of the excavated area were interpreted as features associated with pottery production. The post-pits represented the site of pairs of timber posts. These seem to have been long-standing features which may have been replaced nearby, as perhaps in the case of F1140/F1137 and F1168/F1201, or in the same post-pits when timbers rotted, as with F2154/F2141. F2141 was apparently recut on two occasions by F2129 and F2127, while post-pits F1168 and F1201 may have been replaced by, or been a replacement for, the nearby pair F1140 and F1137. The similar fills of F1168 and F1201, and F2154 and F2141 suggested that they might have been contemporary. Features F2119 and F2159 may have been associated with the post-pit pair on either side. The structures supported by these posts seem likely to have been free-standing. Although it is possible that they served an agricultural purpose, such as drying racks, small granaries, or poultry coops, the presence of pottery production features nearby suggests that they may have been used by the potters, perhaps as drying racks. There was no evidence of any associated structures. The long ditches, F1164 and F2061, seem likely to represent field boundary ditches. These features are discussed further below.

Small quantities of pottery were found in F1198, F1211, F2161, F2164, F2205, F2273 and F2290 from Site 1, Area 1. The latest material from F1211 was second to early third-century tankards. A handful of sherds from F1198, F2161, F2164, F2205 and F2273 represented earlier second-century material. F2290 contained second to early third-century tankards although much of the pottery was early second century. The pits also contained a fragment of first to third-century bottle glass. A small quantity of second-century pottery was found in the post-pits. F2129, the last post pit on the site of F2141, produced a third-century sherd. F2127

contained fragments of a copper alloy bracelet, possibly a child's. A quern fragment came from F1198 and a point sharpener and a second quern fragment from F2167; a stone rubber was found in an upper layer.

Pottery from the ditches derived, with the exception of a single sherd, from F2061. Samian included a stamped vessel dated AD 160–90, and this was accompanied by Severn Valley wares datable to the late second to third century.

Site 2, Area A

The natural subsoil of reddish brown silty clay bonded with greenish grey silty clay was cut by a number of ditches (Fig. 5; Plate 1). The earliest, F125, was a shallow ditch cut into the natural slope and marked by a fill of brown silty clay, 7109 (Fig. 5: S4). To the south was a ditch F115 with clay fills, 7058 and 7064 (Fig. 5: S1). F125 was cut by two field boundary ditches, F109 and F124, with an entrance gap at the corner of the field. F109 also cut F115. The lower fill of F109 was a very compact brown clay, 7090, containing small amounts of Malvernian stone and charcoal. This was sealed by a dark brown silty clay, 7049, also containing Malvernian stone, which lay beneath an upper fill, 7043, of reddish brown sandy clay with large Malvernian stone and flecks of charcoal (Fig. 5: S1). F124 contained a lower fill, 7096, of brown silty clay with charcoal, Malvernian stone and burnt animal bone. Above layer 7091, a very dark brown silty clay flecked with charcoal, and containing Malvernian stone, may mark a recut (Fig. 5: S2). Within the field marked by F109 and F124 was a narrow gully, F119, filled with clay, 7065 (Fig. 5: S3), which ran into F109.

The earlier features, F125 and F115, represent two phases of boundary delineation of which F125 may predate F115. The latter came to a butt end within the excavation, perhaps forming an entrance at the corner of a field with the east boundary outside the area examined. Such an arrangement was replicated in a later layout by F124 and F109, forming the south-east corner of a field enclosure. An entrance at the corner may have been further marked by F119 which may have acted as a drainage ditch alongside a track leading from the entrance.

Pottery from the ditches was late first to mid second century in date. The latest samian sherd, dated Hadrianic or early Antonine, came from F109. Fragments dated AD 100–120 came from F125. An early second-century mortarium was also found. The evidence suggested that the field boundaries had gone out of use by the middle of the second century, with late first and early second-century pottery indicating the period of use of the area. F119 and F124 contained flint flakes.

Site 2, Area B

Above the geological horizon, a layer of hillwash was visible in places. The natural subsoil of silty clay was overlain to the south of the site by a shallow deposit of pale greenish grey clay silt, 7038, 7041, containing flecks of charcoal and occasional sherds of Romano-British pottery in its upper levels. This layer was cut by the features described below.

The north-east corner of a field was marked by ditches F107 and F113 (Fig. 6; Plate 2). These were separated by a gap on

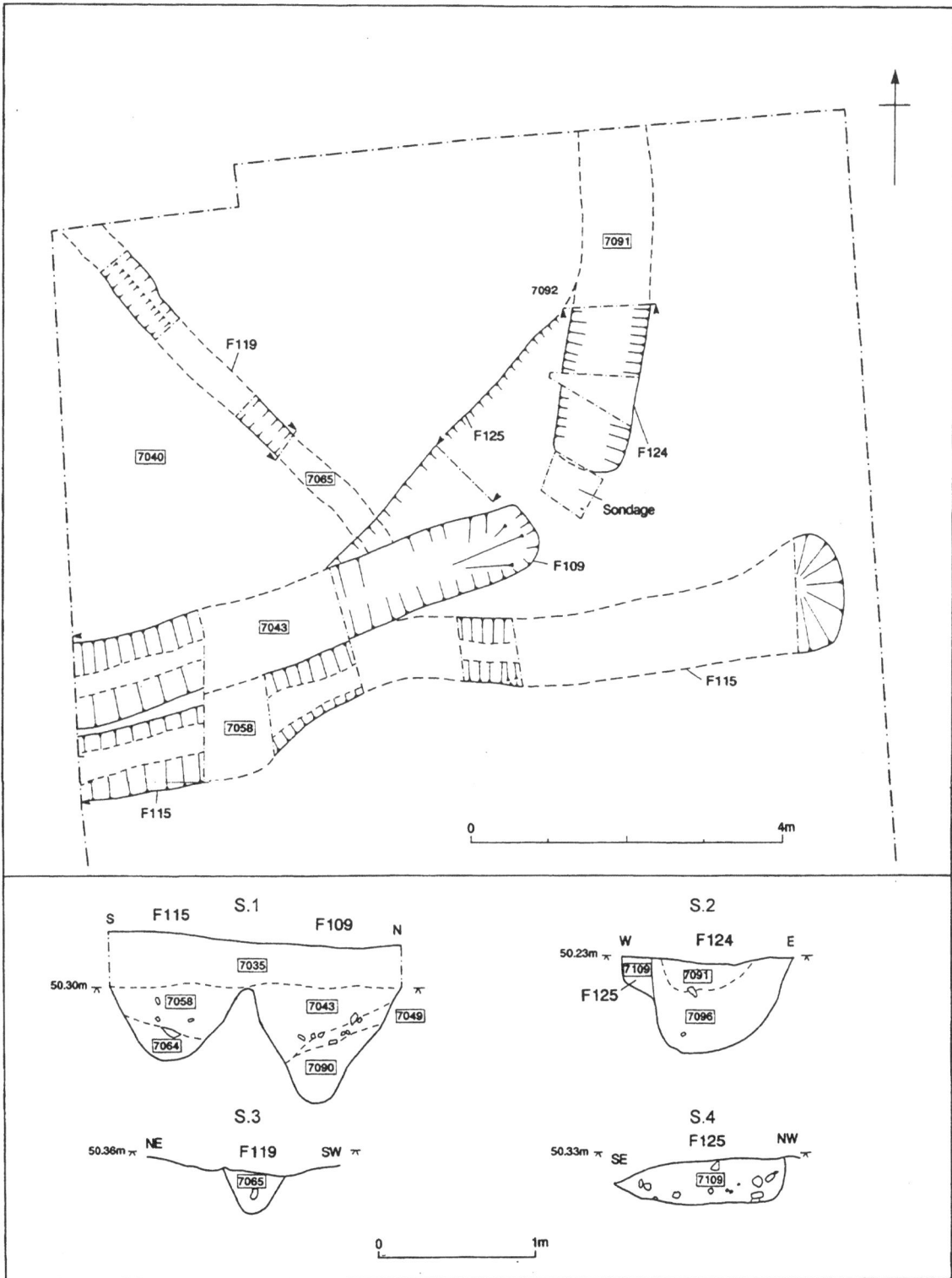

Figure 5: Site 2, Area A, plan and sections; scale 1:80 (plan) and 1:40 (sections)

the east side. F113 was not traced further south across the site. F107 was generally steep-sided with a flat base. Its lower fills were of charcoal-rich silty clay, 7053, in the north–south section, and a very compact, reddish-brown clay, 7083, in the east–west section. The upper fill was a compact brown silty clay, 7033 (Fig. 7: S6, S7). F113 was filled with reddish brown silty clay, 7051, very similar to the natural subsoil, beneath a greyish-brown silty clay, 7048 (Fig. 7: S5).

The remains of a single-flue pottery kiln, F108, were set in a slight flat-based pit near the field boundary (Fig. 8; Plate 3). The pit cut a gully, F149, which was difficult to distinguish in excavation from the kiln itself, but which terminated westward near its centre, and which ran to the east of the kiln. The gully contained a brown silty clay, 7144, and a dump of fragments of fired clay, 7137. The surviving fill of the gully was similar to the overlying layer 7059 filling the kiln. Lines of silt were apparent in its sides.

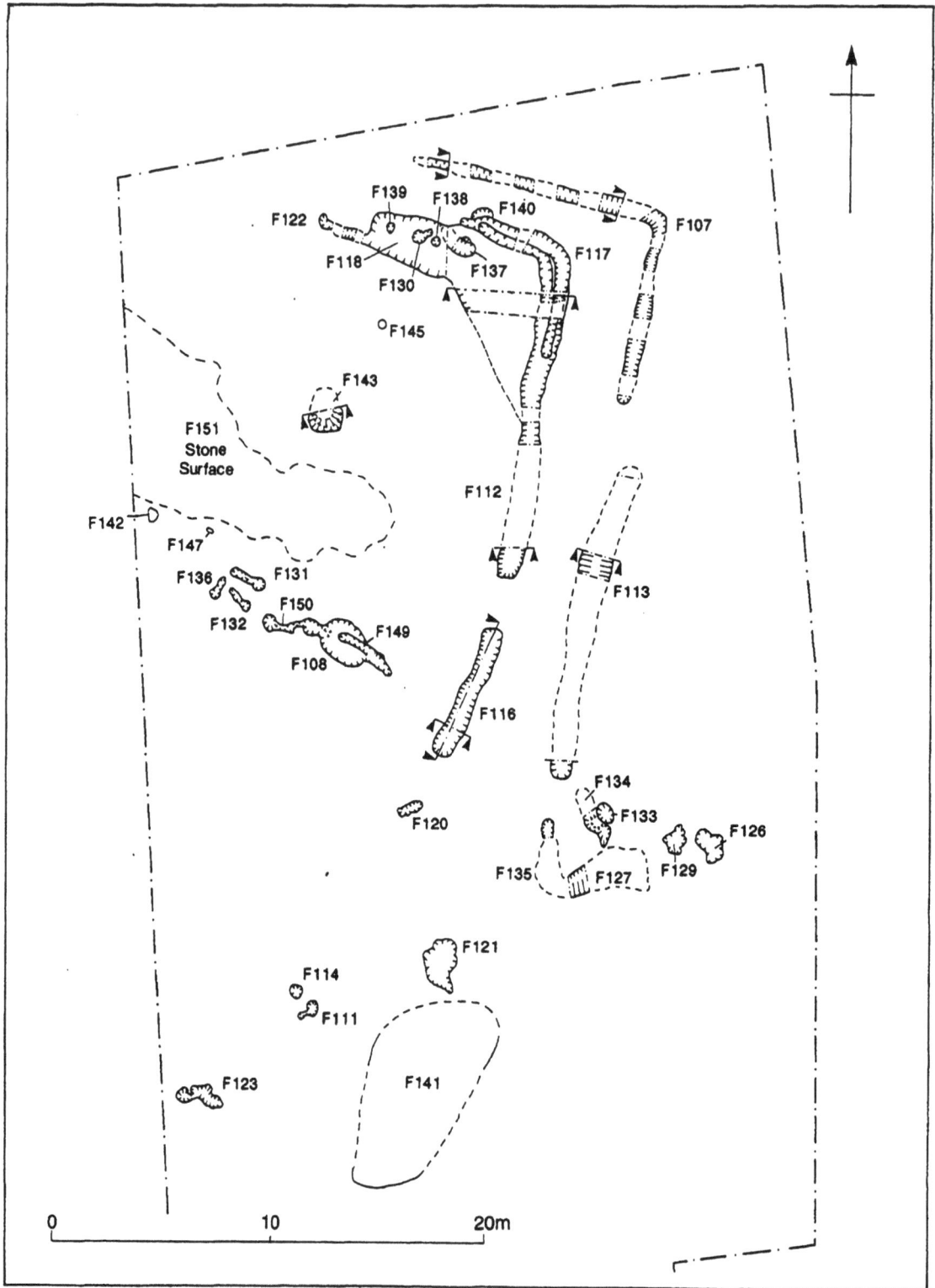

Figure 6: Site 2, Area B, plan; scale 1:200

The central hollow of the kiln contained the truncated remains of its combustion chamber structure, made of lumps of reddish-brown fired clay, 7112, varying in thickness from 0.27m to 0.4m. The chamber structure had four regularly spaced gaps within it. Within the remains of the combustion chamber was a reddish-brown sandy clay, 7111, and lumps of fired clay and charcoal. Two possible flues lay on opposite sides. The eastern flue contained fired clay, charcoal-rich silty clay, 7059, and pottery; patches of its burnt clay sides, 7063,

survived. The shorter flue to the west was filled with a charcoal-rich clay silt, 7034, and a slightly lower area was recorded at the junction of flue and chamber. The gaps to the north and south of the kiln gave the impression in excavation of having been vents. However, these would have been functionally inexplicable at the base of the kiln superstructure. They could be interpreted as later cuts, perhaps plough damage, or the former positions of reinforcing stakes.

8

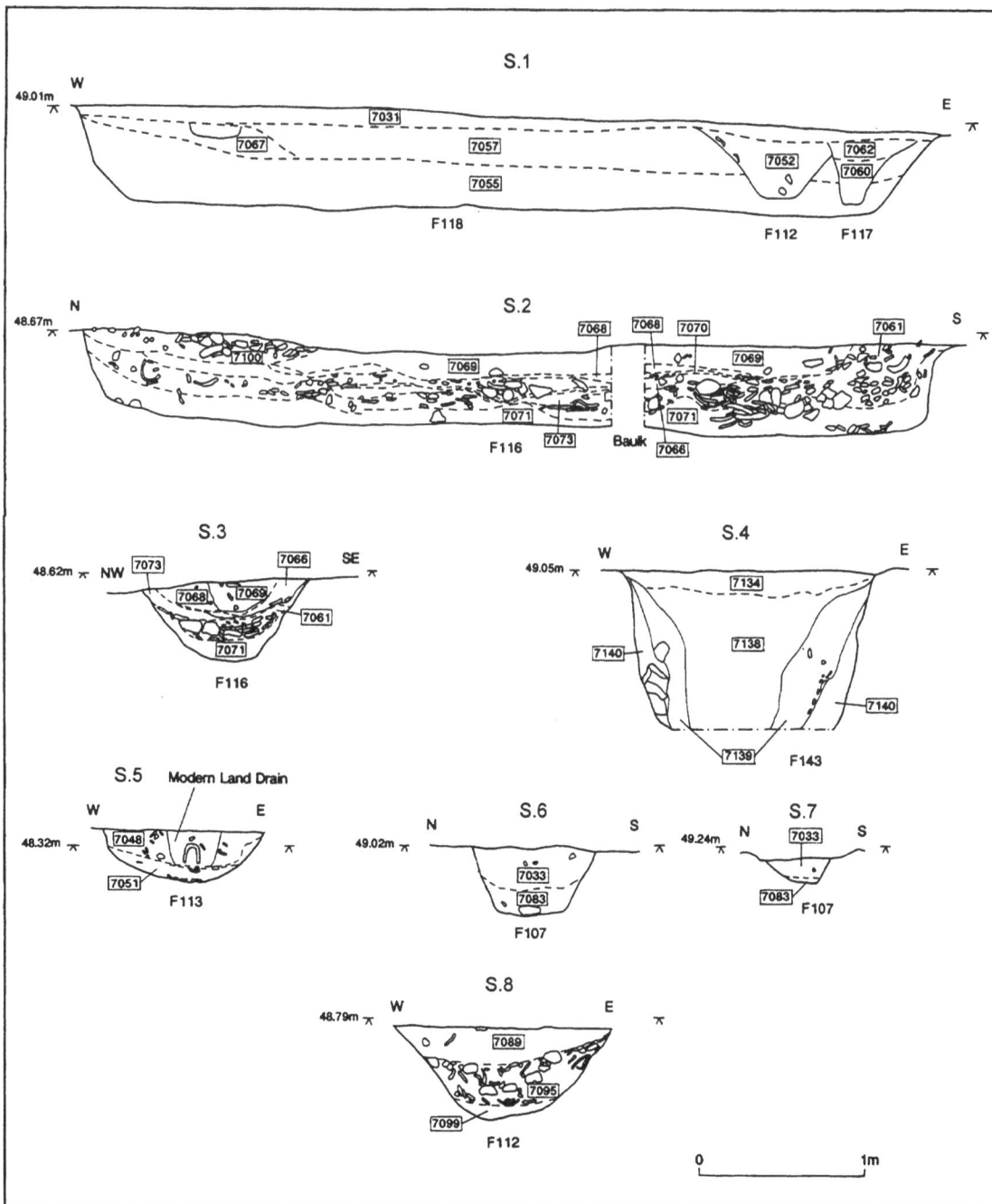

Figure 7: Site 2, Area B, sections; scale 1:40

A group of four keyhole-shaped, hearth-type features, F131, F132, F136, and F150, with large amounts of charcoal in their clay fills, 7113, 7116, 7122 and 7104, lay directly to the west of kiln F108 (Plate 4). These varied in depth from 0.1m–0.15m. To their north was a laid stone surface, F151, of angular Malvernian metamorphic stones incorporating large quantities of Romano-British pottery (Plate 5). To its south was a posthole or small pit, F142, 0.28m deep, filled with dark brown silty clay, 7133, flecked with charcoal, and a small slot, F147, 0.12m deep, with a similar fill to F142. Another possible hearth, F128 (not illustrated), cut trench F112, described below, and was filled with a clay silt, 7087, which contained large amounts of charcoal.

To the north was a circular well-shaft, F143, lined with large angular Malvernian metamorphic stones and red clay, 7140 (Fig. 7: S4). The well was not excavated below a depth of 1m (Plate 6). Its fills comprised a compact reddish brown silty clay, 7139, which had slumped into the shaft and a dark greyish brown silty clay, 7138, containing large Malvernian stones. A layer of dark greyish brown clay silt, 7134, flecked with charcoal, filled a subsidence hollow over the well. Further north again was a posthole, F145, 0.3m deep, filled with a very compact dark brown silty clay, 7141.

To the south of F108, a posthole, F120, 0.35m deep, was filled with dark reddish brown clay, 7081, containing a high concentration of charcoal, beneath a dark brown silty clay,

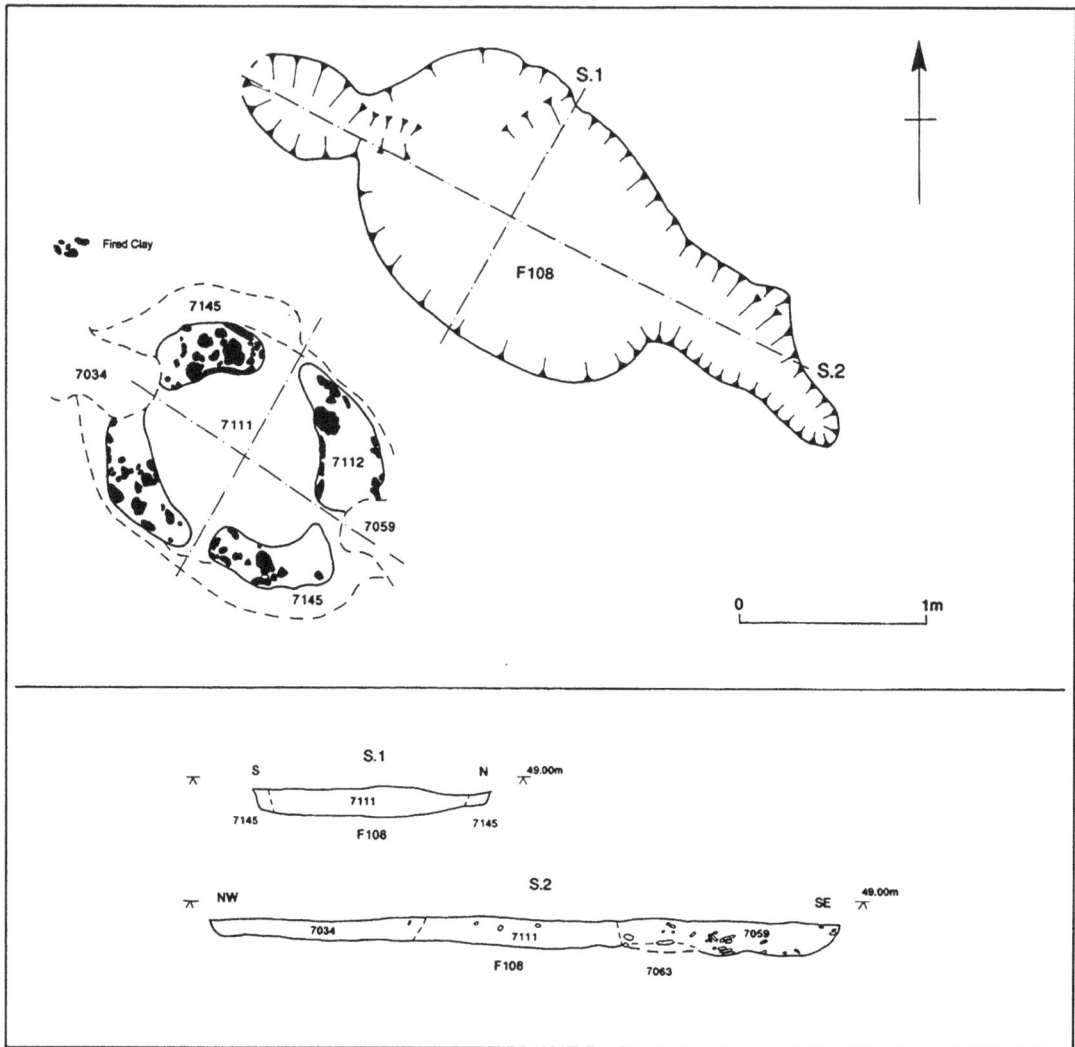

Figure 8: Site 2, Area B, kiln; post and pre-excavation plans and sections; scale 1:40

F148 (not illustrated), contained similar charcoal-rich, silty clay fills, 7054 7046 and 7145 respectively. They varied in depth from 0.25m to 0.13m. A fourth possible hearth, F123, consisted of many shallow irregular hollows up to 0.26m deep, with a similar charcoal and silt fill, 7086.

In the north-east corner of the field, a large pit, F118 (Fig. 7: S1), cut a concave-profiled gully, F122, filled with a brown silty clay, 7088. The base fill of F118, a very compact, reddish-brown clay, 7055, was difficult to distinguish from the natural clay except through the presence of potsherds. It was overlain by a deposit of very dark brown, charcoal-rich silty clay, 7067, with a darker and more silty clay, 7115, in the west part of the feature. These were overlain by a reddish-brown silty clay, 7057. This was cut by two postholes and three possible hearths. Postholes F138 and F139 were 0.5m and 0.45m deep respectively and were filled with similar brown silty clays, 7127 and 7128 respectively. Hearth F137 was 0.28m deep and filled with a charcoal-rich silty clay, 7123. Hearth F140 was 0.22m deep, with vertical sides and a flat base, and a fill of charcoal-rich clay, 7131, underlying a light reddish brown silty clay, 7129. A third possible hearth, F130, was 0.15m deep with similar fills to F140, of charcoal and clay, 7108, and red silty clay, 7105.

F118 and F140 were cut by a trench, F112 (Fig. 7: S1, S8). It was backfilled with numerous fills, 7052, 7074, 7076, 7077, 7078, 7084, 7089, 7095, and 7099, of which 7074, 7077 and 7078 contained large concentrations of charcoal and waster sherds as well as other items listed below. The fills of a second trench to the south, F116, were similar (Fig. 7: S2, S3). Eight separate backfills were recognised, 7061, 7066, 7068, 7069, 7070, 7071, 7073 and 7100, and of these 7061 and 7070 contained large amounts of Romano-British pottery, including wasters, fired clay, slag and charcoal (Plates 7 and 8). Both trench sections had thus been backfilled with waste kiln products. Ditch F112 had been recut by a second trench, F117 (Fig. 7: S1), which was filled with a dark reddish brown clay, 7060, and a dark brown silty clay, 7062, with no evidence of kiln waste.

A layer of grey brown silty clay, 7031, sealed the features overlying F118, and the trenches F112 and F117 (Fig. 7: S1). A similar silt layer, 7047, overlay the stone surface F151. A group of large shallow irregular hollows, F126, F127, F129, F133, F134 and F135, was filled with a similar dark brown silty clay, 7082, 7087, 7098, 7102, 7103, 7118, 7119 and 7120. F141 to its south was a large shallow depression, 0.27m deep, which was also filled with a dark brown silty clay,

10

7132, overlain by a greenish-grey clay silt, 7136, very similar to hillwash deposit 7038.

Layers 7031 and 7047 presumably represent the remains of an overall layer which survived only in the subsidence over features and on the stones of F151. The hollows to the south may have been the remains of truncated features or disturbance by tree roots.

About two-thirds of the total pottery assemblage and all of the kiln debris came from this area, with ditches F112, F116 and F117 and pit F118 containing the great majority of the material recovered. Large sherds were preponderant, as were wasters. The uppermost fill of F116 contained a third or fourth-century sherd amongst an otherwise second to early third-century group. Pottery from F112 was of third to fourth-century date, while its recut, F117, contained only second-century sherds. Other features datable by their fills were F137, dated to the second century, F141, datable to the second to early third century, and F142 which contained a mortarium dated later than c.AD 230 and commonly produced in the second half of the third century or the early fourth. The kiln F108 contained a small group of pottery which included third or fourth-century material. Pottery datable to the late third or early fourth centuries came from the stone surface F151, and from the upper fill of well F143. The pottery from F151 was late third or early fourth century and included an Oxfordshire mortarium dated AD 240–300.

In addition to the potsherds noted above, F112 contained first to third-century bottle glass, two ceramic spindle whorls (Fig. 43.2, 3), a fragment of a copper alloy bracelet and a nail. Amongst the pottery from F112 particular note should be made of a group of four unused mortaria, dated AD 70–120, with a unique application of trituration grits (Fig. 32). These were clearly waste products from a kiln. F116 contained a first- to second-century brooch (Cat. No. 3), F117 a fragment of a copper alloy wire bracelet, and F118 a further fragment of first- to third-century bottle glass. Well F143 contained two iron objects, one possibly a chisel. From the stone spread, F151, came three nails. The layer above, a clay silt, 7047, contained two building nails, a first or second-century brooch (Fig. 43.1), bottle glass of first- to third-century date, as well as a Neolithic stone axe (Fig. 44) and a flint knife (Fig. 45.2). Stone finds comprised a quern fragment and a possible weight from F112, a possible rubber from F116, a whetstone from F117, a possible weight from F118, and, finally, a point sharpener, a whetstone, and a polisher or another whetstone from F151. Analysis of charcoal samples from the kiln showed the use of maple and poplar/willow, the latter a reused timber. A possible fragment of coal was found.

Sherds of later third or early fourth-century date were amongst a number of sherds in 7031 and 7047. Oxfordshire mortaria dated AD 240–300 were found in both layers. Layer 7031 also contained quernstone fragments. F141 contained large quantities of charcoal.

Other findings

There were no Romano-British features worthy of illustration at Site 1, Areas 2–4, as noted above. Deposits of loam were recorded in Areas 2 and 4, the layer in Area 2 containing Romano-British pottery. Two small shallow features were recorded in Area 3.

At Site 2, Area C, a spread of greenish-grey clay silt, 7125, F152, contained concentrations of charcoal and sherds of Malvernian pottery (Fig. 2). The silt appeared to be staining and contamination of hillwash layer 7041, also present in Area B, F141, to a depth of 0.08m. To the south was a line of angular Malvernian metamorphic stones, 7126.

F152 may represent the truncated base of a clay treatment feature. Although charcoal was present there were no indications of the burning that would have been present if this was the site of a surface clamp kiln. Layers 7041 and 7125 contained second and third-century pottery. A large quantity of Romano-British pottery was recovered from the topsoil (7035, 7036 and 7037).

Modern features principally comprising land drains and hop pole holes were recorded in all the excavations. The land drains at Site 1, Area 1, are illustrated (Fig. 3). Romano-British pottery was recovered from the topsoil, which was generally c 0.2m deep, and from some modern features.

Interpretation and discussion

The finding of the kiln, F108, is a major archaeological discovery in the context of previous work in the area, which has been limited to the finding of kiln debris and wasters. The kiln would have been a simple round structure, slightly sunken into the pit, and with a level floor continuing into the flue. Above a low permanent wall the kiln would have been built up at each firing with turves reinforced by withies and sealed with clay. Although gaps may have been left in the temporary upper structure to assist firing, none would have existed in the permanent lower structure. It would seem likley that the western flue replaced that to the east, since no twin-flue kiln producing oxidised pottery is known in Britain (pers. comm. Vivien Swan). The resiting of kiln flues is not uncommon; see for example Hardingstone, Northamptonshire, where Kilns I and VI appear to have had the position of flues changed (Woods 1974), and Fulmer, Buckinghamshire, where the flue of kiln 1 was blocked off and a second flue was constructed on the opposite side (Tarrant and Sandford 1972).

The clay-filled channels F1159, F1211, F1198 and F1164 at Site 1, Area 1, and F112, F116 and F117 at Site 2, Area B, can be interpreted as levigation channels. These are common on kiln sites and were used to allow the impurities to settle out of the liquid clay. The two large pits, F2290 and F118, would also be associated with the channels as water containers and soakaways. They may possibly have originated as clay extraction pits. At Site 2, Area B, gully F149 pre-dated the kiln, providing evidence for an earlier phase of activity. Levigation gullies also post-dated pit F118. The densely packed pottery fills of ditches F112 and F116 may represent the abandonment of potting in this area, the sherds filling the ditches deriving perhaps from a single rubbish dump or midden composed of broken pots. The distinction between levigation ditches and field boundary ditches is not clear-cut but the former seem generally to have poorly defined edges in comparison to the neat execution of the boundary ditches F2061 at Site 1, Area 1, and F107 at Site 2, Area B.

The stone surface F151 may have been intended for unprepared clay or to receive dumps of prepared clay prior to potting. Alternatively it may represent the base of a timber structure. Possible structures are suggested by the postholes found, two of which lie alongside F151, but no individual buildings can be suggested. The small group of stone objects may indicate use as a workshop. Finally the well, F143, would have been the source of the water essential for pottery production.

The ditch features are likely to represent the truncated remains of field boundary ditches. At Site 1, Area 1, the regular sides and alignment of F2061 suggest it was part of a field system. If so, it was part of an agricultural land use later than the post-pits, although it is possible to argue that the pair of post-pits at its south end could be contemporary. At Site 2, Area B, field boundaries were represented by F107 and F113, apparently forming the surviving corner of a field boundary defining the area of pottery production.

The Site 2, Area A evidence seems likely to have related to that from Site 1, Area 1 to the north (Fig. 2). F2061 may represent a continuation of F124 or perhaps of an earlier field layout running north from the east end of F115. F107 from Site 2, Area B, might then have formed a right-angled junction with either suggested ditch line. Alternatively, F107 might have run across Site 1, Area 1, with F2061 and F124 meeting it on either side. It would seem likely that truncation by the plough has removed much of the evidence, leaving occasional survivals where ditches were cut deeper or were protected by a hollow in the ground.

The dating evidence from the pottery production features therefore suggests that those from Site 1, Area 1, were of second-century date. Production was clearly taking place at the same time at Site 2, Area B, but continued at the latter site into the third century. Some later pottery, indicating later third and early fourth-century activity, was found in F151 and the upper fill of F143. This may have been intrusive or, in the case of F151, may be an indication that this was a later structure. The pottery as a whole suggested production took place in the area predominantly in the second and third centuries. It is possible therefore to suggest three phases of activity. The first, in the late-first to mid-second century, was evidenced by the archaeology from Site 2 Area A, and by residual early pottery, including samian, from the other two sites. The second, associated with pottery production, was attested by large quantities of pottery of overwhelmingly second and third-century date at Site 1 and Site 2, Area B. However, there was a small amount of later third and fourth-century pottery from Site 1 and Site 2, Area B, and this must represent a third and final Romano-British phase. At both sites late pottery occurred only in the upper fills of the Phase 2 features. The first and third phases of activity seem to have been primarily domestic in nature, while Phase 2 was dominated by wasters and other material associated with pottery production. This latter phase can be suggested to have occupied a timespan of a century at least, but the conservative forms associated with Severn Valley ware make impossible the recognition of sub-phases within the broad period AD 150 to AD 300.

—◇—

THE ROMAN POTTERY

by C. Jane Evans

with contributions by Brenda Dickinson, Kay Hartley, Joanna Mills,
Kirsty Nichol, and David Williams

Introduction

The pottery discussed in the following report represents the combined assemblages from the 1992 and 1994 excavations and from the evaluation of Site 1 in 1991. The excavations produced a total of 896kg of pottery, 99% of which is thought to have been produced on or near the site. The main product was Severn Valley ware (Webster 1976), but coarsely tempered Malvernian wares (Peacock 1967, 18–28; Peacock 1968, 414–21) were also represented. The assemblage provides the first substantial group of Severn Valley ware to be recovered from a production site, and the first production assemblage to be recorded to modern standards. It is hoped that the publication of the Newland Hopfields assemblage will allow its products to be recognised at future excavation sites and that further work on published and unpublished material will enhance the data published here.

The aim of the pottery analysis was to characterise the pottery industry on the site in terms of:

The date of production on site

The degree of standardisation: reflected in the range of fabrics used, the range of forms produced, and the size of vessels

The level of technology: clay preparation, vessel manufacture (hand-made or wheel-made) and firing (hardness, colour)

The layout of the 'workshop': inferences from spatial analysis

The distribution of its products and an assessment of the kiln's place in Severn Valley ware production as a whole

The size of the assemblage, particularly from Site 2, made it impractical to analyse every sherd, and a sampling strategy was chosen. Only the feature sherds (rims, bases, handles, decorated body sherds and other diagnostic form sherds) in Severn Valley ware were recorded in detail, but all sherds were recorded for other wares. To aid analysis of the pottery, contexts and features from the excavations were divided into nine groups (Table 1). These were then compared. Features associated with pottery production at Site 1, Area 1, and Site 2, Area B (Groups 5 and 7) were separated from features that were only possibly associated with pottery production (Groups 6 and 8). While these groups have been maintained in the tables and charts, no essential differences were seen in the composition of the assemblages. The assemblage is summarised by fabric (Table 2) and spatially (Table 3).

The pottery was recorded by context. Fabrics were analysed using a microscope at X20 magnification. Sherd hardness was noted, but this was probably biased by a tendency to under-fire kiln products, and the abrasive local soil conditions. Based on the evidence from other kiln sites, a wide range of fabric variations was anticipated during recording, only some of which would have wider significance. For this reason, and following discussion with specialists at the County Unit, a site-specific fabric type series was used (Table 4). This was cross-referenced with the existing County Series (Hurst and Rees 1992) when recording was complete. Petrological analysis was undertaken by David Williams, the results being integrated with the fabric descriptions. Rims were classified by both vessel class and precise form, all defined in the form catalogues. The codes used to record vessel classes are listed in Table 5.

Table 1: Feature Groups

	Site 1, Area 1	Site 2, Area A	Site 2, Area B	Site 2, Area C
Group 1	Two posters			
Group 2	Field boundaries			
Group 3		Field boundaries		
Group 4			Field boundaries	
Group 5	Pottery production features			
Group 6	Possible pottery production features			
Group 7			Pottery production features	
Group 8			Possible pottery production features	
Group 9				Miscellaneous

Table 2: Romano-British pottery: summary of the assemblage by fabric (Total assemblage)

Fabric Number	Count	% total count	Wt.	% total wt.	Base EVE	% total base EVE	Rim EVE	% total rim EVE
LOCAL WARES								
O1	*1856		*83670		88.81	23	103.50	21
O2	*109		*6989		4.94	1.3	6.99	1.4
O5	*1725		*53671		75.21	19	91.95	19
O9	*2		*62		0	0	0.06	<1
R1	*447		*14819		22.34	6	21.66	4
R2	*17		*767		1.65	<1	1.32	<1
R5	*17		*262		0	0	1.09	<1
R9	*1		*18		0	0	0	0
Severn Valley ware (Organic)	*4174*		*160258*		*192.95*	*49*	*226.57*	*46.5*
O3	*1450		*60526		70.46	18	88.15	18
O4	*766		*26029		27.72	7	43.13	9
O6	*1296		*38401		56.55	14	67.23	14
O7	*355		*10429		15.37	4	20.23	4
R3	*15		*448		0.76	<1	0.26	<1
R4	*129		*3906		2.80	<1	5.53	1
R6	*15		*395		0.31	<1	0.73	<1
R7	*39		*1004		0.90	<1	1.68	<1
Severn Valley ware (Plain)	*4065*		*141138*		*174.87*	*44.4*	*226.94*	*46.5*
O8	*63		*3156		3.10	<1	3.30	<1
R8	*63		*1328		1.40	<1	2.31	<1
Severn Valley ware (Coarse)	*126*		*4484*		*4.50*	*1.2*	*5.61*	*1*
S.V.W (non-feature sherds)	42495	79.7	538581	60.1	0	0	0	0
Total Severn Valley ware	50860	95.4	844461	94.2	372.32	94.6	459.12	94
R22	1524	2.9	37735	4.2	10.03	2.5	14.16	3
R23	373	<1	5465	<1	4.98	1	6.15	1
R24	107	<1	1589	<1	1.28	<1	2.06	<1
Total Malvernian ware	2004	3.8	44789	5.0	16.29	4.1	22.37	4.6
TOTAL LOCAL	52864	99.2	889250	99.2	388.61	98.7	481.49	99
SOURCE UNKNOWN								
O25	3	<1	15	<1	0	0	0	0
R25	39	<1	759	<1	1.10	<1	0.50	<1
R26	91	<1	2492	<1	0	0	0	0
TOTAL SOURCE UNKNOWN	133	<1	3266	<1	1.10	0.3	0.50	<1
TRADED WARES								
R21	172	<1	1714	<1	0.69	<1	3.15	<1
R27	9	<1	793	<1	0	0	0.07	<1
M1	5	<1	126	<1	0.20	<1	0.15	<1
M2	7	<1	212	<1	0	0	0.27	<1
M3	1	<1	17	<1	0	0	0.08	<1
W1	8	<1	41	<1	0	0	0	0
W2	2	<1	16	<1	0	0	0	0
TOTAL TRADED	204	<1	2919	<1	0.89	0.2	3.72	<1
IMPORTED WARES								
O43.1	14	<1	205	<1	0	0	0.77	<1
O43.2	67	<1	761	<1	3.02	<1	1.12	<1
O43.3	1	<1	36	<1	0	0	0	0
TOTAL IMPORTED	82	<1	1002	<1	3.02	0.8	1.89	<1
TOTAL POTTERY	53283		896437		393.62		487.60	

* NB Rim and base EVES are representative of the assemblage as a whole. The sherd counts and weights shown for individual Severn Valley ware variants represent only the feature sherds, but the counts and weights for other fabrics represent the total quantities present.

Table 3: Romano-British pottery: summary of the assemblage by Site, Area, and Feature Group

Site	Area	Group	Feature type	Count	% total count	Wt.	% total wt.	Base EVE	% total base EVE	Rim EVE	% total rim EVE
1		1	Two posters	*34		*1029		1.59	<1	1.05	0.2
1		2	Field boundaries	*134		*7510		6.64	1.7	4.88	1.0
1		5	Pottery production	*131		*4716		7.22	1.8	4.85	1.0
1		6	? Pottery production	*12		*399		0	0	0.43	0.1
1		None	Other contexts	*455		*14307		17.42	4.4	20.80	4.3
			Total Site 1	3392	6.3	53345	5.9	32.87	8.3	32.01	6.6
2	A	3	Field boundaries	*742		*19234		12.85	3.3	16.01	3.3
2	B	4	Field boundaries	*388		*8905		7.84	2.0	12.50	2.6
2	B	7	Pottery production	*5776		*239992		260.71	66.2	305.18	62.6
2	B	8	? Pottery production	*510		*11886		14.44	3.7	22.45	4.6
2	C	9	Miscellaneous	*489		*9364		10.72	2.7	13.61	2.8
2		None	Other contexts	*1824		*		59.49	15.1	72.73	14.9
			Total Site 2	49594	93.1	835966	93.3	353.20	89.7	442.48	90.7
			Unstratified	298	<1	7143	<1	7.75	2.0	13.11	2.7
			Total pottery	53284		896454		393.82		487.60	

Rim and base EVES are representative of the assemblage as a whole, but the quantities and weights by feature group, marked *, are based only on the feature sherds.

14

Table 4: Romano-British pottery: pottery fabrics

Fabric Number	Fabric Name	WCM Fabric Code (Hurst and Rees 1992)	References (National Roman Fabric Reference Collection code, and page number for Tomber and Dore 1998)
	Severn Valley ware		Webster 1976; Rawes 1982; Timby 1990; Tyers 1996, 197-9 (SVW OX1, SVW OX2, 148-150)
O1/R1	Fine charcoal-tempered ware	12.2/12.3	
O2/R2	Coarser charcoal-tempered ware	12.2/12.3	
O3/R3,	Plain Severn Valley ware	12/12.1	
O4/R4	Plain Severn Valley ware	12.6/	
O5	Charcoal-tempered variant	12.2	
O6/R6	Plain Severn Valley ware	12/12.1	
O7/R7	Plain Severn Valley ware	12/12.1	
O8	Coarser-gritted variant	-	
O9	Organic-tempered variant	12.2	
R21	South-east Dorset BB1	22	Farrar 1973; Williams 1977; Tyers 1996 182-6 (DOR BB 1, 127)
R22	Hand-made Malvernian metamorphic ware	3	Peacock 1968, 414-21, Group A; Morris 1981; Morris 1983, 112-6, figs. 4.15 and 4.16 (MAL REA, 147)
R23	Wheel-made Malvernian metamorphic ware	19	Peacock 1967, 18-28
R24	Hand-made Malvernian metamorphic ware variant	3	
O25	Oxidised sandy ware	13	
R25	Reduced sandy ware	14/15	
R26	Coarse, grog-tempered ware	16 and 16.2	
R27	Savernake ware	-	Swan 1975; Tyers 1996, 195-6 (SAV GT, 191)
O43.1	Samian, South Gaulish	43	(LGF SA, 28)
O43.2	Samian, Central Gaulish	43	(LEZ SA 2, 32-3; LMV SA, 30-1)
O43.3	Samian, East Gaulish	43	(RHZ SA, 39)
M1	Mancetter-Hartshill Mortaria	32	Hartley 1973, 143-7; Tyers 1996 (MAH WH, 189)
M2	Oxfordshire white ware mortaria	33	Young 1977, 56-79; Tyers 1996, 129 (OXF WH, 174-5)
M3	Oxfordshire white colour-coated mortaria	-	Young 1977 (OXF WS, 176-7)
W1	Mancetter-Hartshill white ware	-	(MAH WH, 189)
W2	Oxfordshire white ware	38	Young 1977, 93-112 (OXF WH, 174-5)

O = oxidised wares, R = reduced wares, M = mortaria, W = white wares

Where possible, jars and bowls were subdivided into functional categories, but general categories (J and B) were assigned to jars and bowls that could not be more closely defined. During analysis, individual forms were grouped into broad form types, also defined in the catalogues. Forms were also recorded for handles, bases and, where appropriate, body sherds. These are not, however, discussed in detail in the publication text.

Decoration was recorded where possible, but most sherds (64%) were very abraded. This high level of abrasion probably reflects a number of factors. The heavy, slightly acid clay adhered to the pottery, making washing difficult, and much of the pottery came from gullies which, owing to the poor drainage on the site, would have been regularly waterlogged. Sherds seemed also to be predominantly underfired and therefore soft.

A variety of other characteristics was considered and recorded where present. These related to manufacture (presence of string marks, method of applying handles etc); firing (colour variations; hardness; waster types, warped or with air bubbles; and a broad assessment of the micaceous content of fabrics); vessel use (eg sooting, limescale, wear marks) and repair (eg perforations, lead rivets). Obvious cross-joins between contexts were noted, but it was not practical in the time available to make a detailed study.

During the assessments (Buteux 1992; Evans 1995), total counts and weights of pottery had been recorded by context for both site assemblages. During analysis different methodologies were applied to the Severn Valley wares and the other fabrics represented. All non-Severn Valley wares were recorded in detail. Only feature sherds were recorded in Severn Valley ware. Using the sherd count and weight data it was possible to produce a broad quantification of the pottery from the two sites (Table 3). It was also possible to calculate the total count and weight by fabric for all non- Severn Valley wares, and for Severn Valley ware as an overall group (Table 2). Counts and weights for individual Severn Valley ware fabrics, however, are based only on the feature sherds. This data is not reliable statistically as the decorated body sherds introduce an uncertain element of bias. They could, for example, be more common in one fabric than another, so that a higher proportion of the fabric would have been recorded as feature sherds. They are also subject to varying levels of abrasion, so that fewer decorated sherds would have been

Table 5: Romano-British pottery: vessel classes

Vessel class	Code
Flagons or handled jars	F
Cups	C
Tankards	T
Jars	J
Jars/cook pots	JC
Narrow-mouthed jars	JNM
Medium-mouthed jars	JM
Wide-mouthed jars	JWM
Large storage jars	JLS
Bowls	B
Cooking bowls	BC
Table ware bowls	BT
Dishes	D
Platters/dishes	PD
Mortaria	M
Lids	L
Spouted strainers	VST
Crucibles	VC
Tettinas	VTT

recorded from more disturbed contexts. More detailed statistical analysis was possible using EVEs, summing the percentage of the rim or base extant. This provided the most reliable method for quantifying the feature sherds. Although both rim and base EVEs were recorded, base EVEs have only occasionally been presented.

In the following report, the pottery is presented by ware. These are arranged by source. The locally produced wares are presented first, with Severn Valley ware followed by the Malvernian wares. Next are the wares of uncertain source, followed by the non-local, 'traded' wares, and finally the imported wares. Each section comprises a general discussion followed by fabric descriptions and a catalogue of illustrated forms, with their parallels. These sections are followed by discussions of the ceramic dating and functional evidence. Selected information relating to the date or function of specific features or areas has been integrated into the site narrative. A broader overview of the assemblage and its significance is presented in the overall discussion at the end of the report. Material was selected for illustration as a form type series. Features associated with the kiln (group 7) were recorded first, and the majority of pottery illustrated is derived from these.

—✧—

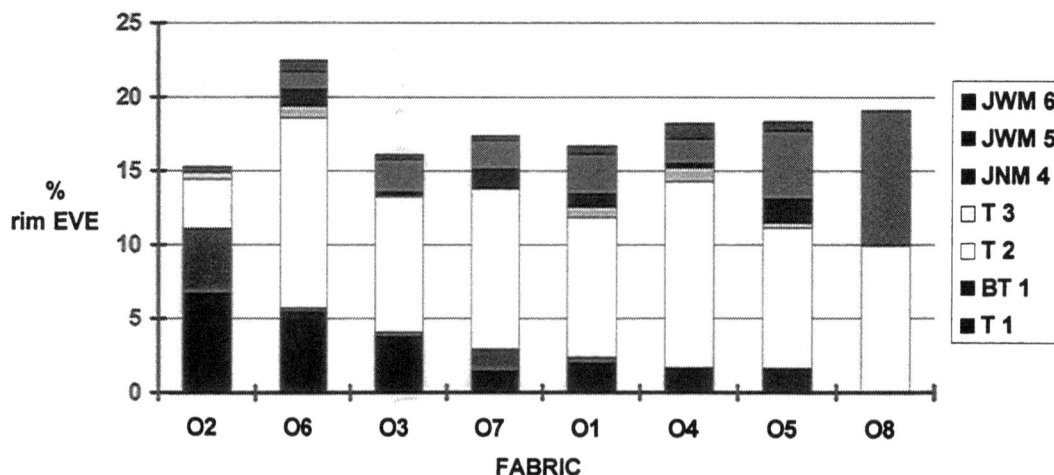

Figure 9: Severn Valley ware: seriation of fabrics by form type (% rim EVE)

SEVERN VALLEY WARE
with Kay Hartley, Kirsty Nichol and David Williams

Introduction
Severn Valley wares accounted for about 95% of the assemblage (Table 2). The great majority of the pottery was oxidised, although reduced variants of most fabrics occurred in small quantities. Only 24 sherds from the assemblage displayed evidence of use, such as sooting or limescale, and there was no evidence of repair.

Fabrics
with David Williams

The nine fabrics were, with the exception of the sandier variant Fabric O8, divisible into plain and organic-tempered wares. Thirteen samples were sent to David Williams for petrological analysis. These were compared with existing thin sections from a variety of kiln sites in the Malvern area made by Roberta Tomber (Tomber 1980). The fabrics were broadly similar, especially to those from previous fieldwalking at the Newland Hopfields site, with the exception of three samples (fabrics O1, O2 and O5). These had inclusions of carbonised wood, which, although an obvious by-product of kiln firing, is not a commonly found inclusion in pottery of any period, and had not previously been noted in the Malvern material.

The carbonised wood was distinctive in thin section. Charcoal would not have burnt out, even at high temperatures, so its presence or absence is unlikely to reflect variations in the firing temperature. Its presence in this assemblage may reflect variations in the preparation of a specific batch or batches of clay. The coarser fabric (O2) in particular was only common in two feature groups, and seems to be an earlier variant. Charcoal in organic-tempered Severn Valley wares may be more common than the current evidence suggests. During petrological analysis, Tomber noted charcoal fragments in one of the Severn Valley ware fabrics from Worcester (Darlington and Evans, 1992, 45, Sidbury fabric 12.6). The Sidbury fabric was difficult to distinguish macroscopically, however, and was not separated out from the organic Severn Valley ware. No source was proposed for it, but the sherds were considered identical to Gloucester fabric TF17 (Hurst 1985, 81). A similar fabric was also noted at Beckford, Worcestershire, thought to be from the lower Severn basin or north Wiltshire area (Beckford fabric 50, pers. comm. Helen Rees). Neither of the Sidbury or Beckford fabrics is included in the County series.

Analysis of the more closely datable forms suggests some chronological differences between the fabrics (Fig. 9). The coarser charcoal-tempered ware (Fabric O2) was datable to the first and second centuries by the relatively higher proportion of tankards (T type 1) and carinated bowls (BT type 1) of this date. The ware seemed to be going out of production during the second century, when the moderately splayed tankards (T type 2) superseded the earlier type. A few characteristically third- to fourth-century forms were noted, but less than in other variants. Organic-tempered Severn Valley wares have been identified as early fabrics

elsewhere, for example Worcester (Darlington and Evans 1992, 41), so the evidence from Newland Hopfields confirms a general pattern. The only form noted in the organic-tempered ware (Fabric O9) was a fragmentary rim from a large storage jar. It seems likely, however, that this is contemporary with Fabric O2.

The finer charcoal-tempered wares (Fabrics O1 and O5) appear to date predominantly to the second to third century. They include fewer examples of the early forms, and second- to third-century tankards (T type 2) are most common. Small numbers of the most splayed tankards (T type 3) and other characteristically third- to fourth-century forms are also present (JNM type 4, JWM types 5 and 6). The plain wares (Fabrics O3, O4, O6, O7) also appear to date predominantly to the second to third century, although they also include some earlier and later forms. Fabrics O3 and O6 produced slightly higher proportions of the early forms, while Fabric O5 produced slightly higher proportions of the later forms. The sandier variant (Fabric O8) is perhaps the latest fabric. No diagnostically early forms were represented. The proportion of characteristically later forms was also higher, although the range of later forms was much narrower.

The reduced variants of these wares, occurring in much smaller quantities, followed the same general pattern and there were no forms which did not also occur in the oxidised variants. There were no diagnostically 'grey-ware' forms, such as the earlier, rusticated jars known to have been produced at Malvern and found at Worcester (Darlington and Evans 1992, 48). The only possible exceptions were the medium-mouthed jars and cook-pots, but these were often oxidised, The reduction, therefore, seems in the majority of cases to have been accidental rather than deliberate. Most of the Severn Valley ware fabrics were thus broadly contemporary, with the exception perhaps of fabrics O2 and O8.

Forms
Analysis of vessel classes by fabric showed some interesting variations (Fig. 10), perhaps reflecting deliberate choices by the potter. Some may result from technological factors, while others may reflect other, less easily identifiable factors such as the working methods of individual potters. The coarse, charcoal-tempered ware (O2) included very low proportions of narrow-mouthed and medium-mouthed jars, but exceptionally high proportions of large storage jars. The latter, having thick walls, presumably required the coarser temper to survive the firing. Bowls were also common in this fabric, but it was not used for the production of flagons. The need for a coarser temper might also explain the high proportion of large storage jars produced in the sandier fabric (O8), which produced the highest proportion of jars overall. Flagons were more common in this fabric than in any of the others; presumably the potters were emulating the sandy oxidised wares used for the production of flagons elsewhere. Bowls were very poorly represented in this ware.

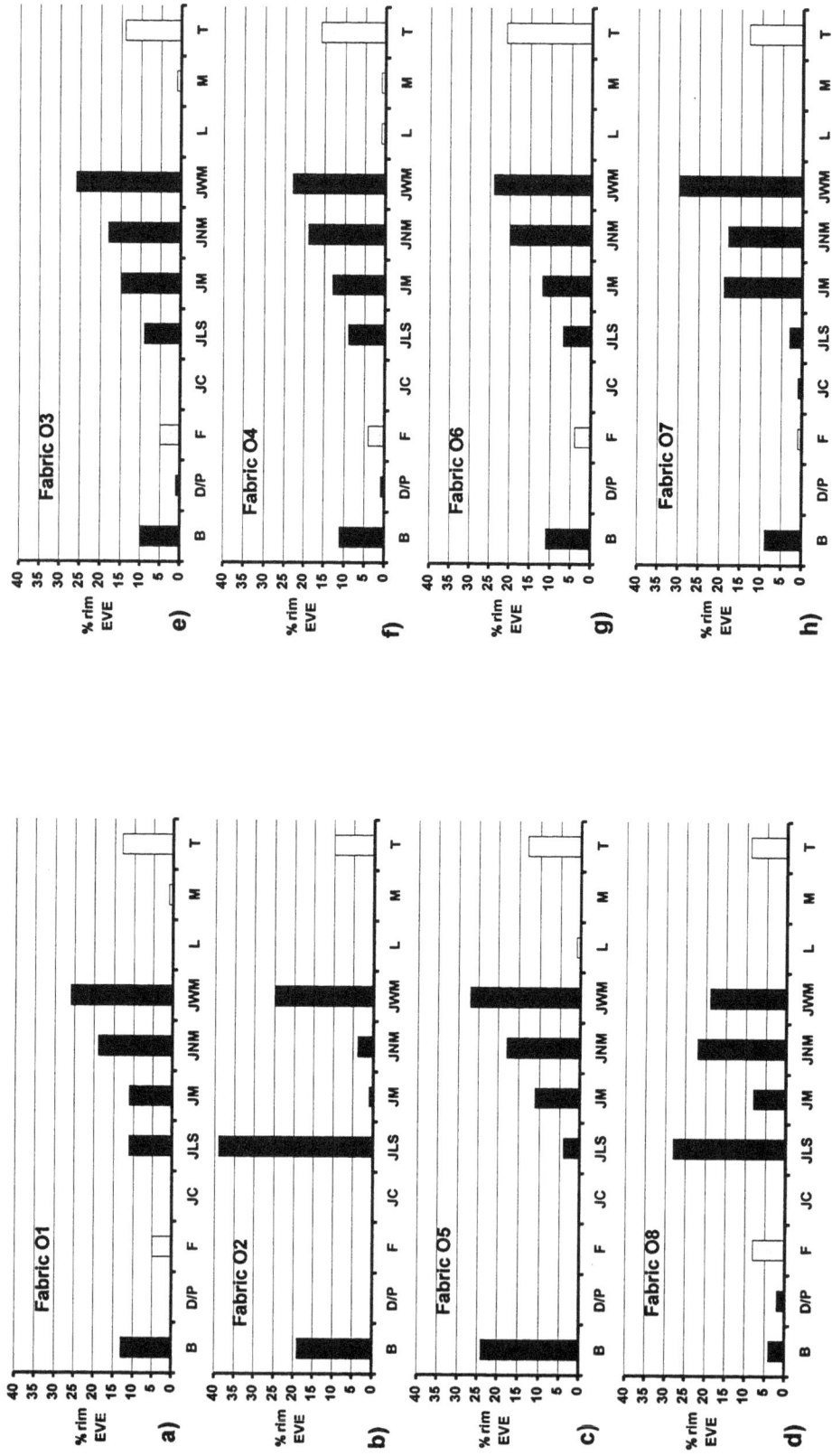

Figure 10:   Severn Valley ware: vessel classes by fabric (% rim EVE).

a - c: Organic Severn Valley ware;   d: Coarse Severn Valley ware;   e -h: Plain Severn Valley ware.

Key: B - bowl;   D/P - dish/platter;   F - flagon;   JC - jar/cookpot;   JLS - large storage jar;   JM - medium-mouthed jar;   JNM - narrow-mouthed jar;   JWM - wide-mouthed jar;   L - lid;   M - mortarium;   T - tankard.

18

The very fine fabric (O7), not surprisingly, produced the lowest proportion of large storage jars and the highest proportions of wide-mouthed and medium-mouthed jars. Fabric O5 seemed to be most commonly used for bowls, but few jars, particularly large storage jars, were produced. Fabric O6 seemed most commonly to be used for tankards.

Newland Hopfields products

The principal Newland Hopfields products can be defined by quantifying the forms produced in the ware as a whole (Fig. 11a). Jars were by far the main vessel class produced, followed in roughly equal proportions by tankards and bowls. Flagons were the only other single class to represent more than 1% of the assemblage. Other forms included lids, dishes or platters, mortaria, and more unusual miscellaneous forms such as the *tettina* and spouted bowl. The composition of the assemblage, therefore, broadly reflects the pattern noted on consumption sites in the area, such as Sidbury (Darlington and Evans 1992, 41) and Deansway in Worcester (Buteux and Evans forthcoming).

Amongst the jars, those with wide-mouths were most common, followed by narrow-mouthed jars, medium-mouthed jars, and large storage jars. These were probably all intended as storage vessels, although the medium-mouthed jars could perhaps be classified as food-preparation vessels on the basis of their similarity to BB1 cook-pot forms. The narrow and wide-mouthed jars mostly had simple, thickened or slightly overhanging rims (Fig. 12c, JNM types 1 and 2; Fig. 12e, JWM types 1 and 2). Some of the narrow-mouthed jars, however, had hooked rims (Fig. 12c, JNM type 3), and this was the most common rim form found on large storage jars (Fig. 12f, JLS type 2). The most common medium-mouthed types copied second-century BB1 forms, and had near-upright or gently everted rims (Fig. 12d, JM type 2.1). The most common tankard type, also the single most common individual form, had moderately splayed walls (Fig. 12b, T type 2). Tankards have been broadly classified here as serving vessels, and could have served as drinking vessels or measures.

The bowls were sub-divided into three categories. Most common were the medium to large bowls (Fig. 12g, B types 2 and 3). These have been classified as food preparation vessels, firstly because of their larger size, and secondly because they tend to have heavy rims, similar to mortaria. The next most common category was the table wares. This included the small to medium bowls (Fig. 12g, B types 1, 4, 5, 6 and 7), and any bowls not obviously fitting into any other category. The most common individual type was medium to large flange-rimmed bowls with reeded rims (Fig. 12g, BT type 3). The only other bowls present in any quantity were small to medium bowls with beaded or everted rims (Fig. 12g, BT type 4), and medium to large flange-rimmed bowls (Fig. 12g, BT type 2).

A high proportion of the pottery, many of the wasters, and most of the kiln debris came from four features, F112, F116, F117 and F118 near the area B kiln F108. These features, therefore, were considered the most likely to produce good evidence for the products of the excavated kiln, and their assemblages were analysed in detail. However, the pottery deposited in these features may have been dumped for some time in waster heaps, and could include the products of neighbouring kilns. The kiln itself, F108, produced very little kiln debris, indicating that it had been cleared out at some point after its final use. It produced a small assemblage of pottery, which was fairly fragmentary and included few wasters. It did not, therefore, appear to represent kiln products *in situ*. The pottery was analysed in detail, however, for comparison with its neighbouring features.

The composition of the assemblage from the five features, based on vessel class, is very similar to that for the Severn Valley ware assemblage as a whole (Fig. 11a and b). In the overall assemblage narrow-mouthed jars were slightly more common in relation to medium-mouthed jars, and large storage jars were also fractionally more common, while tankards and flagons were fractionally less so.

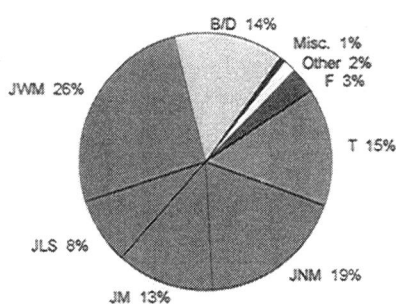

a) Vessel classes - whole assemblage

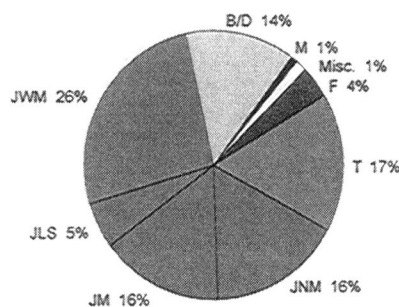

b) Vessel classes - five selected features

Figure 11: Severn Valley ware: vessel classes a) from the overall assemblage and b) from five selected features (% rim EVE)

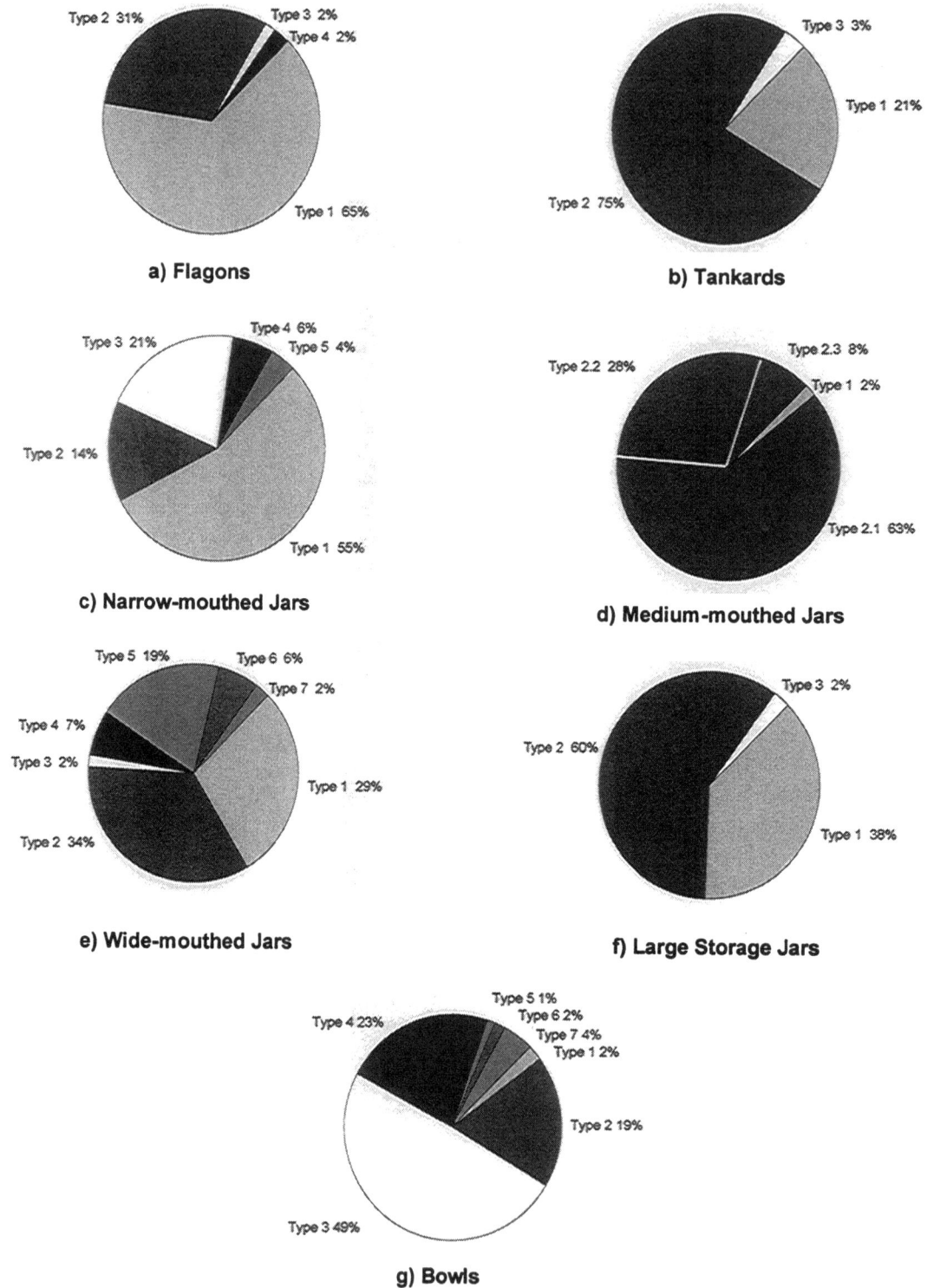

a) Flagons — Type 2 31%, Type 3 2%, Type 4 2%, Type 1 65%

b) Tankards — Type 3 3%, Type 1 21%, Type 2 75%

c) Narrow-mouthed Jars — Type 4 6%, Type 5 4%, Type 3 21%, Type 2 14%, Type 1 55%

d) Medium-mouthed Jars — Type 2.3 8%, Type 1 2%, Type 2.2 28%, Type 2.1 63%

e) Wide-mouthed Jars — Type 5 19%, Type 6 6%, Type 7 2%, Type 4 7%, Type 3 2%, Type 1 29%, Type 2 34%

f) Large Storage Jars — Type 3 2%, Type 2 60%, Type 1 38%

g) Bowls — Type 5 1%, Type 6 2%, Type 7 4%, Type 1 2%, Type 4 23%, Type 2 19%, Type 3 49%

Figure 12: Severn Valley ware: vessel classes by form type (% rim EVE)

20

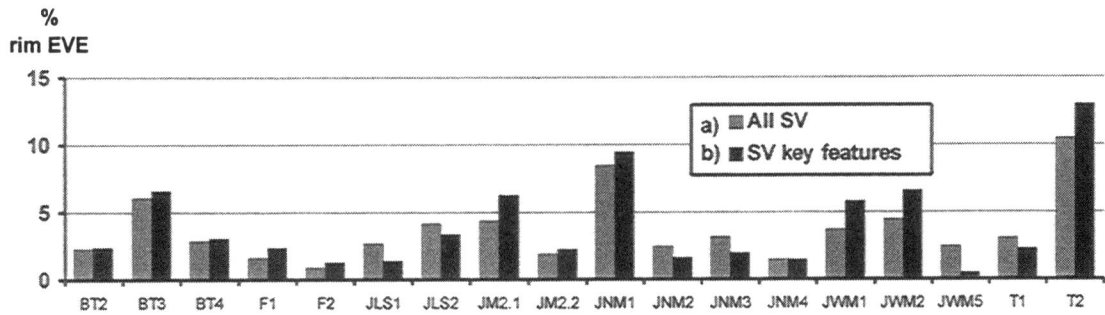

Figure 13: Severn Valley ware: Occurrence of form types, a) in overall assemblage, and b) in five selected features (% rim EVE >1%)

Only minor variations were noted between the form types from the five features and those for Severn Valley ware as a whole (Fig. 13 a and b). Amongst the jars, hooked-rim, narrow-mouthed types (JNM type 3) were rather less common. The later short-necked type (JWM 5) was even more poorly represented in the assemblage from the five features. There were also proportionally slightly fewer first- to second-century upright-walled tankards (type 1); and while type 1 was again the most common flagon variety, type 2 also represented just over 1% of the assemblage.

Considering the five feature assemblages individually (Fig. 14), broad similarities are evident between the pit F118 and the gullies. Once again, the generally most common Severn Valley ware forms prevail. Some variations can be seen in the relative proportions of vessel classes, for example, medium-mouthed jars were particularly common in gully F117, and noticeably less common in pit F118; tankards were very common in pit F118, but relatively poorly represented in gully F112. Variations could also be seen in the individual forms; for example bowl type 3 is less common in gully F116

than in gullies F112 and F117 and pit F118; and one of the late wide-mouthed jar types (type 5) is absent or poorly represented in features F116, F117 and F118, but represents more than 1% in F112. These variations could reflect differences between kiln loads, but could be totally random.

Variations are apparent when comparing the pit and gully assemblages with the assemblage from the kiln F108. The proportions of vessel classes in the latter are very different. Flagons and large storage jars are absent, tankards very poorly represented, and wide-mouthed jars are proportionately twice as common as in the other features. The assemblage also contains a higher proportion of later types; the most common forms being third- to fourth-century jars (JWM type 5; JNM type 4).

In assessing the degree of standardisation of the kiln products it is important to realise that most of the sherds in the assemblage were present on site because they derived from pots rejected by the potters. Although some vessels had very obvious faults, many did not, and these may have been underfired vessels discarded because they were too porous.

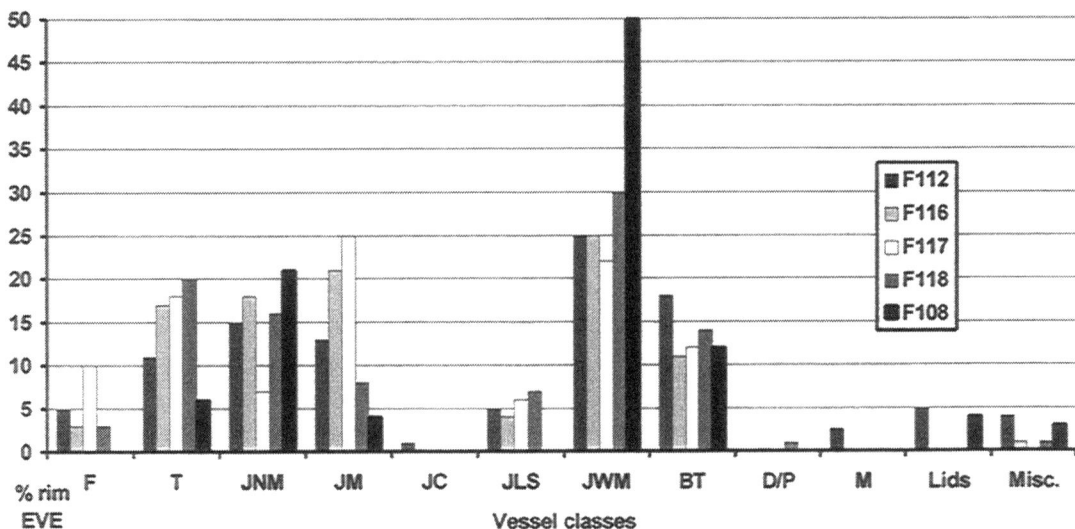

Figure 14: Severn Valley ware: vessel classes from five selected features (% rim EVE)

Table 6: Romano-British pottery: Severn Valley ware rim diameters by form type (cms)

Form Type	Overall diameter range	Most common range	Mean diameter	Modal diameter
F type 1	7-20	12-20	14	12
F type 2	7-13	7-13	9	9
F type 3	single sherd		7	7
F type 4	three sherds			8, 12, 14
T type 1	8-22	12-18	15	14
T type 2	8-25	12-20	15	14
T type 3	10-20	10-20	15.5	14, 16
JNM type 1	10-24	12-18	15.5	14
JNM type 2	11-22	14-18	16	14
JNM type 3	10-24	14-20	16	14
JNM type 4	10-20	12-18	15	16
JM type 1	13-20			
JM type 2	10-26	10-26	17	16 (then 18)
JWM type 1	16-38	24-32	28	30
JWM type 2	12-38	20-32	26	24
JWM type 3	22-40	22-40	29.5	24 (then 32, 34, 40)
JWM type 4	14-31	16-28	23	24
JWM type 5	11-37	24-30	25	24
JWM type 6	22-36	22-36	29	30
JWM type 7	8-32	12-20	17	20
JLS type 1	20-40	24-36	31	32
JLS type 2	16-40	24-36	29	28
JLS type 3	26-36	26-36	31	36
BT type 1	10-18	10-18	14	11, 18
BT type 2	12-46	18-36	27	18 (then 26 and 32)
BT type 3	14-45	20-34	26	24
BT type 4	9-26	12-16	15	14
BT type 5	14-26	14-26	20	24
BT type 6	9-24	22	19	22
DP type 7	14-28	14-18	17	14

Others may simply have been broken during or after firing. If the potters were concerned with standardisation, however, it is possible that the assemblage contains vessels rejected because they did not match the standard requirements. The ware is generally very uniform (Webster 1976, 18), but some minor variations were noted at Newland Hopfields. The abandonment of coarse charcoal as a temper perhaps reflects an increased control of firing conditions in the kiln. The remaining fabrics are fairly standard, with only minor variations. These may reflect the use of batches of clay from slightly different sources, or prepared in slightly different ways.

The great majority of vessels in Severn Valley ware fall within a very standardised range of forms; predominantly a narrow range of jar types (Webster 1976, classes A and C), tankards (ibid class E), and a limited range of bowls (ibid. class D, F, G and H). Other forms were produced in smaller quantities (ibid. classes B, I, J, K and L). The Newland Hopfields assemblage is composed mainly of the standard types, but contains a few less typical forms. The presence of some 'oddities' is very typical of kiln assemblages. They often include forms made for very local sale; one-offs, perhaps made to special order or as experiments, and forms

imitating those in popular fabrics (Peter Webster pers. comm.). Flagons, for example, are not a standard Severn Valley ware form. The two main types produced at Newland Hopfields (F types 1 and 2) perhaps reflect more local influences. Some of the other less standard forms could also be considered Malvern types. Most notable are the mortaria (Fig. 31, MT1, 2, 4 and 7). One of the small to medium bowl types (BT type 4), although found in Gloucestershire, is considered there to be a Malvern type (Rawes 1982, fig. 5.90). The type 1 medium-mouthed jar is very similar to the Malvernian tubby cook pots, and perhaps represents an experiment in wheel production of this form. A variety of other less standard types was also produced, for example BB1 copy jars (JM type 2), various bowls, dishes and platters (BT types 6 and 7) and miscellaneous forms such as the tettina and spouted bowl.

Although no detailed statistical analysis has been undertaken of vessel sizes, based on diameters, basic analysis by vessel class often shows fairly broad ranges, with clusters around one or two peaks (Fig. 15). Flagons, for example, fell into two categories, for which there are fairly standard size ranges (Table 6). For tankards, there does appear to be a mathematical correlation between the diameter and vessel height of the tankards (Fig. 16, Table 7). The tankards

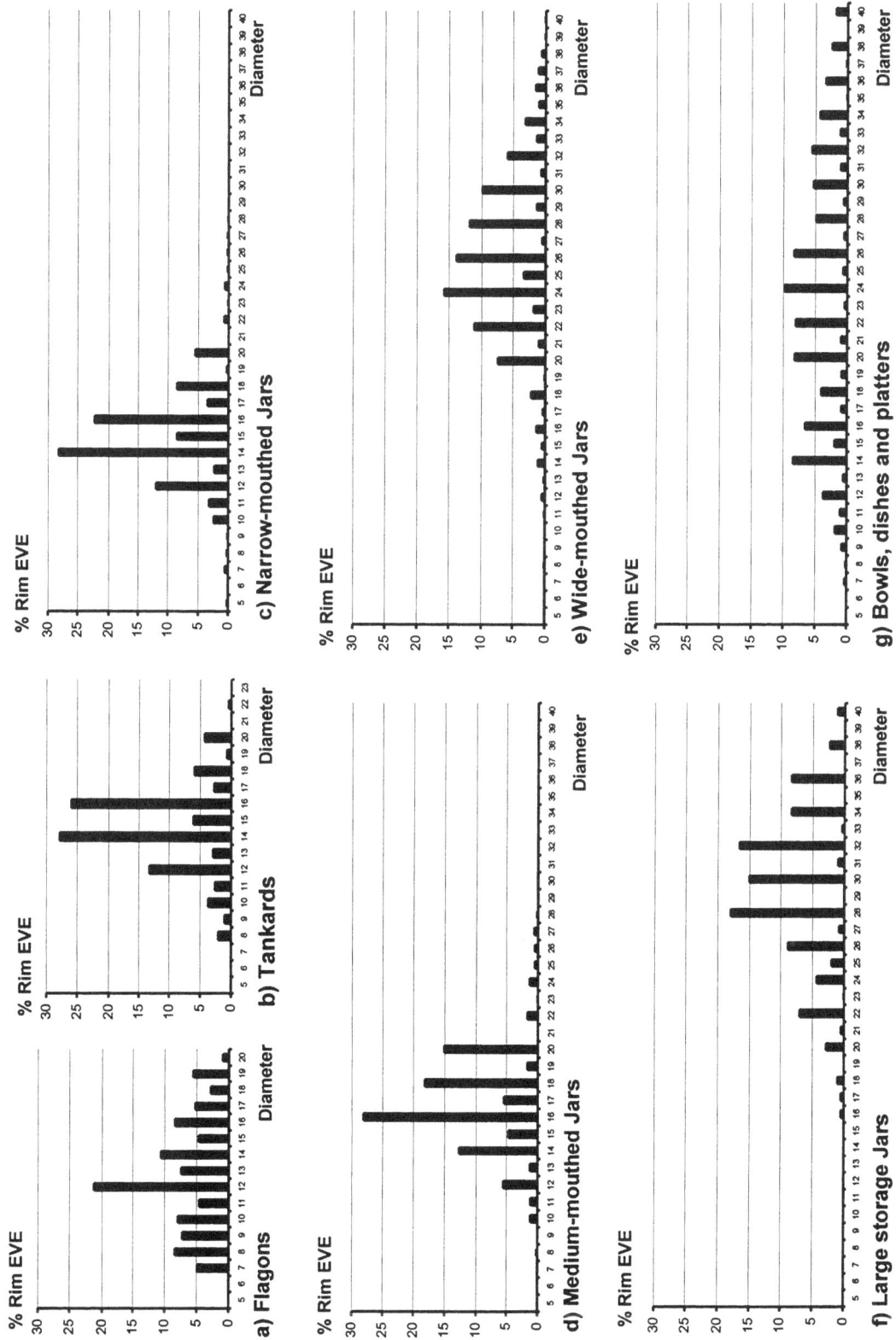

Figure 15: Severn Valley ware: rim diameters by vessel class (% rim EVE)

considered to be unusually large at Astley (Walker 1959, 46,fig. 7.33–4) had diameters of *c*.180mms, and would therefore also be at the larger end of the range produced at Newland Hopfields. At Alcester (Lee *et al.* 1993, fiche M2:C12) the larger tankards had diameters averaging 157mm, the mean average at Newland Hopfields, and the smaller tankards 107mms. The tankards and jars from Great Buckmans Farm (Waters 1976, 66–7) were in size ranges of standardised capacity, which was thought to indicate a fairly sophisticated level of organisation during the manufacturing process (Tomber 1980, 35). A few of the tankards from Newland Hopfields were sufficiently complete for capacities to be estimated, but it was not possible to reconstruct profiles for the jars, as the majority of body sherds were not analysed in detail. The data for tankards are presented in Table 7. These can be compared with the data from Alcester (Lee *et al.* 1994, fiche M6), where eight larger tankards had capacities ranging from 1.19 litres to 1.62 litres, and three smaller ones ranged from 0.28 to 0.64 litres.

Kiln technology

Analysis of the pottery allowed an assessment of the degree of control over firing. Its colour can reflect the amount of carbon in the clay, the duration of the firing, the amount of oxygen in the kiln, and the speed of cooling (Orton *et al.* 1993, 133). The majority of the Severn Valley ware was oxidised, with sherds most commonly having a reduced core (Fig. 17a). A few were patchily fired, perhaps having one oxidised and one reduced surface, lenses of different colours, or variations in colour across one surface. These must reflect variations from the normal firing atmosphere, and perhaps more rapid cooling of the pots. The least common category was the reduced sherds which are probably all misfired.

Analysing the firing colour by fabric (Fig. 17b), certain patterns are evident. The charcoal-tempered wares (Fabrics O1, O2 and O5) most commonly have a reduced core, or at least reduced patches. This primarily reflects their high carbon content. The fact that some sherds are oxidised throughout, however, indicates variations either in the amount of oxygen entering the kiln, or the duration of firing. The two sherds of organic-tempered ware are not included in the graph, but also had reduced cores. A much higher proportion of the plain wares (Fabrics O3, O4, O6, and O7) were oxidised throughout, as might be expected given that these fabrics contained no visible charcoal. However, about half were still partially reduced, so there was obviously a fair degree of variation in the firing conditions. The firing of the sandy variant (Fabric O8) seemed very variable.

The hardness of the pottery (Fig. 17c, d) should reflect whether the pottery was generally over or under-fired, although soil conditions may also have been a significant factor, as at Usk (Webster 1993, 286). Certainly, the majority of sherds were classed as either very abraded (64% by count) or abraded (32%), with evidence for surface treatment having usually been lost. Some sherds were very hard or over-fired. Most of these were classified as wasters, and the majority were reduced. Relatively few of the

Table 7: Romano-British pottery: Severn Valley ware, capacity of tankards (based on 13 near-complete vessels)

Height (cms)	Radius – rim (cms)	Radius – base (cms)	Capacity (litres)
10	6	5	0.95
11	7	4.5	1.16
12	6	5	1.14
12	8	5.5	1.74
13	8	5.5	1.88
13	7.5	6	1.87
13	8	5	1.76
13.5	9	6	2.42
14	8	5.5	2.03
15	9.5	5	2.56
4	5	2	0.16
8	4	3.5	0.35
9	6	4	0.72

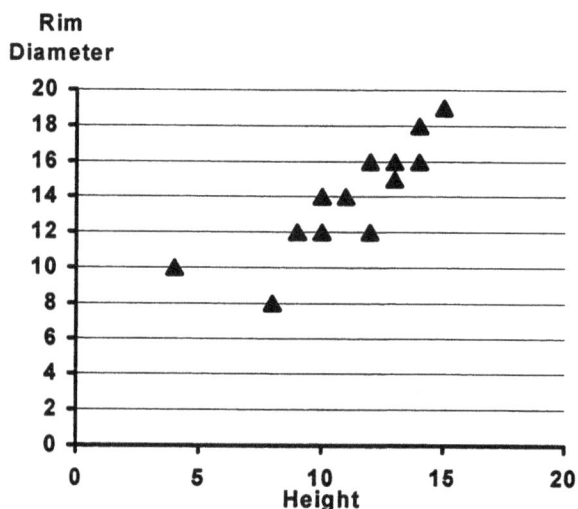

Figure 16: Severn Valley ware: relationship of height and diameter for tankards (based on 13 vessel profiles)

other sherds, in contrast, were reduced. The tendency, therefore, seems to have been to under, rather than over, fire.

Less than a quarter of the assemblage was classified as wasters (Fig. 18a). The bias towards reduced sherds being over-fired (Fig. 18b) supports the suggestion that the reduced wares are usually mis-fired, rather than deliberate grey wares. This is evident when the wasters are quantified by fabric (Fig. 18c), the reduced variants generally producing higher proportions of wasters than their oxidised counterparts. The only exception to this appears to be the sandy variant (Fabric O8).

a) Firing colour for all Severn Valley ware (% sherd count)

Patchy 10%
Reduced 6%
Oxidised (reduced core) 50%
Oxidised 34%

b) Firing colour by fabric (% of each total fabric by sherd count)

Legend: □ Oxidised ■ Oxidised (reduced core) □ Patchy

% sherd count

Fabric

c) Sherd hardness for all Severn Valley ware (% sherd count)

Very hard 17%
Soft 20%
Hard 63%

d) Sherd hardness for oxidised and reduced Severn Valley ware (% sherd count)

Legend: □ % Oxidised ■ % Reduced

% sherd count   Soft   Hard   Very hard

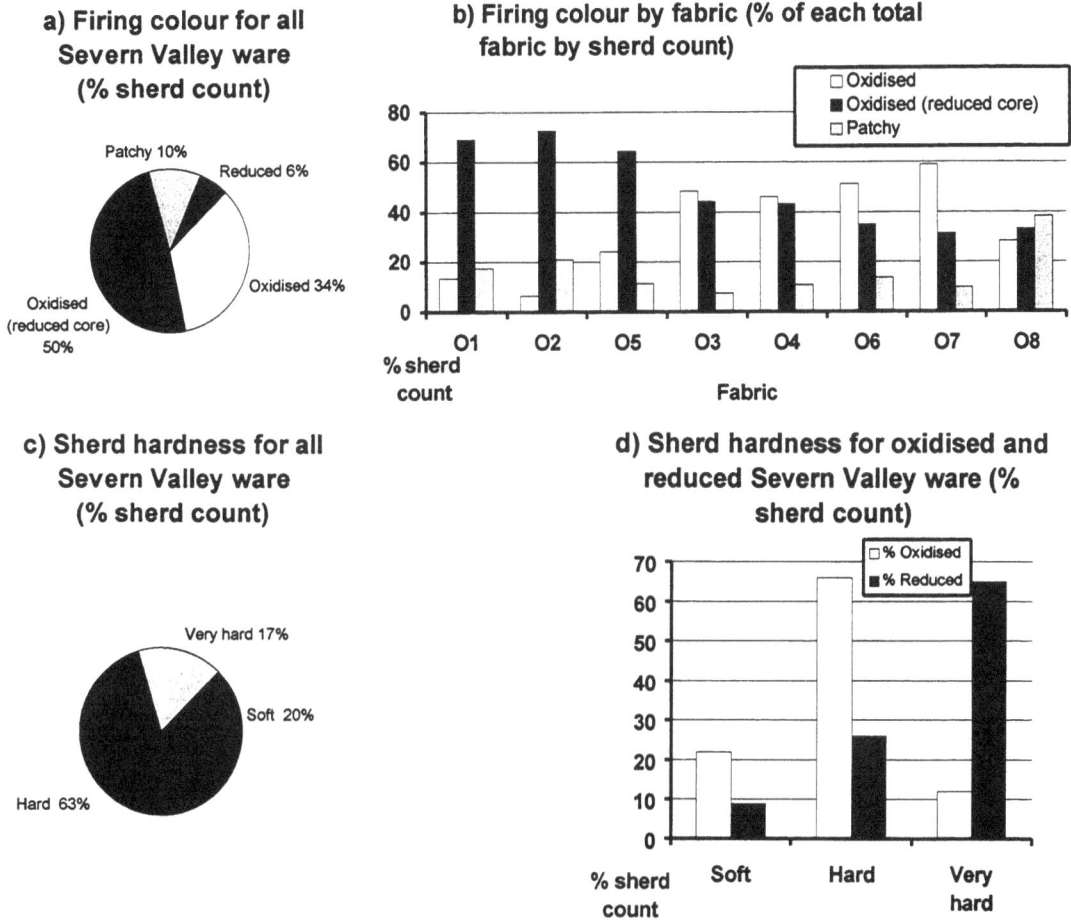

Figure 17: Severn Valley ware: firing data a) and b) from colour, c) and d) from hardness

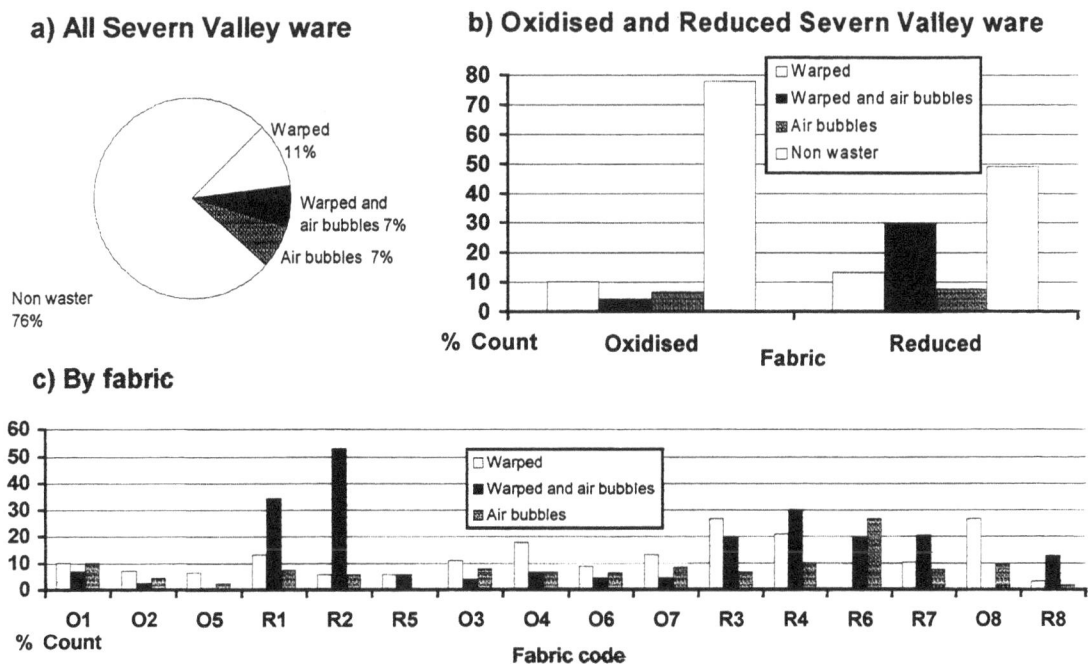

a) All Severn Valley ware

Warped 11%
Warped and air bubbles 7%
Air bubbles 7%
Non waster 76%

b) Oxidised and Reduced Severn Valley ware

Legend: □ Warped ■ Warped and air bubbles ▦ Air bubbles □ Non waster

% Count   Oxidised   Fabric   Reduced

c) By fabric

Legend: □ Warped ■ Warped and air bubbles ▦ Air bubbles

% Count   O1 O2 O5 R1 R2 R5 O3 O4 O6 O7 R3 R4 R6 R7 O8 R8   Fabric code

Figure 18: Severn Valley ware: wasters (% sherd count)

Description of fabrics
with Kirsty Nichol and David Williams

Plain Severn Valley ware
During recording, eight variants were identified on the basis of coarseness and sometimes firing: O3, O4, O6 and O7, and their reduced counterparts R3, R4, R6, R7. None of these variations was significant petrologically, however, and the plain Severn Valley wares were therefore grouped together for the purposes of statistical analysis.

Fabric O3: Plain, oxidised ware (Fabric R3: reduced variant)
Hard, slightly sandy fabric with small glistening flecks of mica. Usually reddish-yellow throughout (Munsell 5YR 7/6), but may have a grey core (Munsell 5Y6/1). The smooth outer surface may appear paler (Munsell 7.5YR 7/6 – 7/8). Thin sectioning shows little else but silt-sized quartz grains and flecks of mica, together with a little iron ore and a few small clay pellets. Includes two sherds of mortaria analysed by David Williams, thin section samples 12 and 13.

Fabric O4: Fine, plain, oxidised ware (Fabric R4: reduced variant)
Either oxidised, red (2.5YR 5/6), with reddish-yellow surfaces (5YR 6/6), or with a reduced, light to dark grey core (10YR 6/1 to 5YR 4/1). Similar to Warwickshire fabrics 025/027. It has been defined as the Malvern-Link Severn Valley ware noted in Alcester (pers. comm. Jeremy Evans). Thin section sample 8.

Fabric O6: Coarser, plain, oxidised ware (Fabric R6: reduced variant)
Oxidised, with yellowish-red core and margins (5YR 5/6), and paler, reddish-yellow surfaces (5YR 6/6). Thin section sample 6.

Fabric O7: Very fine, plain, oxidised ware (Fabric R7: reduced variant)
Usually oxidised, yellowish-red (5YR 5/6) throughout, with paler surfaces (7.5YR 6/6), though sometimes with light, yellowish-brown, reduced patches (10YR 6/4). Thin section sample 7.

Charcoal-tempered Severn Valley ware
Fabrics O1, O2, O5, O8 and O9 and their reduced counterparts R1, R2, R5, R8, and R9 were distinguished by containing charcoal. David Williams notes that the quantity of carbonised ?wood present in fabric O2, at least, indicates that it was most likely deliberately introduced to the clay by the potter. He suggests that it was perhaps intended to produce a harder-fired vessel, resulting from the separate combustion of the wood in the clay during firing.

Fabric O1: Fine, oxidised charcoal-tempered ware (Fabric R1: reduced variant)
A hard, smoothish, slightly sandy fabric with small glistening flecks of mica. The surfaces are reddish-yellow (Munsell 5YR 6/6), and the core varies from light grey (Munsell 5Y6/1) to light, yellowish brown (Munsell 2.5Y N6/0). David Williams describes the sample sherd as slightly vesicular, best seen in fresh fracture using a binocular microscope (x40). In some of the vesicles small black fragments of carbonised material are still remaining, which may be burnt wood. In thin section, well-sorted silt-sized quartz grains and flecks of mica can be seen throughout the clay matrix. Also present are a few slightly larger grains of quartz, just below 0.20mm in size, iron oxide, clay pellets and a few small pieces of siltstone. There is a number of voids scattered throughout the clay matrix. Similar to Warwickshire fabric 036 (pers. comm. Jeremy Evans). Thin section sample 1.

Fabric O2: Coarser, oxidised charcoal-tempered ware (Fabric R2: reduced variant)
Similar in the hand-specimen and in thin section to fabric O1. Distinguished by a more frequent range of inclusions, including voids containing carbonised ?wood, which makes the fabric slightly coarser. Surfaces oxidised, reddish-yellow (Munsell 7.5YR 6/6) with a reduced, grey core (Munsell 5Y 6/1, 2.5Y N6/0). Thin section sample 2.

Fabric O5: Oxidised, charcoal-tempered ware (Fabric R5: reduced variant)
A hard, somewhat rough, slightly sandy fabric, with flecks of mica and small voids, some of the latter containing carbonised ?wood. The hand specimen characteristically had a laminar fracture. Sherds usually had reddish-brown margins and surfaces (Munsell 5YR 5/4), and a reduced, grey core (Munsell 5Y 5/1 – 6/1), but 'buff' sherds (Munsell 7.5YR 6/6 reddish-yellow) with pink surfaces (Munsell 7.5YR 7/4) were also noted. Thin sectioning showed a fairly clean matrix containing moderately sparse silt-sized quartz grains and some flecks of mica. Also present are voids, clay pellets and iron oxide. This may be a slightly finer version of fabric O1, perhaps less well-made. Sample 4 was noted by David Williams to be closer-bodied, reflected in the narrower-shaped voids. Thin section samples 3 and 4.

Fabric O9: Oxidised, organic-tempered ware (Fabric R9: reduced variant)
Soft, fairly smooth fabric, with yellowish-red margins and surfaces (Munsell 5YR 5/6), and a reduced, grey core (Munsell 5Y 5/1). David Williams notes that this is quite a vesicular fabric in the hand specimen, especially noticeable in fresh fracture. No carbonised wood can be seen, either in the hand specimen or in thin section. Moreover, the variable size and shape of the vesicles suggests some other form of organic material was introduced to the clay, ie chopped chaff or grass. In thin section, the clay matrix can be seen to contain a great many voids. The clay itself has well-sorted silt-sized quartz grains and flecks of mica, together with some clay pellets. Thin section sample 5.

Other Severn Valley ware

Fabric O8: Coarser-gritted, oxidised ware (Fabric R8: reduced variant)
Very hard, smoothish, somewhat sandy fabric with scattered sparse quartz grains and the odd fragment of fine-grained sandstone visible. Can be oxidised throughout, yellowish-red (Munsell 5YR 5/6) with paler, reddish-yellow surfaces (Munsell 7.5YR 6/6), but may have a grey core (Munsell 10YR 6/1). Thin sectioning shows frequent grains of quartz, ranging up to about 0.80mm across, though the majority are silt-sized and just above. Also present are flecks of mica, iron oxide and some pieces of fine-grained sandstone. Thin section sample 11.

A somewhat unusual base sherd of mortarium in fabric O8, which had two different layers of clay joined together one on top of the other, was also sent for petrological analysis. David Williams reported as follows:

'The outer surface is composed of a hard, smooth, slightly micaceous, close-bodied, fine-textured fabric, light-reddish-brown in colour (Munsell 5YR 6/3). The inner surface, which also contains the trituration grits, is much more coarse and open-bodied, and has moderately frequent grains of quartz and some scattered pieces of fine-grained sandstone. It is reddish-yellow in colour (Munsell 5YR 7/6).

Thin sectioning confirms the use of two clays of different texture. The finer outer surface clay is very similar to many of the fabrics described above, with a groundmass of frequent, well-sorted, silt-sized quartz grains and flecks of mica. Also present are some slightly larger quartz grains, iron oxides and a few small pieces of siltstone. The coarser inner surface clay also contains a groundmass of frequent silt-sized quartz grains and flecks of mica but, in addition, there are moderately frequent, ill-sorted grains of quartz, ranging up to 0.60mm in size. Also present is a little quartzite and fine-grained sandstone.

On this evidence, it looks as if only one type of clay may actually have been used for the vessel, with the inner layer being additionally tempered with sand. This may have been an experimental piece to see if a coarser inner layer of clay would strengthen the vessel against the regular pounding or grinding that mortaria receive. No other mortaria sherds with two layers of clay have been recovered from the site, so the experiment may not have been successful or was perhaps too labour intensive'. Thin section sample 10.

CATALOGUE OF ILLUSTRATED FORMS

Fig. 19

Flagons or handled jars
(not included in the Severn Valley ware forms noted by Webster 1976)

Type 1: Flagons or handled jars with open mouths and cordons, or carinations, on the neck
The majority of flagons recovered from the site belonged to this category, and are defined by the presence of cordons or carinations on the neck, encompassing a range of variations. Decoration, where evident, comprised zones of burnishing, usually with horizontal burnish on the rim and from the shoulder down, with a zone of vertical burnish on the neck. Handles, with one exception, were strapped.
The type seems to be derived from the collared flagons often found on military sites. A collared pitcher with a similar neck cordon included in the Usk fortress assemblage was identified as a local copy of a continental type (Greene 1993, fig. 4, type 9). Parallels from military contexts at Wroxeter and Brompton, both in Shropshire, are also noted below. The type was known previously to have been produced at Great Buckmans Farm, Malvern (Waters 1976), but has not been noted from any of the other kiln sites in the area (Tomber 1980). Related forms are found in other assemblages in the region. A Severn Valley ware pitcher similar to the Usk type was noted at Alcester (Lee *et al.* 1994, fig. 22.O46). Excavations in Alcester also produced reduced-ware jars with 'dished-moulded rims' similar to the Malvern flagons with carinated necks (*ibid.* fig. 1.R19, R20). A related type was noted in the first- to second-century organic-tempered Severn Valley ware assemblage from Deansway, Worcester (Buteux and Evans forthcoming, fab 12.2) and other parallels from Worcester are noted below. A large flagon in 'buff-orange ware', included in the second-century assemblage from Hawford, Worcestershire, is also of a broadly similar type (Fennell 1964, fig. 5.34), and a parallel from Gloucestershire is also noted below. Similar mouldings are found on certain amphorae types, for example Dressel 28 (Peacock and Williams 1986, 149, class 31), and seem ideal for securing a cover in place, perhaps of leather or cloth. These open-mouthed forms lack the narrow neck typical of true flagons and may have had a very different function, not necessarily involving liquids. The Usk pitchers are thought to have been used as containers for locally produced, perishable liquids, such as milk, and this is a possible function for the Malvern vessels.

A number of variations was produced at Newlands Hopfields. Some had hooked rims and carinated (F1) or cordoned necks (F2-F4), some triangular rims (F5-F9), and some flattened-bead rims (F10).

Type 1.1: With a hooked rim and a pronounced carination on the neck. Total rim EVE 0.27

F1   With a pronounced hook rim and a carinated neck, giving the effect of a cordon externally; waster; Fabric O3. Site 2, area B, group 7, F116, layer 7061

Type 1.2: With hooked rim and applied cordon on the neck, similar to a type produced at Great Buckmans Farm (Waters 1976, fig. 4.19). Total rim EVE 4.15

F2   Fabric O3. Site 2, area B, group 7, F116, layer 7061

F3   With a less-pronounced hooked rim; hints of vertical burnishing on the neck, and horizontal burnish around the rim, the most common individual flagon form; Fabric O1. Site 2, area B, group 7, F116 layer 7061

F4   With two cordons on the neck; Fabric R1. Site 2, area B, group 7, F117, layer 7062

Type 1.3: With a thickened, usually triangular rim, with either applied cordons or a carination on the neck. Similar to a flagon or jar noted by Rawes (1982, fig. 2.2) from a second-century context at Brockworth. Similar forms were included in the military assemblage from Wroxeter (Timby *et al.* 2000, fig. 140. F5.61), produced in the local sandy fabric, and in the predominantly Flavian assemblage from the fort and *vicus* at Brompton, Shropshire, produced in Severn Valley ware (Evans forthcoming, fig. P2 F3.3). Total rim EVE 3.55

F5   Complete profile of vessel, with two opposing rod handles; rounded rim and applied cordon on neck; decorated with vertical burnishing from the neck to the shoulder, just below the handle, then with horizontal burnishing below; Fabric O4. Site 2, area B, group 7, F137, layer 7123

F6   Triangular rim, carinated neck; Fabric O3. Site 2, Area B, group 7, F116, layer 7061

F7   With two cordons, similar to F4; Fabric R1. Site 2, area B, group 7, F118, layer 7079

F8   One strap handle survives; Fabric O1. Site 2, area B, group 7, F118, layer 7079

F9   With triangular rim and short neck; Fabric O5. Site 2, area B, layer 7047

Type 1.4: With a flattened-bead rim and a carinated neck. The mouth is cupped internally, perhaps to seat a lid. Similar examples in Severn Valley ware were noted in Worcester at Sidbury (Darlington and Evans 1992, fig. 16.8) and Deansway (Buteux and Evans forthcoming, fabric 12). Total rim EVE 0.78

F10   Decorated with vertical burnishing on the neck; Fabric O3. Site 2, area B, group 7, F112, layer 7052

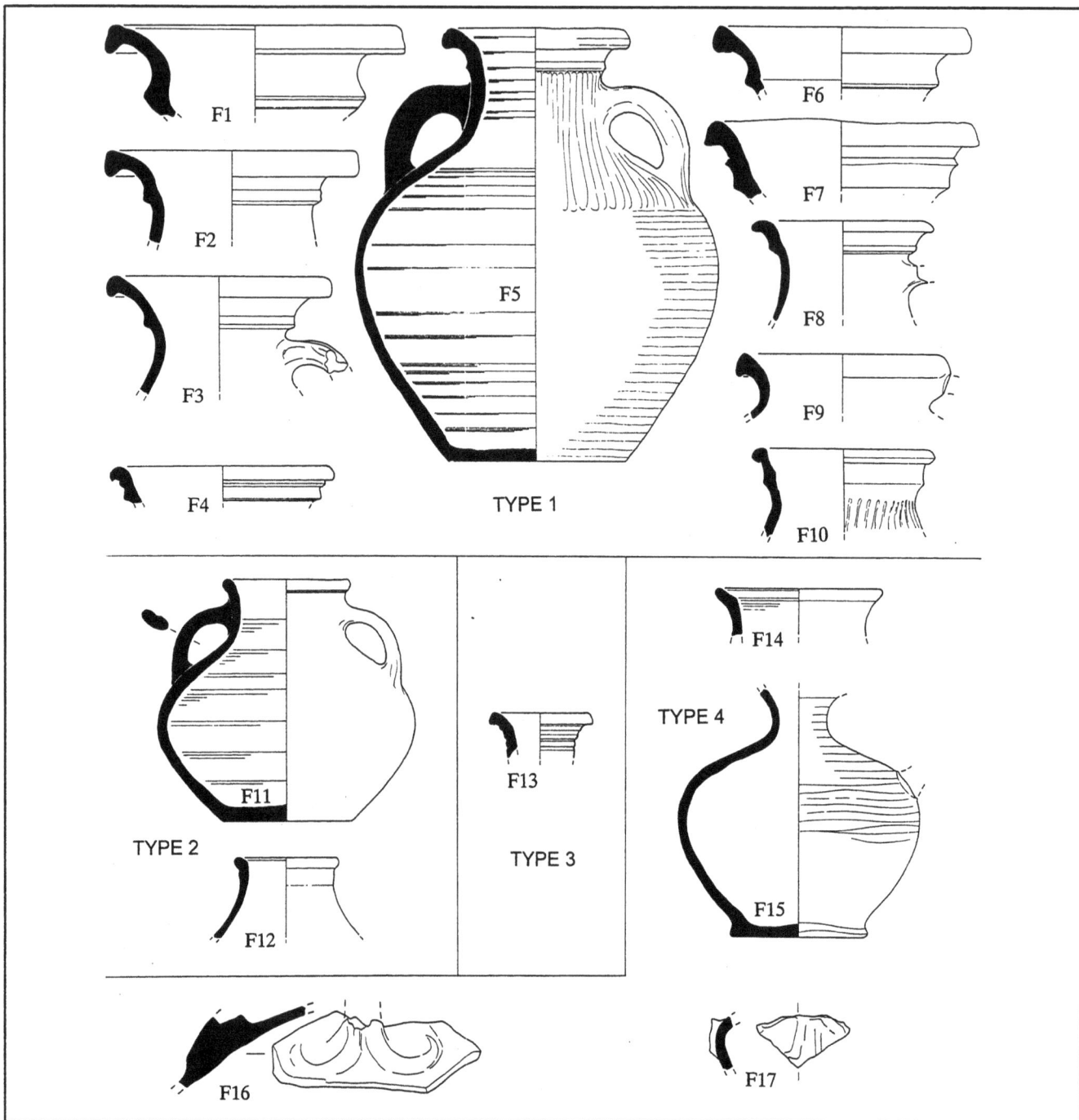

Figure 19: Severn Valley ware: flagons or handled jars; scale 1:4

Type 2: Open-mouthed flagons or handled jars with bead rims
This comprised the second most common category. Decoration again comprised horizontal burnish on the rim and from the shoulder down, with a zone of vertical burnish on the neck. Handles were strapped. These had more restricted mouths than the previous category.

Similar types were produced at Great Buckmans Farm (Waters 1976, fig. 4.18), and at Marley Hall, near Ledbury (Tomber 1980, fig. 3.21). The form is found at both Sidbury (Darlington and Evans 1992, fig. 16.10) and Deansway in Worcester (Buteux and Evans forthcoming, fabric 12), and at a number of other Worcestershire sites, such as the Old Bowling Green, Droitwich (Rees 1992, fig. 28.5), the early second to early third-century enclosure at Astley (Walker 1959, fig. 8.37–9), and the second-century enclosure at Hawford (Fennell 1964, fig. 4.18). The type is also found at Alcester. Total rim EVE 4.16

F11   Complete profile, with strap handles; Fabric O6. Site 1, trench 2000, F2061, layer 2165

F12   Everted-bead rim; Fabric O1. Site 2, area B, group 7, F112, layer 7052

Type 3: Ring-necked flagons
These were not at all common in the assemblage. They are not noted in any of the other Malvern kiln assemblages (Tomber 1980). Total rim EVE 0.22

F13   With pronounced upper ring, and poorly defined neck rings, a second-century type; the only example recorded had a diameter of 70mm; Fabric O1. Site 2, area B, group 4, F113, layer 7048

Type 4: Miscellaneous types

Type 4.1: Flagons with cupped rims. Total rim EVE 0.43

F14   Cupped rim from a flagon, from which only a short profile survives, perhaps related to form F9/F10; only three rims were noted; Fabric O3. Site 2, area B, group 7, F118, layer 7031

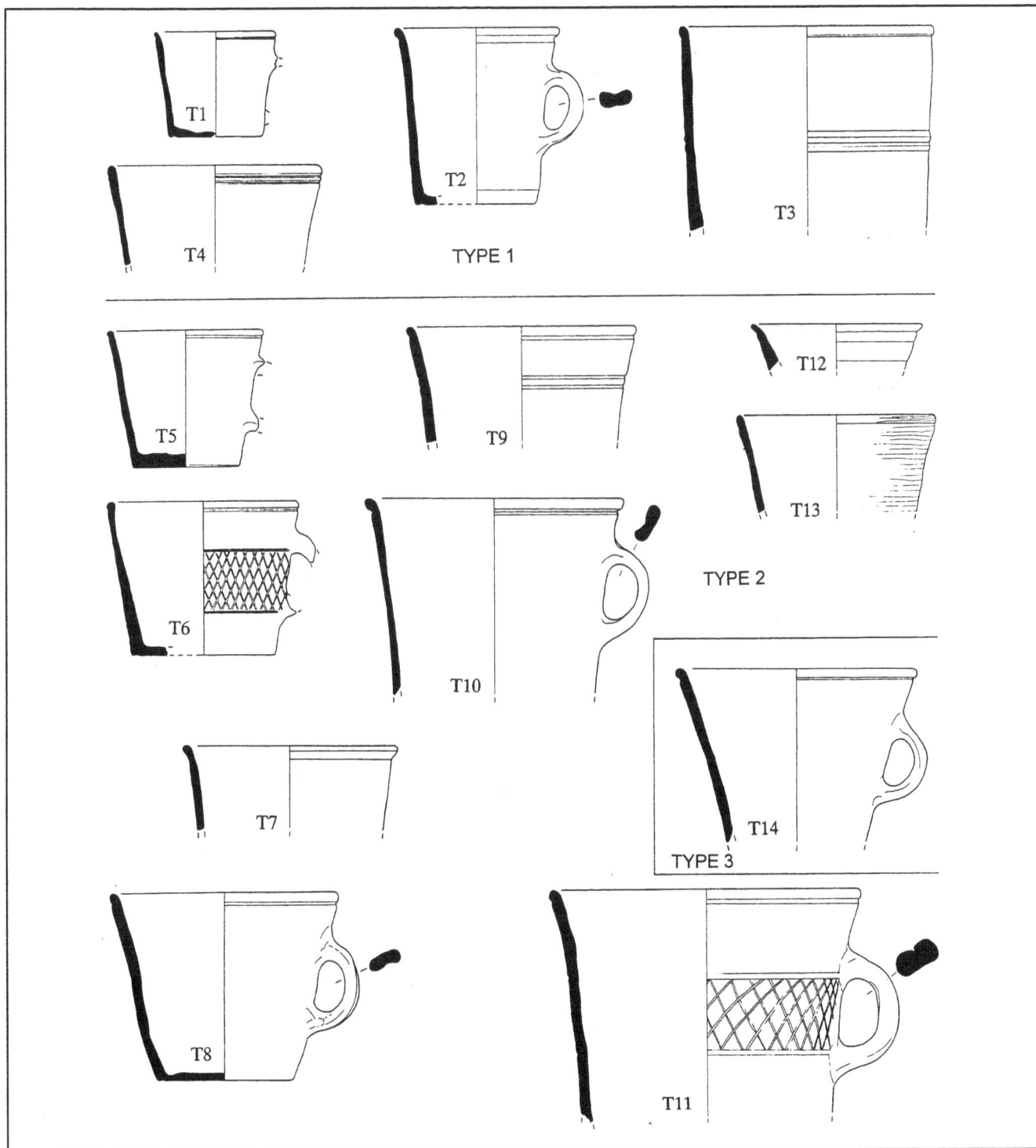

Figure 20: Severn Valley ware: tankards; scale 1:4

Type 4.2: Incomplete forms

F15   Globular form, rim missing; with vertical burnish on the neck, and horizontal burnish round the girth; Fabric O1. Site 2, area B, group 7, F117, layer 7060

F16   Handle scar; Fabric O1. Site 1, trench 1000, layer 1191 and F1178, layer 1177

F17   Handle scar; Fabric O4. Site 2, area B, group 7, F112, layer 7074

The assemblage also included fragments from splayed-neck flagons and narrow-necked flagons (not illustrated).

Fig. 20

Tankards
(Webster 1976, Group E)

Type 1:   Tankards with upright or near-upright walls and beaded rims
Similar to Webster types E38 and 39, dating to the first and second centuries (Webster 1976, fig. 7). Decoration, where it survived, consisted mainly of plain burnish, with occasional sherds having a cross-hatch pattern burnish. A number of sherds had single or multiple incised grooves, which were sometimes used to delineate zones of burnish. Handles were all strapped, with single grooves. These were the second most common tankard type, but are not found at any of the other Malvern kiln sites (Tomber 1980). Total rim EVE 13.31

T1   Complete profile of squat, straight-sided tankard, slight bead suggested by groove below the upright rim; strap handle, and flat base with single groove; Fabric O3. Site 2, area A, group 3, F115, layer 7064

T2   Walls curving out slightly towards rim, with all-over, horizontal burnish and handle scars; Fabric O3. Site 2, area B, group 7, F116, layer 7061

T3   Fabric O2. Site 1, trench 2000, F2164, layer 2163

T4   With two grooves below the rim; Fabric O6. Site 2, area A, group 3, F115, layer 7058

Type 2:   Tankards with moderately splayed walls

Type 2.1:   With a beaded rim. Similar to Webster types E40 and 41, dating broadly from the second to third or early third centuries (Webster 1976, fig. 7). Surviving decoration again comprised mainly plain burnish, usually horizontal but occasionally vertical. Only 23 sherds were noted with pattern burnish, which was mainly cross-hatched, although two sherds had diagonal burnish, perhaps rather similar to an example from Worcester, Deansway (Buteux and Evans forthcoming, fabric 13). The bead rims were usually marked by a groove, and some sherds had burnished zones bordered by grooves. Handles were all strapped with single grooves. This type had been noted previously from the Newland Hopfields site, and also appears to have been produced at Great Buckmans Farm and Marley Hall (Tomber 1980, fig. 13.184). Total rim EVE 42.94

T5   Small, undecorated tankard; Fabric O3. Site 2, area B, group 7, F116, layer 7061

T6   With a band of cross-hatch burnish, bordered above and below by a zone of plain, horizontal burnish; Fabric O5. Site 2, area B, group 7, F117, layer 7062

T7   Elongated, bead rim and vertical burnish; Fabric O1. Site 2, area B, group 7, F116, layer 7061

T8   With all-over horizontal burnish, and a strap handle with a single groove; Fabric O4. Site 2, area B, group 7, F117, layer 7062

T9   With double grooves separating bands of plain burnish; Fabric O6. Site 2, area B, group 7, F112, layer 7052

T10   Plain tankard; Fabric O3. Site 2, area A, group 3, F109, layer 7043

T11   With a band of cross-hatch burnish, bordered above and below by a zone of plain, horizontal burnish; Fabric O4. Site 2, area B, group 7, F116, layer 7061

Type 2.2:   Variant with tapering, everted rim. Decoration comprised plain burnish and incised grooves, sometimes bordering a central zone. Total rim EVE 3.22

T12   Similar to Worcester, Deansway form 80 (Buteux and Evans forthcoming, fab 12); Fabric O4. Site 2, area B, group 7, F112, layer 7052

Type 2.3:   Variant with plain or only very slightly beaded rim. Decoration comprised plain burnish and incised grooves, sometimes bordering a central zone. No associated handles were noted. Total rim EVE 1.68

T13   Plain or only very slightly beaded rim; Fabric O1. Site 2, area B, group 7, F116, layer 7061

Type 3:   Tankards with increasingly splayed walls (T14)
Similar to Webster types E42 and E43, probably dating to the late second or third centuries (Webster 1976, fig. 7). Decoration comprised plain burnish and single or multiple incised grooves, sometimes bordering a central zone. Of the three associated strap handles , two had single grooves and one was plain. Similar types were produced at Grit Farm and Marley Hall (Tomber 1980, fig. 200). Total rim EVE 2.13

T14   Bead rim, with plain, horizontal burnish; Fabric O1. Site 1, trench 2000, F2061, layer 2021

Jars

(Webster 1976, Groups A, B, C)
Narrow-mouthed, necked jars.

Fig. 21

Type 1:   Globular jars, with simple or very slightly thickened, out-curving rims (JNM1-JNM5)
Similar to Webster type A1, very broadly dated from the mid-first to the fourth century (Webster 1976, fig. 1.1). These were by far

the most common narrow-mouthed jars represented. Decoration consisted of cordons and grooves, bordering zones of either plain-horizontal or pattern burnish, the latter either cross-hatched or vertical lines. Total rim EVE 38.79

Webster notes a number of parallels for this form, including Malvern kiln II, and simple-rimmed jars were also found at Grit Farm and Marley Hall (Tomber 1980, fig. 4.49). The variant with the thickened, angular rim is very similar to types produced at both Marley Hall and Swan Inn. Examples are also known from Droitwich, Old Bowling Green, from the early second to mid third-century phase 5 (Rees 1992, fig. 29.3), but, interestingly, no close parallels were noted at Worcester.

JNM1   Decorated on the shoulder with applied cordons and grooves; Fabric O1. Site 2, area B, group 7, F116, layer 7061

JNM2   With a slightly beaded rim, decorated with zones of plain and cross-hatch burnish, demarcated by cordons and grooves; Fabric O3. Site 2, area B, group 7, F116, layer 7061

JNM3   Rim slightly flattened, decorated with zones of plain and vertical burnish, demarcated by cordons and grooves; Fabric O4. Site 2, area B, group 7, F116, layer 7061

JNM4   With a thickened, angular rim; Fabric O3. Site 2, area B, group 7, F116, layer 7061

JNM5   Thickened, near-triangular rim; Fabric O3. Site 2, area B, group 7, F116, layer 7061

Type 2:   Jars with triangular or slightly over-hanging rims (JNM6-JNM8)
Similar to Webster types A3–5, common in the second century and continuing in use into the third (Webster 1976, fig. 1). No pattern burnish was noted, the only decoration being plain burnish, cordons and grooves. Similar forms were produced at Great Buckmans Farm (Waters 1976, fig. 4.16). Total rim EVE 10.23

JNM6   Triangular rim, similar to Webster type A4, which continues in use into the fourth century; Fabric O1. Site 2, area B, F118, layer 7031

JNM7   Waster; Fabric O1. Site 2, area B, group, F112, layer 7052

JNM8   Fabric R1. Site 2, area B, group 7, F112, layer 7052

Type 3:   Hook-rimmed jars (JNM9 and JNM10, JNM11)

Type 3.1:   Similar to Webster types A6 and A8 (Webster 1976, figs. 1 and 2), dated to the second to third, and third centuries respectively. This was the only other variety to represent 20% or more of the narrow-mouthed jars. Cordons, grooves and plain burnish were the only types of decoration noted. Broadly similar forms were produced at Grit Farm and Marley Hall (Tomber 1980, fig. 5.73). Total rim EVE 14.25

JNM9   Gently hooked, triangular rim; Fabric O1. Site 2, area B, group 7, F116, layer 7070

JNM10   More-sharply hooked rim; Fabric O1. Site 2, area B, group 7, F112, layer 7089

Type 3.2:   Variant with rolled-over rim. Total rim EVE 0.65

JNM11   This and four of the other five sherds of this form, are wasters, so the pronounced roll of the rim may not have been intentional. However, a similar form was noted at the Swan Inn kiln site (Tomber 1980, fig. 7.91); Fabric O1. Site 2, area B, group 7, F112, layer 7052

Type 4:   Pulley-rimmed jar (JNM12-JNM16)
A third- to fourth-century type, similar to Webster types B9 to B13 (1976, fig. 3). Apart from plain burnish and a single sherd with incised grooves, no decoration was noted. Similar forms were noted in all the Malvern kiln assemblages, with the exception of that from Swan Inn (Tomber 1980, fig. 6.83, 84), and the type is noted at Worcester (Buteux and Evans forthcoming, fabric 12.2). Total rim EVE 4.29

JNM12   Single groove, waster; Fabric O1. Site 2, area B, group 7, F116, layer 7061

JNM13   Single groove with internal lid seat; similar to a type noted at Worcester, Sidbury (Darlington and Evans 1992, fig. 18.4); Fabric O1. Site 2, area B, group 7, F116, layer 7100

JNM14   With pronounced pulley rim, single groove, and splayed neck; Fabric O1. Site 1, trench 1000, F1178, layer 1177

JNM15   Fabric O1. Site 2, area B, layer 7124

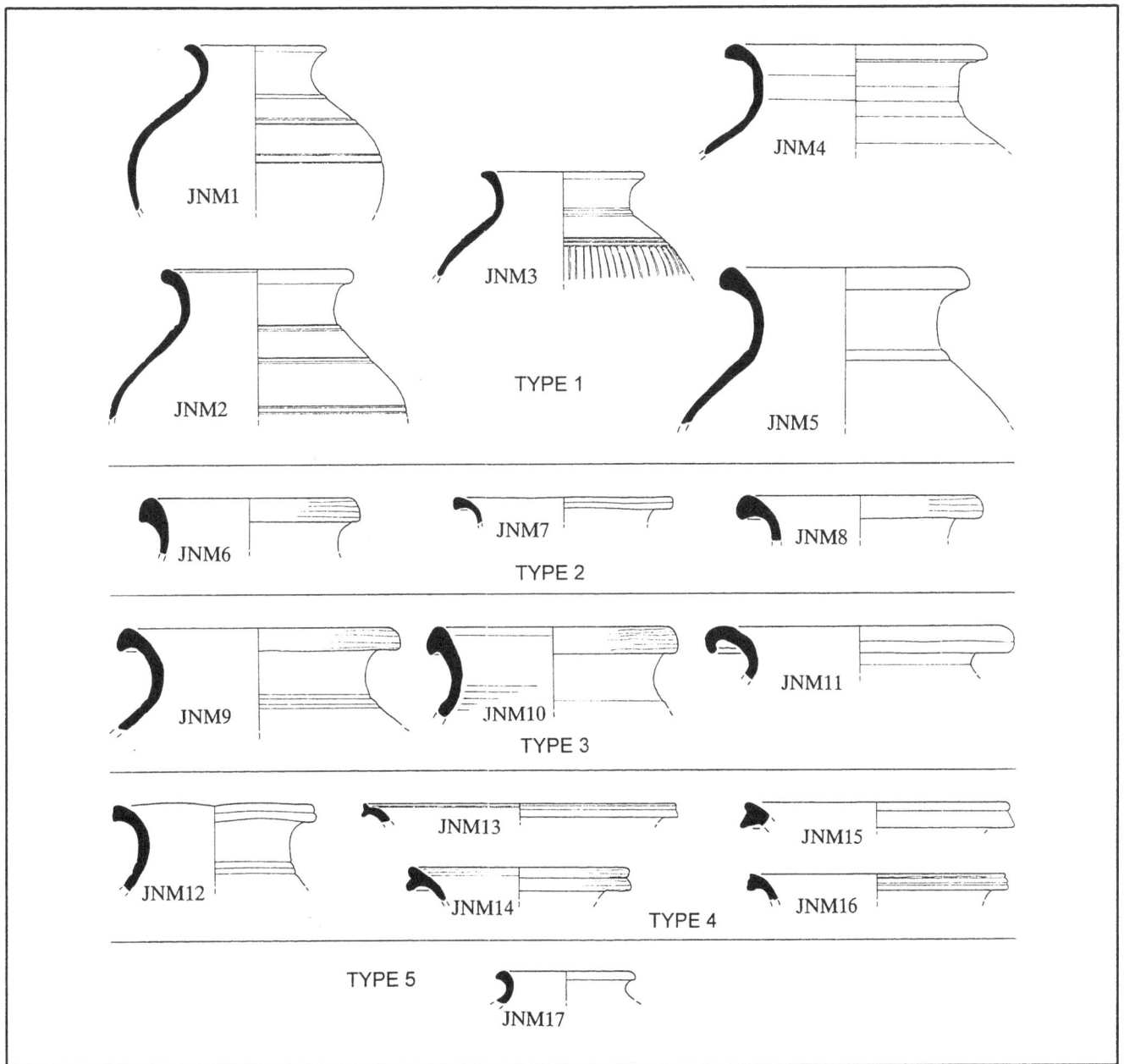

Figure 21: Severn Valley ware: narrow-mouthed jars; scale 1:4

JNM16 Double grooves; Fabric O3. Site 2, area B, group 7, F112, layer 7052

Type 5: Very short-necked jar. (JNM17) Total rim EVE 2.78
JNM17 With a plain, out-curving rim; Fabric R1. Site 2, area B, group 7, F108, layer 7112

Fig. 22

Medium-mouthed jars. Neckless jars, with slightly more-open mouths, similar to the cook-pot forms produced in coarser fabrics. These are not typical Severn Valley ware forms, and are types more normally associated with grey wares.

Type 1: Jar with in-turned, bead rims
This is the tubby cooking pot form normally produced in the handmade, Malvernian-metamorphic fabric (Fig. 37, JC1–11). Represented by only four rims. Only plain burnish was noted. Total rim EVE 0.51
JM1 Fabric O5. Site 2, area B, group 7, F112, layer 7052

Type 2: Neckless jars with everted rims
This was the main form in this class. The only decoration comprised zones of plain burnish and incised grooves. Varieties with near-upright or gently everted rims were more common than the increasingly splayed types. If these forms are copying BB1

types, then type 2.1 probably dates to the second century and types 2.2 and 2.3 to the third century and later. Similar forms were produced at Great Buckmans Farm (Waters 1976, fig. 71. 31, 33), and were found at Worcester, Sidbury (Darlington and Evans 1992, fig. 18.6). Total rim EVE 28.34

Type 2.1: Near-upright or gently everted rims. Total rim EVE 18.80
JM2 Slightly everted rim; Fabric O4. Site 2, area B, group 7, F118, layer 7079
JM3 Gently everted rim; Fabric O3. Site 2, area B, group 7, F112, layer 7052
JM4 Slight groove, suggesting pulley rim; Fabric O3. Site 2, area B, group 7, F116, layer 7061

Type 2.2: More-sharply everted rims. Total rim EVE 8.48
JM5 Sharply everted rim; Fabric O3. Site 2, area B, group 7, F112, layer 7052
JM6 Splayed neck, near triangular at tip, with groove on neck; Fabric O3. Site 2, area B, group 7, F118, layer 7079
JM7 Tapering, everted rim; Fabric O4. Site 2, area B, group 7, F141, layer 7132
JM8 With a heavy, angular rim and grooves at the base of the neck; Fabric O3. Site 2, area B, group 7, F112, layer 7052

31

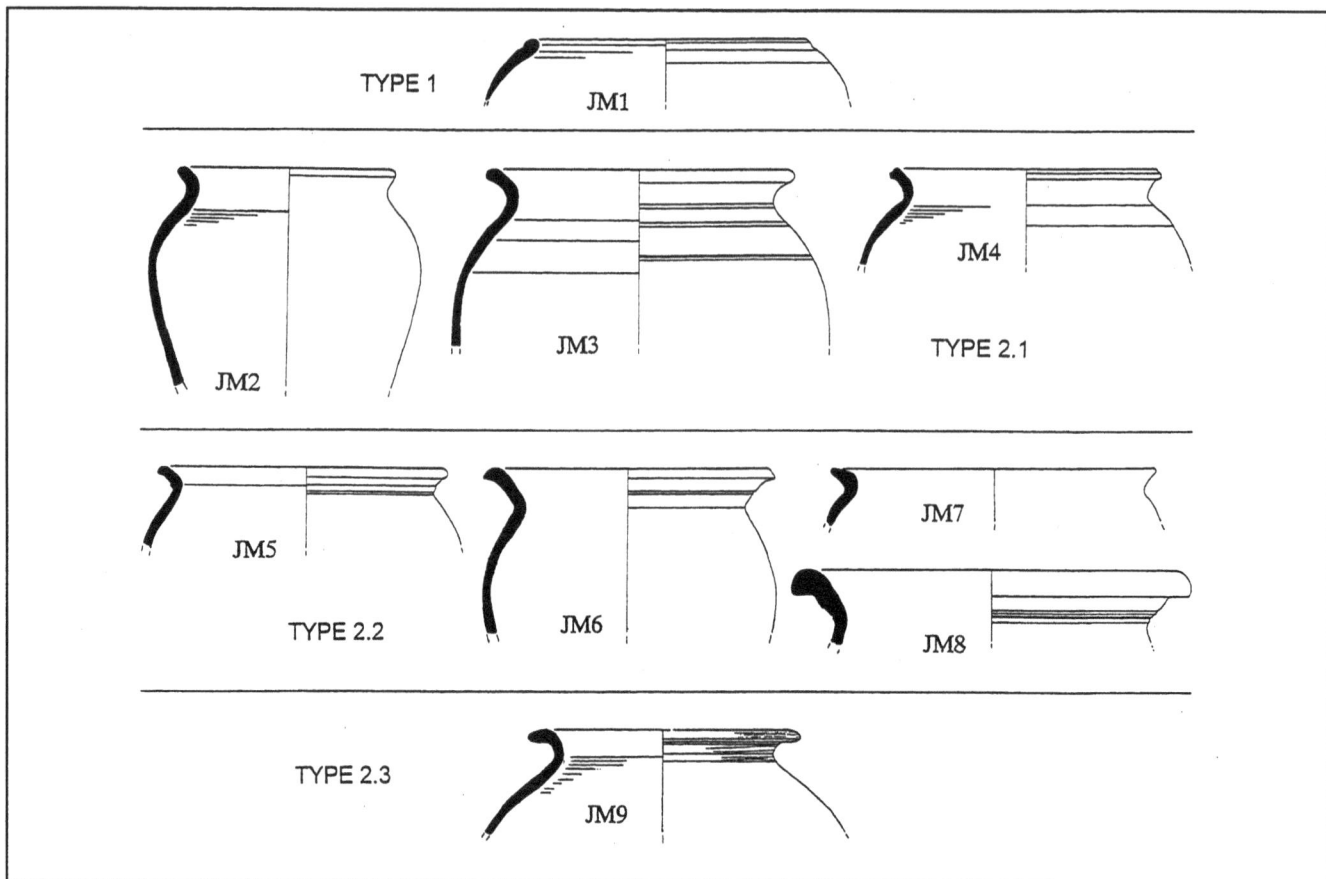

Figure 22: Severn Valley ware: medium-mouthed jars; scale 1:4

Type 2.3: Splayed, out-curving rim. Total rim EVE 2.28
JM9   Fabric O3. Site 2, area B, group 7, F116, layer 7061

Fig. 23

Wide-mouthed jars or bowls. Necked jars or bowls with open mouths. The girth usually varies from slightly wider than near-equal, to slightly narrower.

Type 1:   Medium to long-necked jars of wide girth, with rims ranging from simple to thickened and sometimes slightly overhanging
Similar to Webster type C20, and loosely similar to his type C21, although the latter is of narrow girth (Webster 1976, fig. 4). Type C20 is dated first to second century and type C21 to the mid to late second century. Also similar to Rawes type 67 (Rawes 1982, fig. 4.67), broadly dated to the second century. Decoration comprised plain burnish and incised grooves. Related forms were produced at the Swan Inn site (Tomber 1980, fig. 98) and Great Buckmans Farm (Waters 1976, fig. 3.7), and various parallels from Worcester are noted above. Total rim EVE 17.65
JWM1   Upright, slack neck with no clear division between it and the shoulder. Surface abraded. Loosely similar to types noted at Worcester, Sidbury (Darlington and Evans 1992, fig. 18.7); Fabric O3. Site 2, area B, group 7, F108, layer 7059
JWM2   Upright neck. Angle at base of neck and shoulder clearly defined; with plain, horizontal burnish on the shoulder and rim; Fabric O3. Site 2, area B, group 7, F112, layer 7052
JWM3   Out-turned neck and slightly overhanging rim, similar to types noted at Worcester, Sidbury (Darlington and Evans 1992, fig. 18.9). Typologically a later form than JWM1 and JWM2 above (Peter Webster, pers. comm.); Fabric O7. Site 2, area B, group 7, F116, layer 7066

Type 2:   Medium to long-necked jars of narrow girth, with rims ranging from simple to thickened and sometimes slightly overhanging
Encompassing Webster types C21 to C23, the former dated mid to late second century, and the latter mid second to late third century

(Webster 1976, fig. 5). Also similar to Rawes types 55, 56, 57, 58 and perhaps 59 (Rawes 1982, fig. 4), dated from the late second into the third, and perhaps fourth centuries. With the exception of a single sherd decorated with a cordon, the only decoration comprised plain burnish and incised grooves. Total rim EVE 20.97
JWM4   Everted rim, thickening at the tip, decorated with a zone of horizontal burnishing delineated by grooves; Fabric O3. Site 2, area B, group 7, F117, layer 7062
JWM5   Surface abraded; Fabric O3. Site 2, area B, group 7, F116, layer 7061
JWM6   Complete profile, with bead rim; Fabric O4. Site 2, area B, group 7, F116, layer 7061
JWM7   Pronounced triangular rim. Plain, horizontal burnish on the shoulder and rim; Fabric O1. Site 2, area B, group 7, F116, layer 7061
JWM8   Out-turned neck and plain rim, surface abraded; Fabric O1. Site 2, area B, group 7, F116, layer 7061

Type 3:   Medium-to-long-necked jars of narrow girth, with pronounced, hook rims
Similar to Webster types C24 to C29 (Webster 1976, figs. 5 and 6), and Rawes type 60 (Rawes 1982, fig. 4), all ranging in date from the late second to the fourth century. Only twelve sherds were noted in this form. Plain burnish was the only decoration noted. Similar forms were produced at Grit Farm (Tomber 1980, figs. 10.140, 11.145, 146) and Marley Hall (ibid. fig. 10.135, 137–9), both dated to the third to fourth centuries. Total rim EVE 1.10
JWM9   Fabric O1. Site 2, area B, group 7, layer 7072

Type 4:   Fine, hook-rim jars of uncertain girth
Plain burnish was the only decoration noted. Total rim EVE 4.19
JWM10 Relatively fine-walled vessel with slight internal cup and hooked rim. Plain, horizontal burnish on the neck and rim; Fabric O4. Site 2, area B, group 4, F107, layer 7033
JWM11 With very pronounced hooked rim; Fabric O4. Area B, group 4, F107, layer 7033

32

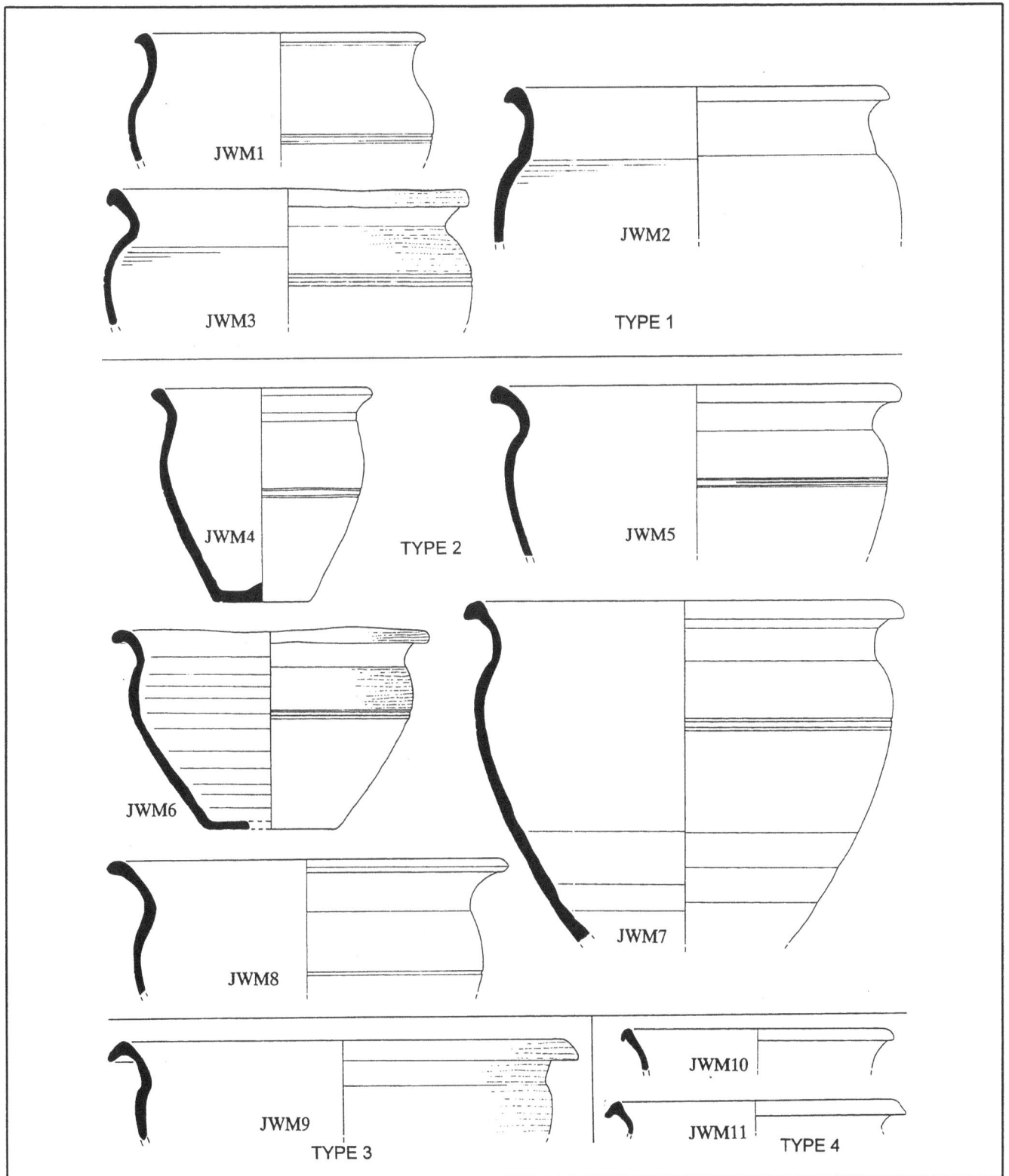

Figure 23: Severn Valley ware: wide-mouthed jars or bowls, types 1–4; scale 1:4

Fig. 24
Wide-mouthed jars or bowls (cont.)

Type 5: Short-necked jar or bowl of near-equal or narrow girth, with rims ranging from simple to thickened and sometimes slightly overhanging

No good parallels are published by Webster, but Rawes includes some similar forms from Gloucester (Rawes 1982, fig. 4.61, 68, 69), the first dated to the third or fourth century, and the other two to the second century. Apart from a single sherd decorated with rouletting, plain burnish was the only decoration noted.

These were one of the main forms produced at the Hygienic Laundry site, dated by Peacock to the fourth, or possibly third, century (Peacock 1967, fig. 3. 32–51). They are also present at Grit Farm (Tomber 1980, fig. 9.121) and Marley Hall (*ibid.* fig. 9.117, 118), both third- to fourth-century sites. No good parallels are published from Worcester. Total rim EVE 12.07

JWM12 Fabric O4. Site 1, trench 4000, layer 4011

JWM13 With near-triangular rim. Rouletted decoration below the neck; Fabric O1. Site 2, area B, group 7, F108, layer 7059

JWM14 Near-triangular rim; Fabric O1. Site 2, area B, group 7, F108, layer 7059

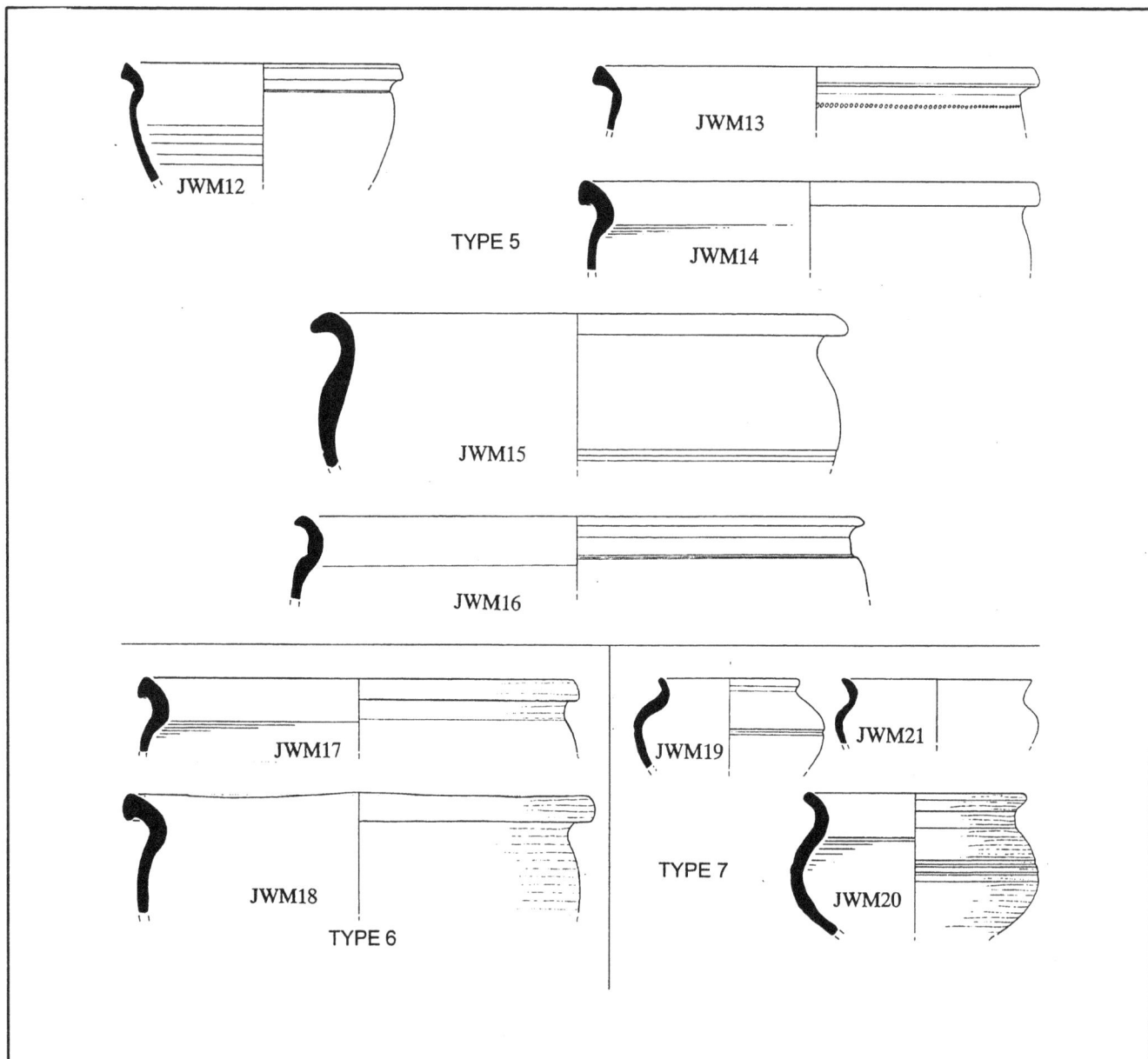

Figure 24: Severn Valley ware: wide-mouthed jars, types 5–7; scale 1:4

JWM15 With plain, flange rim; plain, horizontal burnish on the shoulder, neck and rim, and a groove below the shoulder; Fabric O3. Site 2, area B, group 7, F116 ,layer 7061

JWM16 Fabric O1. Site 2, area B, group 4, F113, layer 7051

Type 6: Short-necked jar or bowl of narrow girth, with hooked rims
Webster types C32 and C33, dated to the fourth century (Webster 1976), fig. 7). No good parallels are published by Rawes. Plain burnish was the only decoration noted. These were also produced at the Hygienic Laundry site (Peacock 1967, figs. 3.52–4, 4.55–60), and have been found in Worcester (Buteux and Evans forthcoming, fabric 12). Total rim EVE 3.9

JWM17 Fabric O3. Site 2, area B, group 7, F145, layer 7141

JWM18 Fabric O5. Site 2, area B, layer 7130

Type 7: Neckless, globular, jar or bowl, with gently everted rims
Variants of Webster types C19 and C20, dating from the mid-first to the second century (Webster 1976, fig. 4). Incised grooves around the belly were the only decoration noted. Amongst the Malvern Link kilns, only the Swan Inn site produced this form, but similar forms are noted from Worcester (Darlington and Evans 1992, fig. 18.7; Buteux and Evans forthcoming, fabric 12.3). Total rim EVE 1.39

JWM19 With plain, horizontal burnish and a shoulder groove; Fabric O4. Site 2, area B, group 7, F112, layer 7052

JWM20 Fabric O4. Site 1, trench 1000, F1211, layer 1217

JWM21 Fabric O1. Site 2, area B, group 7, F141, layer 7132

Fig. 25

Large storage jars
(Webster 1976, Group A)

Type 1: Narrow-mouthed, necked jars, with thickened, near-triangular or slightly overhanging rims
Similar to Webster types A3–5, common in the second century and continuing in use into the third (Webster 1976, fig. 1). Plain burnish and incised grooves were the only decoration noted. Total rim EVE 12.23

JLS1 Very short profile survives; Fabric O3. Site 2, area B, group 7, F118, layer 7079, and F112, layer 7088

JLS2 Slight groove inside rim, perhaps unintentional; Fabric O6. Site 2, area B, group 7, F118, layer 7079

JLS3 Slightly over-hanging rim with two grooves; Fabric O3. Site 2, area B, group 7, F116, layer 7061

Type 2: Narrow-mouthed, necked jars with markedly hooked rims
Similar to Webster types A6 and A8 (Webster 1976, figs. 1 and 2) dated to the second to third and third centuries respectively. Apart from plain burnish, the only decoration noted was a single rim

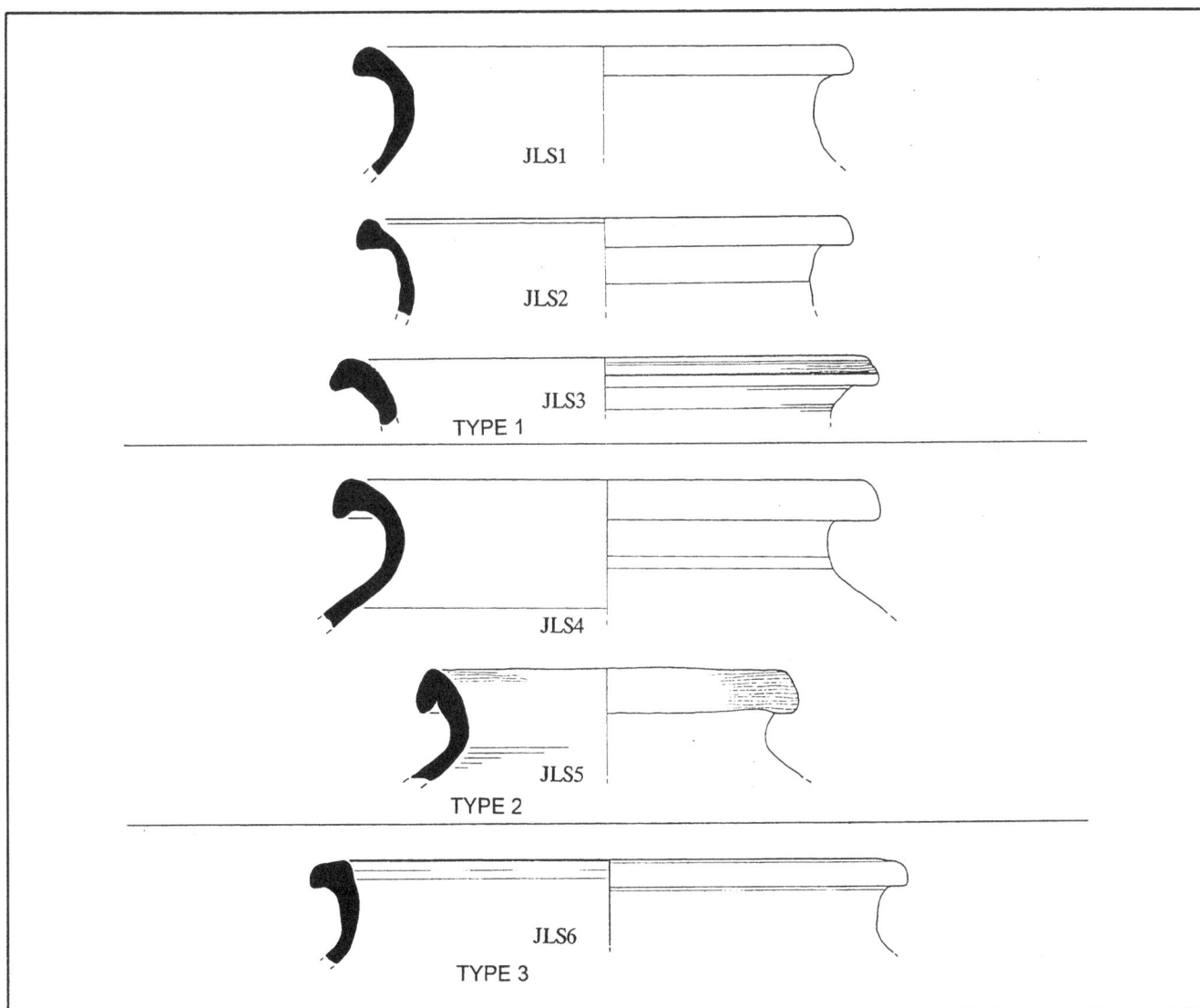

Figure 25: Severn Valley ware: large storage jars; scale 1:4

with a wavy, burnished line inside the mouth (not illustrated). Similar forms were common in the Grit Farm assemblage. They were also found at Great Buckmans Farm, Marley Hall and the Swan Inn site, although they were not considered to be a kiln product at the latter (Tomber 1980, figs. 5.61, 6.86, 88, 89). They are also found at Worcester (Buteux and Evans forthcoming, fabric 12.2). Total rim EVE 19.18

JLS4 With hooked rim; Fabric O3. Site 2, area B, group 7, F112, layer 7052

JLS5 Rim folded over close to neck; Fabric O1. Site 1, trench 2000, group 2, F2061, layer 2021

Type 3: Narrow-mouthed, necked jars with squared, slightly down-turned rims
Perhaps an unusual variant of type 2. Total rim EVE 0.79

JLS6 Waster; Fabric O3. Site 2, area B, group 7, F112, layer 7052

Bowls, dishes and platters
(Webster 1976, Groups D, F, G, H, I and K)

Vessels were classified as bowls, dishes or platters using the rough ratios of height to rim diameter defined by Graham Webster (1976, 17-19). The Severn Valley ware bowls were classified as table wares (BT) because of the fine, oxidised fabric used.

Fig. 26

Type 1: Small to medium sized, carinated bowls with bead rims (Webster 1976, type H, fig. 9.59, 60)

Dated by Webster to the first to second centuries. The Swan Inn site is the only other Malvern kiln to produce this form (Tomber 1980, fig. 15.219, 220), which is found in plain and organic-tempered Severn Valley ware at both Worcester, Sidbury (Darlington and Evans 1992, figs. 18.11, 21.5) and Deansway (Buteux and Evans forthcoming, fabrics 12 and 12.2). This class is found in Gloucestershire in first and early second-century contexts and, according to Rawes, continued to be made there as an undecorated type later in the second century (Rawes 1982, 46, fig. 7.152–4). Decoration comprised combinations of plain burnish, incised grooves and applied cordons. Total rim EVE 1.41

BT1 With concave walls above the carination, and plain, horizontal burnishing; Fabric O6. Site 2, area B, group 7, F112, layer 7052

BT2 With straight, out-turned walls above the carination, undecorated; Fabric O7. Site 2, area B, group 7, F116, layer 7073

BT3 With a double-bead rim; Fabric O2. Site 1, trench 1000, F1211, layer 1217

BT4 With straight wall above the cordoned carination, and a bead rim, applied ring base. Fabric O1. Site 2, area A, group 3, F109, layer 7043

Type 2: Medium-sized to large, flanged bowls with an internal lip and curving walls (Webster 1976, type F, fig. 8.45–50, fig. 9.51–2)
A type produced throughout the Roman period (*ibid.* 31–3). The form derives from a long-lived military type, associated mainly with legionary sites (Greene 1993, 38-9, fig. 6 type 22). Similar bowls were produced at Great Buckmans Farm, and in small numbers at Grit Farm (Tomber 1980, figs. 16.246, 17.248). The form has been found at Worcester, Deansway (Buteux and Evans forthcoming, fabric 12.2) and Worcester, Sidbury (Evans and

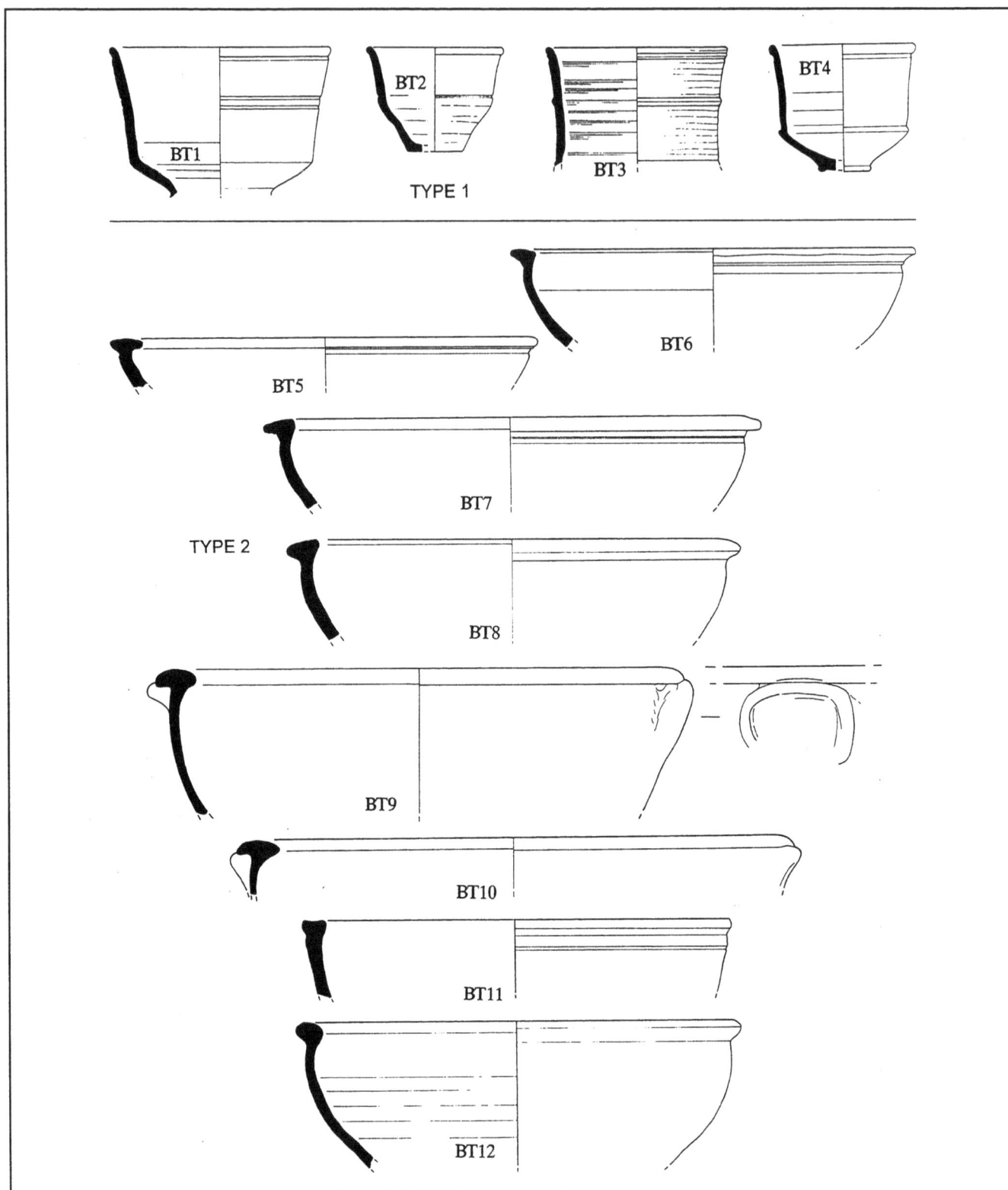

Figure 26: Severn Valley ware: bowls, types 1–2; scale 1:4

Darlington 1992, fig. 23.10). The latter was in a reduced, charcoal-tempered Severn Valley fabric, WSM 12.6, identical to Gloucester TF17. Similar bowls have also been noted at Droitwich, at Old Bowling Green (Rees 1992, fig. 30.4) and the nearby Bays Meadow site, in contexts dated to the late second century to *c*.. AD 289–96 (Barfield forthcoming). Other examples are known from Astley, from contexts dated to the early second to early third century (Walker 1959, fig. 10.61), and the third to fourth century (*ibid.* fig. 13.101), and Alcester (Lee *et al.* 1994, fig. 34.O.345–56). Rawes notes the internal projection as a characteristic of the Gloucester bowls and, like Greene (*op. cit.*) suggests that it is intended to prevent spillage (Rawes 1982, 37,

45). Greene proposed that this form had an important function in military cooking (*op. cit.*), perhaps for making stews or as a large milk bowl. The heavy flange rim would be useful for lifting, like mortaria, as would the handles, where these occur. Diameters were spread fairly evenly between 180 and 360mm. Plain burnish and incised grooves were noted, but there was no evidence for the wavy, burnished lines noted by Webster on this type (Webster 1976, 31).

Type 2.1: With a very pronounced T-shaped rim. Total rim EVE 0.16

BT5   Similar to a type noted by Rawes from Portway, Gloucestershire (1982, fig. 6.135), and to a type found in third-century contexts at

36

Gloucester, East Gate (Ireland 1983, 101, fig. 71.234); Fabric O4. Site 2, area A, group 3, F115, layer 7058

Type 2.2: With a less pronounced internal bead, broadly paralleled by bowls found in Gloucestershire (Rawes 1982, fig. 6.108, 109, 121, 130). The most common type in this group. Total rim EVE 8.37

BT6   Rim slightly up-turned. Similar vessels are noted from Worcester, Sidbury (Darlington and Evans 1992, fig. 19.9, 10) and at Wroxeter (Timby *et al.* 2000, B9.11); Fabric O3. Site 2, area B, group 7, F116, layer 7061

BT7   With a slightly down-turned rim, crude bands of horizontal burnishing inside and below the rim; Fabric O1. Site 2, area B, group 7, F116, layer 7061

BT8   Heavy, slightly down-turned rim; Fabric O1. Site 2, area B, group 7, F116, layer 7061

BT9   With curving rim, tooled underneath, and horizontal lug handle applied below the rim; Fabric O1. Site 1, trench 2000, group 2, F2061, layer 2162

BT10   With scar of a twisted handle; Fabric O5. Site 2, area B, layer 7047

Type 2.3: Concave, T-shaped rim. Total rim EVE 0.35
BT11   Straight, near-upright walls and beaded rim, suggested by external groove; Fabric O5. Site 2, area B, group 7, F112

Type 2.4: With heavy, bead-shaped rim. Total rim EVE 2.35
BT12   Slight internal bead; Fabric O3. Site 2, area B, group 7, F112, layer 7052

Fig. 27

Type 3: Medium-sized to large, flanged bowls with reeded or grooved rims, and curving walls (Webster 1976, type G, fig. 9.54–8). Broadly second- to third-century types (*ibid.* 33).

Type 3.1: T-shaped, 'reeded' rim with two grooves.
A form produced at Great Buckmans Farm (Waters 1976, fig. 5.28). Not noted at Worcester Sidbury, and only related forms, rather than exact parallels, noted at Deansway (Buteux and Evans forthcoming, fabric 12). Similar to forms found at Portway, Gloucestershire (Rawes 1982, fig. 6.128). This was the single most common bowl form produced on the site. Total rim EVE 13.45

BT13   With an up-turned rim and a slightly less pronounced internal bead, and with plain, horizontal burnishing on and just below the rim; Fabric O1. Site 2, area B, group 7, F112, layer 7052

BT14   With a horizontal handle below the rim; Fabric O5. Site 2, area B, group 7, F112, layer 7052

BT15   Slightly down-turned rim with a broad central band, large external bead and small internal bead; Fabric O3. Site 2, area B, group 7, F116, layer 7061

BT16   Flat rim with a narrow central band; Fabric O5. Site 2, area B, group 7, F112, layer 7052

BT17   Distinguished by an external groove just below the rim. A similar type is noted from Wroxeter (Timby *et al.* 2000, B16.21); Fabric O3. Site 2, area B, group 7, F116, layer 7061

BT18   Stubby, only slightly thickened variant; Fabric O5. Site 2, area B, group 7, F112, layer 7031

BT19   Wall more upright than type BT19, rounded internal bead and external grooves below the rim; Fabric O4. Site 2, area B, group 7, F118, layer 7031

Type 3.2: Slightly T-shaped reeded rim with two grooves. Total rim EVE 0.56
BT20   Very fragmentary and abraded; Fabric O5. Site 2, area C, group 9, layer 7041

BT21   With very pronounced central ridge; Fabric O5. Site 2, area B, group 7, layer 7072

BT22   With two grooves inside rim; Fabric O5. Site 2, area B, layer 7047

Type 3.3: Slightly T-shaped, reeded rim with three grooves. Total rim EVE 0.22
BT23   Markedly down-turned rim, grooves on shoulder; the illustrated example is deliberately perforated before firing, perhaps for attaching a handle that became detached during firing; Fabric O1. Site 2, area B, group 7, F118, layer 7079

Type 3.4: Flange rims with two grooves
Flat rim, usually with a broad central band. Similar to types produced at Great Buckmans Farm (Waters 1976, fig. 5.28). No parallels were found at Worcester, Sidbury, but similar forms were noted at Worcester, Deansway (Buteux and Evans forthcoming, fabric 12), and, as an unstratified form (318), from Droitwich, Bays Meadow (Barfield forthcoming). They probably date from the second to third centuries. The rim on some is reminiscent of characteristically Flavian/Trajanic military reed-rim types, from which they, and perhaps the other Severn Valley reed-rim bowls, may have evolved. The third most common type in this group. Total rim EVE 3.64

BT24   Similar to Webster type G56 which is dated to the third century and noted at Whitchurch and Wroxeter (Webster 1976, fig. 9); Fabric O1. Site 2, area B, group 7, F112, layer 7052

BT25   Elongated, up-turned flange, thickened at the tip; Fabric O1. Site 2, area C, group 9, layer 7041

BT26   Elongated flange, thickened at the tip. broad central band and two shallow grooves. Perhaps a late first to early second-century type, similar to Webster type G54 (Webster 1976, fig. 8); Fabric O5. Site 2, area B, group 7, F117, layer 7062

BT27   Small bowl or dish, with a flat rim with a narrow central band; Fabric O4. Site 2, area B, group 7, F112, layer 7052

BT28   Frilled, pie-crust, edge to flange; broadly similar to types noted at Droitwich (Rees 1992, fig. 30.11) and Alcester (Lee *et al.* 1994, fig. 35.O.361, O.362), which seem to be associated with third and fourth-century contexts; Fabric O6. Site 2, area B, group 7, layer 7072

Fig. 28

Type 3.5: Small bowl, with markedly up-turned rim, two grooves with a broad central band
Similar to Webster type G58, which he dates to the second to third centuries (Webster 1976, 33, fig. 9). The example from Astley which is illustrated by Webster, however, is a collander rather than a flat-based bowl. Total rim EVE 0.50
BT29   Fabric O4. Site 2, area A, group 3, F115, layer 7058

Type 3.6: Flange rim with three grooves. Total rim EVE 0.13
BT30   A tapering, slightly down-turned rim; Fabric O6. Site 2, Area A, group 3, F115, layer 7058

Type 3.7: Flange rim with internal lid seat. Total rim EVE 0.49
BT31   Pulley rim with marked, internal lid seat; Fabric O3. Site 2, area B, group 7, F108, layer 7112

Type 3.8: Bowl with curved walls and flange rim with single groove
A similar vessel is dated to the third century by Webster (1976, fig. 8.57). Similar forms were produced at Great Buckmans Farm, and were found in small quantities at Grit Farm (Tomber 1980, fig. 17.252, 257, 259) and Marley Hall (*ibid.* fig. 17.256)

Type 3.9: Heavy, up-turned flange higher than the inturned bead rim. The fourth most common type in this group. Total rim EVE 3.21
BT32   Small internal bead. No good parallels from Worcester, Sidbury or Deansway, but similar to a type noted in a mid third to late fourth-century context at Droitwich, Old Bowling Green (Rees 1992, fig. 30.8); Fabric O3. Site 2, area B, group 7, F108, layer 7059

BT33   With pie-crust rim; Fabric O6. EV1, F103, layer 102

BT34   Rounded flange; Fabric O5. Site 2, area B, group 7, F117, layer 7062

BT35   Fabric O5. Site 2, area B, layer, layer 7047

Type 3.10: Straight-sided, flanged bowl with pulley rim. Total rim EVE 0.56
BT36   T-shaped rim, with a single groove, very similar to a Sidbury example (Darlington and Evans 1992, fig. 18.4). Decorated internally with incised cross-hatch. A fragmentary, flange rim with similar decoration is illustrated in the Droitwich, Old Bowling Green archive form series (HWCM 600, form 95.034, 536) but is not included in the publication and the fabric is not noted; Fabric O4. Site 2, area B, group 7, F112, layer 7052

Type 3.11: With flange lower than the in-turned bead rim. The second most common type in this group. Total rim EVE 4.9

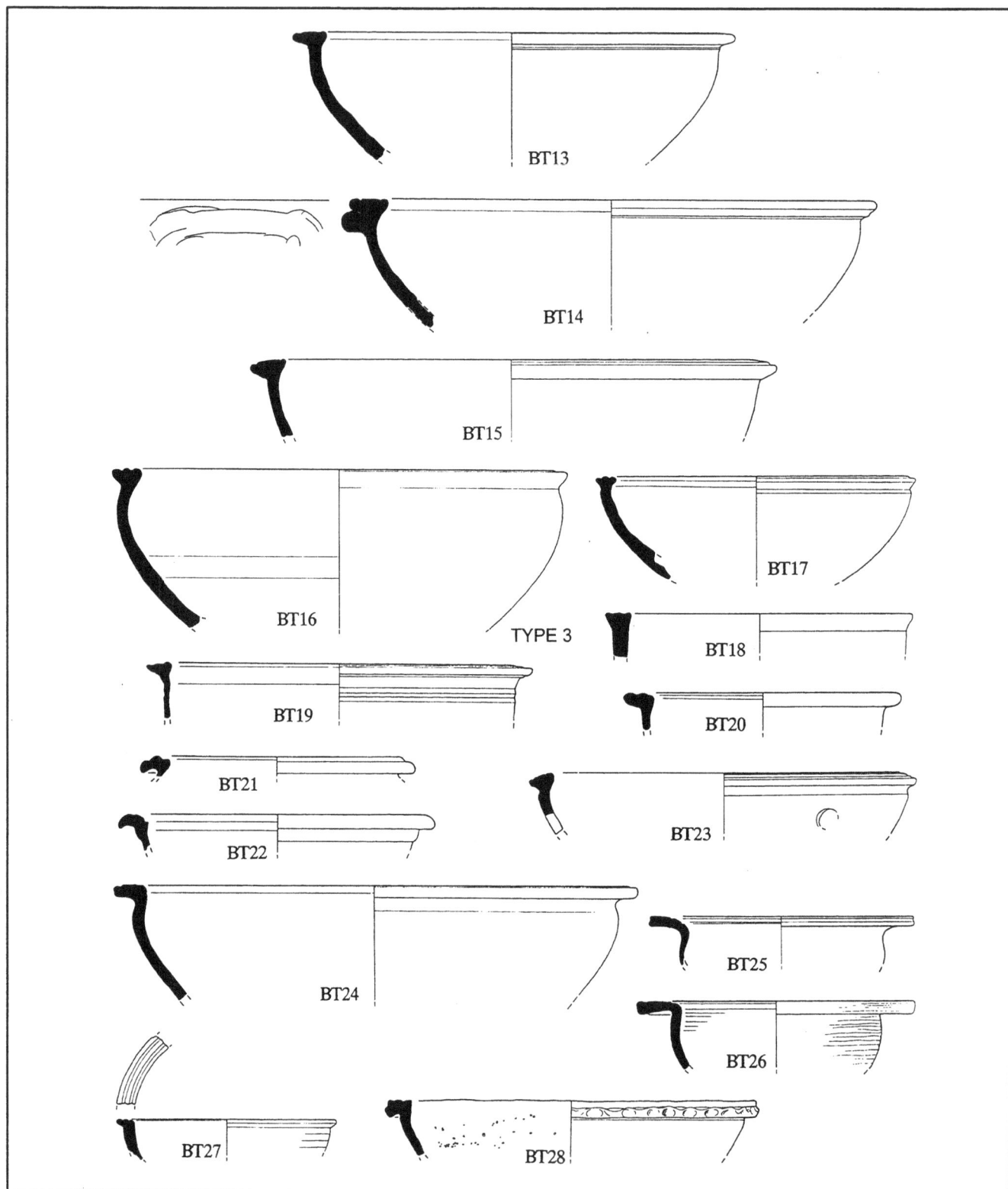

Figure 27: Severn Valley ware: bowls, type 3, BT13–28; scale 1:4

BT37 Flange folded over; Fabric O7. Site 2, area B, group 7, F116, layer 7061

BT38 Waster, slightly warped; Fabric O1. Site 2, area B, layer 7047

BT39 Variant with down-sloping, T-shaped rim, giving the effect of a small external flange; Fabric O4. Site 2, area A, group 3, F125, layer 7109

BT40 With pie-crust decoration on tip of flange; very abraded; Fabric O4. EV1, F119, layer 118

BT41 Fabric O1. Site 1, trench 1000, layer 1191

Type 3.12: With flange lower than upright bead. Total rim EVE 1.25

BT42 With stubby flange and poorly defined bead; Fabric R8. Site 2, area B, group 7, F118, layer 7031

BT43 With down-curving flange and ring base; Fabric O6. Site 2, area B, group 7, F117, layer 7062

Fig. 29

Type 3.13: Bowls with flanged rims, external grooves, and curving walls
A variety of forms with no good parallels found from the other Malvern kilns, or from Worcester. Total rim EVE 1.07

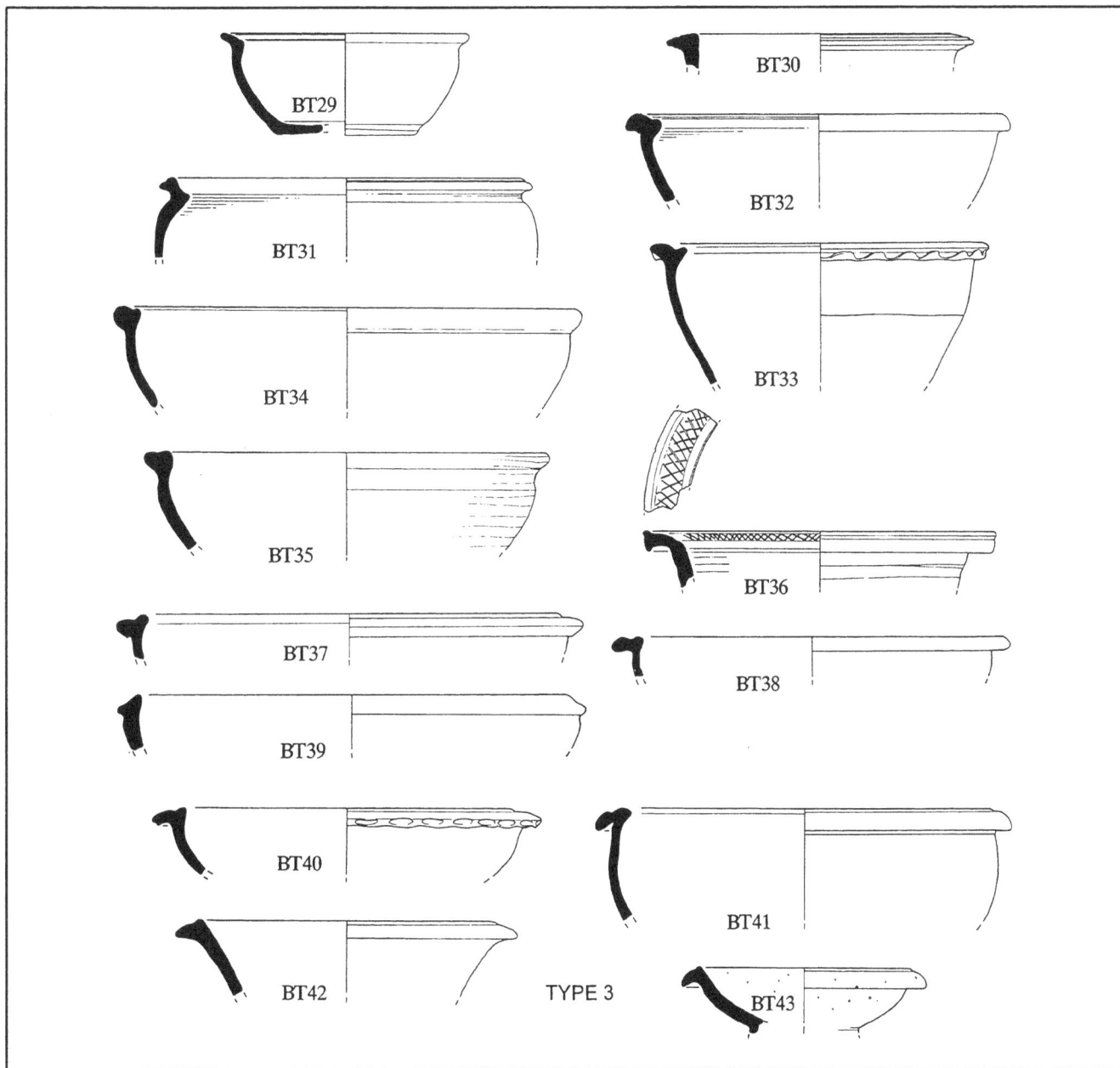

Figure 28: Severn Valley ware: bowls, type 3, BT29–43; scale 1:4

BT44   Bead-and-flange rim with grooves below; Fabric O3. Site 2, area B, group 7, F115, layer 7058

BT45   Small flange rim, exaggerated by external groove, and internal lip; Fabric O4. Site 2, area B, group 7, F116, layer 7061

BT46   Very angular internal projection; Fabric O6. Site 2, area B, group 7, F118, layer 7079

BT47   Up-turned flange rim with single groove, heavy internal bead and small external flange; Fabric O4. Site, area B, group 7, F112, layer 7052

BT48   Pronounced internal bead formed by pushing rim in, and straight walls; Fabric O3. Site 2, area B, group 7, F116, layer 7069

Type 3.14: Bowls with decorated flanges
BT49   Fabric R5. EV4, F407, layer 406.

Type 4:   Small to medium-sized, hemispherical bowls with beaded or everted rims (Webster 1976, type D)
The type is broadly dated by Webster to the second to fourth centuries (*ibid.* fig. 7.34–6)

Type 4.1: Bead-rimmed bowls with in-turned mouths. Total rim EVE 9.02
No exact parallels are published by Webster or Rawes, although the form is known from other Malvern kilns at Great Buckmans Farm (Waters 1976, fig. 3.11, 12) and Marley Hall (Tomber 1980,

fig. 16.237). The form was found at the Worcester, Sidbury site (Darlington and Evans 1992, fig. 19.1, 4), but not at Deansway. Similar types are known from a third-century context from Wroxeter (Timby *et al.* 2000, fig. 155. B7.12), and from Alcester (Lee *et al.* 1994, fig. 36. O.364, O.367, O.369, O.374)

BT50   Bead clearly defined, plain horizontal burnishing externally; Fabric O1. Site 2, area B, group 7, F112, layer 7052

BT51   Fabric O3. Site 2, area B, group 7, F112, layer 7061

BT52   With poorly defined bead; Fabric O5. Site 2, F116, layer 7061

BT53   With a heavier rim; Fabric O3. Site 2, area B, group 7, F112, layer 7052

BT54   With more upright and elongated bead rim, clearly defined by an external groove; Fabric O1. Site 2, area B, group 7, F116, layer 7061

BT55   Variant, with two grooves externally, suggesting bead rim, and internal lid seat; similar to a type noted from Worcester, Sidbury (Darlington and Evans 1992, fig. 19.6); horizontal burnish externally; Fabric O7. Site 2, area B, group 7, F112, layer 7052

BT56   Slight bead suggested by external grooves; Fabric O3. Site 2, area B, group 7, F116, layer 7061

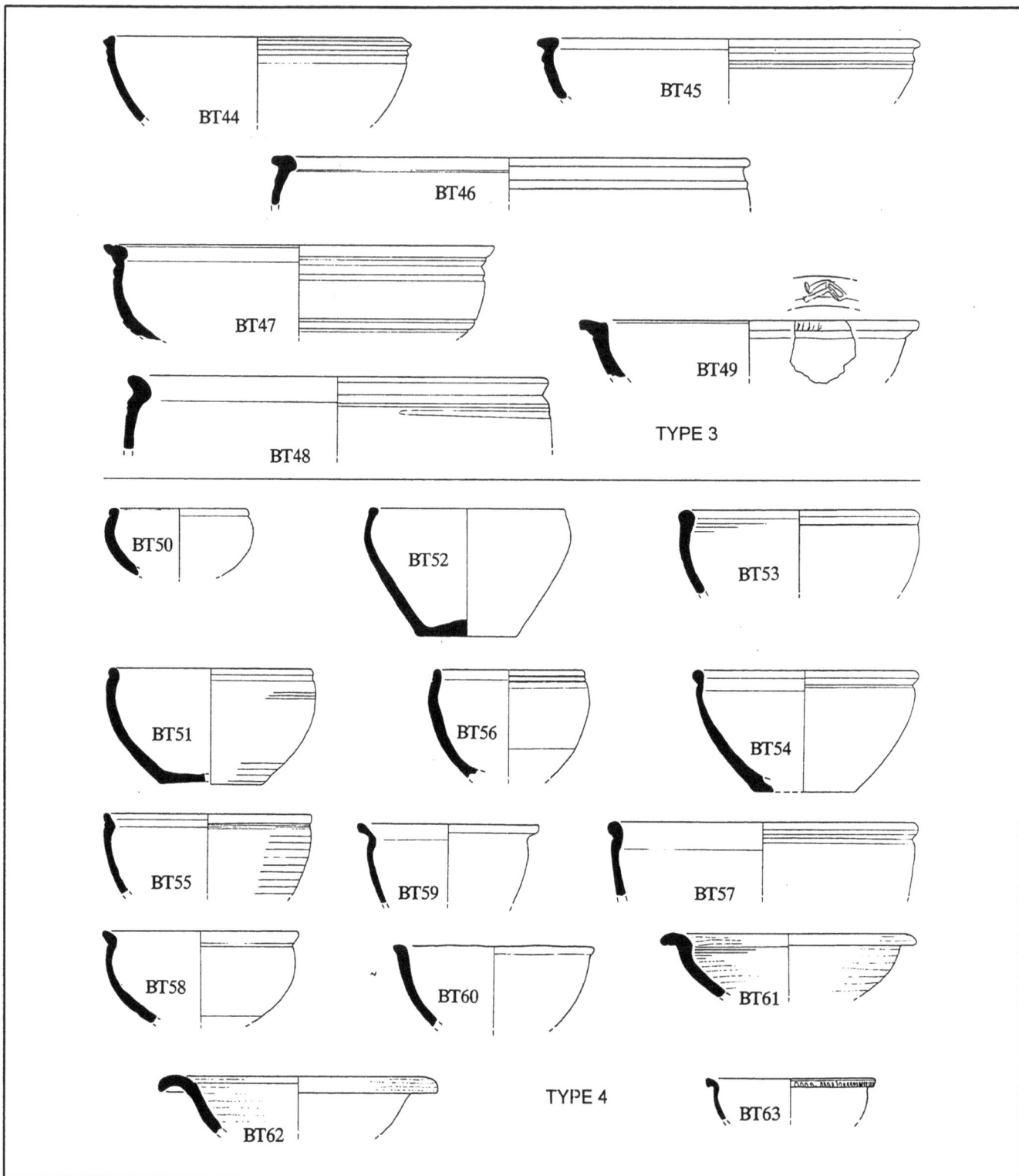

Figure 29: Severn Valley ware: bowls, type 3, BT44–9, type 4; scale 1:4

BT57 With horizontal burnishing externally; Fabric O3. Site 2, area B, group 7, F116, layer 7061

Type 4.2: Bowls with up-turned flange rims

Webster (1976) types D34–36. An example from Gloucestershire is identified by Rawes as a Malvern, rather than a Gloucestershire, type (Rawes 1982, fig. 5.90). This is a form also produced at Great Buckmans Farm (Waters 1976, fig. 3.10,11), Grit Farm and the Swan Inn site (Tomber 1980, fi. 16.236). It is found at Worcester, Sidbury (Darlington and Evans 1992, fig. 19.5), at Droitwich, from a mid third to late fourth-century context (Rees 1992, fig. 30.21), and at Alcester (Lee *et al.* 1994, fig. 36.O.365, O.366, O.370, O.371). Total rim EVE 4.1

BT58 Up-turned flange rim (Buteux and Evans forthcoming, fabric 12); Fabric O4. Site 2, area B, group 7, F116, layer 7061

BT59 With an elongated flange, similar to Webster type D36; Fabric O5. Site 2, area B, layer 7124

BT60 Stubbier rim, on a less hemispherical profile; Fabric O1. Site 2, area B, group 7, F116, layer 7061

BT61 Hemispherical bowl with gently up-turned, curving flange rim; Fabric O4. Site 2, area B, group 7, layer 7072

Type 4.3: Bowls with fine, up-turned flanges. Total rim EVE 0.43

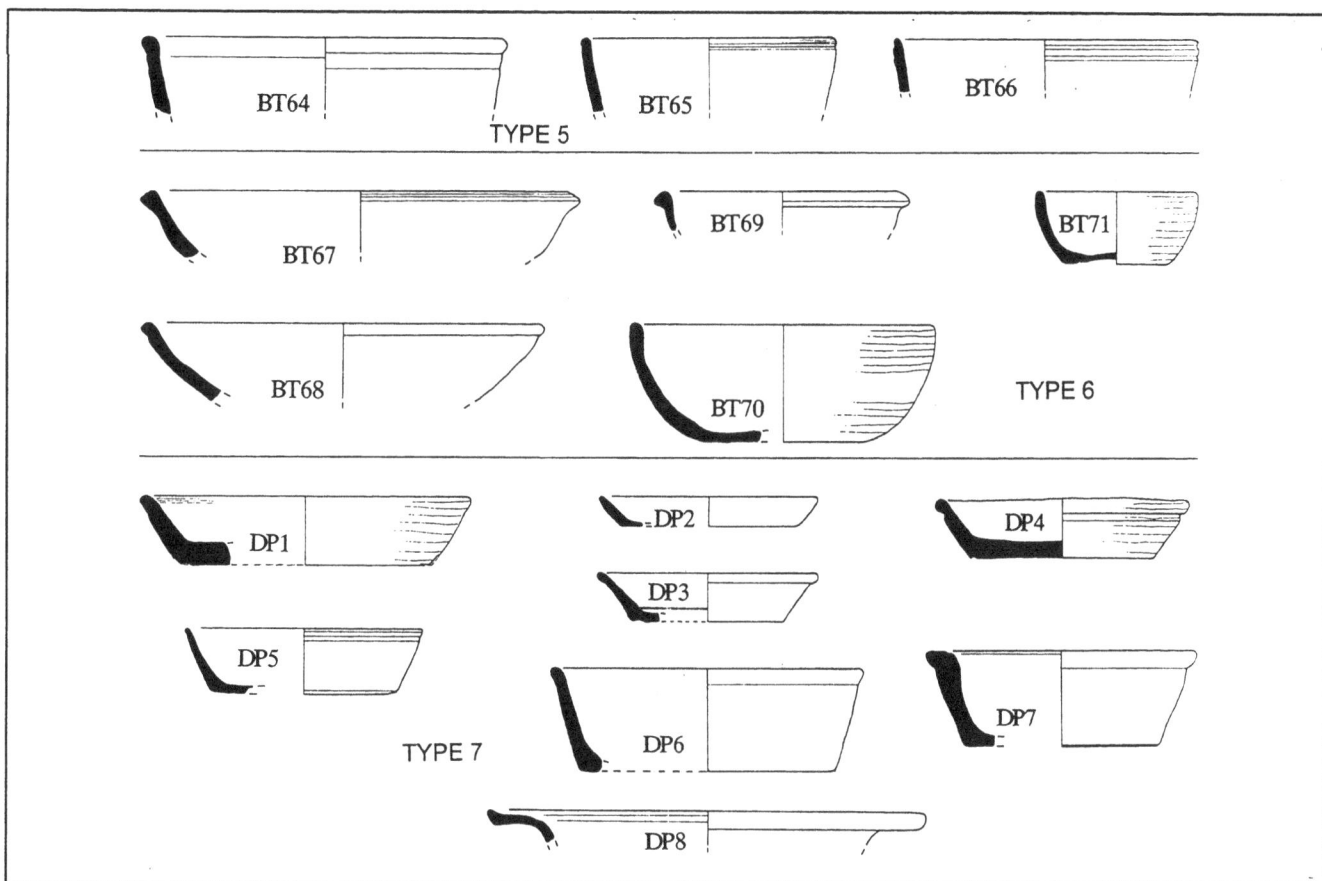

Figure 30: Severn Valley ware: bowls, dishes and platters, types 5–7; scale 1:4

BT62 Flange curving upwards, with internal lid seat; Fabric O1. Site 2, area B, group 7, F116, layer 7061

BT63 With wavy decoration on edge of rim; Fabric O7. Site 2, area B, group 7, F142, layer 7133

Fig. 30

Type 5: Small to medium-sized bowls, reminiscent of samian forms, Webster type I (1976, fig. 9.61–64)
Bead-rim bowls with upright rims, perhaps copying samian form 37. Total rim EVE 0.79

BT64 Upright wall; Fabric O1. Site 2, area B, group 7, F118, layer 7031

BT65 Curving walls, more delicate form with slight bead rim; Fabric R5. Site 2, area B, group 7, F118, layer 7031

BT66 Grooved or double-beaded rim, similar to forms noted at Wroxeter (Timby *et al.* 2000, B7.43) or at Sidbury (Darlington and Evans 1992). Fabric O1. Site 2, area B, group 7, F108, layer 7059

Type 6: Miscellaneous bowls or dishes

Type 6.1: Shallow bowl, rim slightly thickened with two grooves. Total rim EVE 0.09

BT67 Everted walls and slightly thickened, down-sloping rim; Fabric O4. Site 2, area A, group 3, F119, layer 7065

Type 6.2: Shallow bowl or dish with curving walls and bead rim. Total rim EVE 0.19

BD68 Fabric O3. Site 2, area B, group 7, F141, layer 7132

BD69 Fabric O1. Site 2, area B, layer 7047

Type 6.3: Plain rimmed bowls/dishes. Total rim EVE 0.61

BT70 Fabric O1. Site 2, area B, group 7, F118, layer 7031

BT71 With curving walls; Fabric O1. Site 2, area B, group 7, F118, layer 7079

Type 7: Dishes or platters (Webster 1976 type K, fig. 10).

Type 7.1: Plain or slightly bead-rimmed, straight-walled dishes and platters. Total rim EVE 2.25

DP1 Splayed walls, with an internal groove at the junction of the wall and base, very abraded; ht 35mm. No exact parallels are published by Webster or Rawes, although both date a range of similar vessels to the first or second centuries. A similar vessel came from a late second-century context at Alcester (Lee *et al.* 1994, fig. 37.O.427); Fabric O5. Site 2, area B, group 7, F116, layer 7061

DP2 With carinated wall; Fabric O1. Site 2, area B, layer 7085

DP3 With bead rim; Fabric O4. Site 2, area B, layer 7035

DP4 Platter or shallow dish with splayed walls, a flat, grooved base and a pronounced bead rim; Fabric O3. Site 2, area B, group 7, F118, layer 7031

DP5 Finer variant, with slight bead rim and splayed walls; Fabric O1. Site 2, area B, group 7, F118, layer 7067

DP6 Dish, with less splayed walls and a slightly beaded rim; Fabric O6. Site 2, area B, group 7, F118, layer 7031

Type 7.2: Reeded-rim dishes. Total rim EVE 0.29

DP7 Reed rim with two grooves, perhaps copying a BB1 form or derived from an early military type; Fabric O3. Site 2, area B, group 7, F116, layer 7061

Type 7.3: Shallow dishes or platters with flange rims
Flange rim, up-turned at the tip. Perhaps derived from samian form Curle 15, a predominantly second-century type, common in the pre-Antonine period. Similar forms have been noted from Worcester: in Severn Valley ware, from the Deansway site (Buteux and Evans forthcoming, fabric 12), and in sandy grey ware, from Sidbury (Darlington and Evans 1992, fig. 28.11). Parallels can also be found from Droitwich (Rees 1992, fig. 30.24). No similar forms are known from the other Malvern kilns, but they are comparable to the flange-rimmed forms produced at Portway, Gloucestershire during the second century (Rawes 1982, 45, fig. 6.126–9). Total rim EVE 0.71

DP8 Fabric O6. Site 2, area A, group 3, F115, layer 7058. Total rim EVE 0.05

41

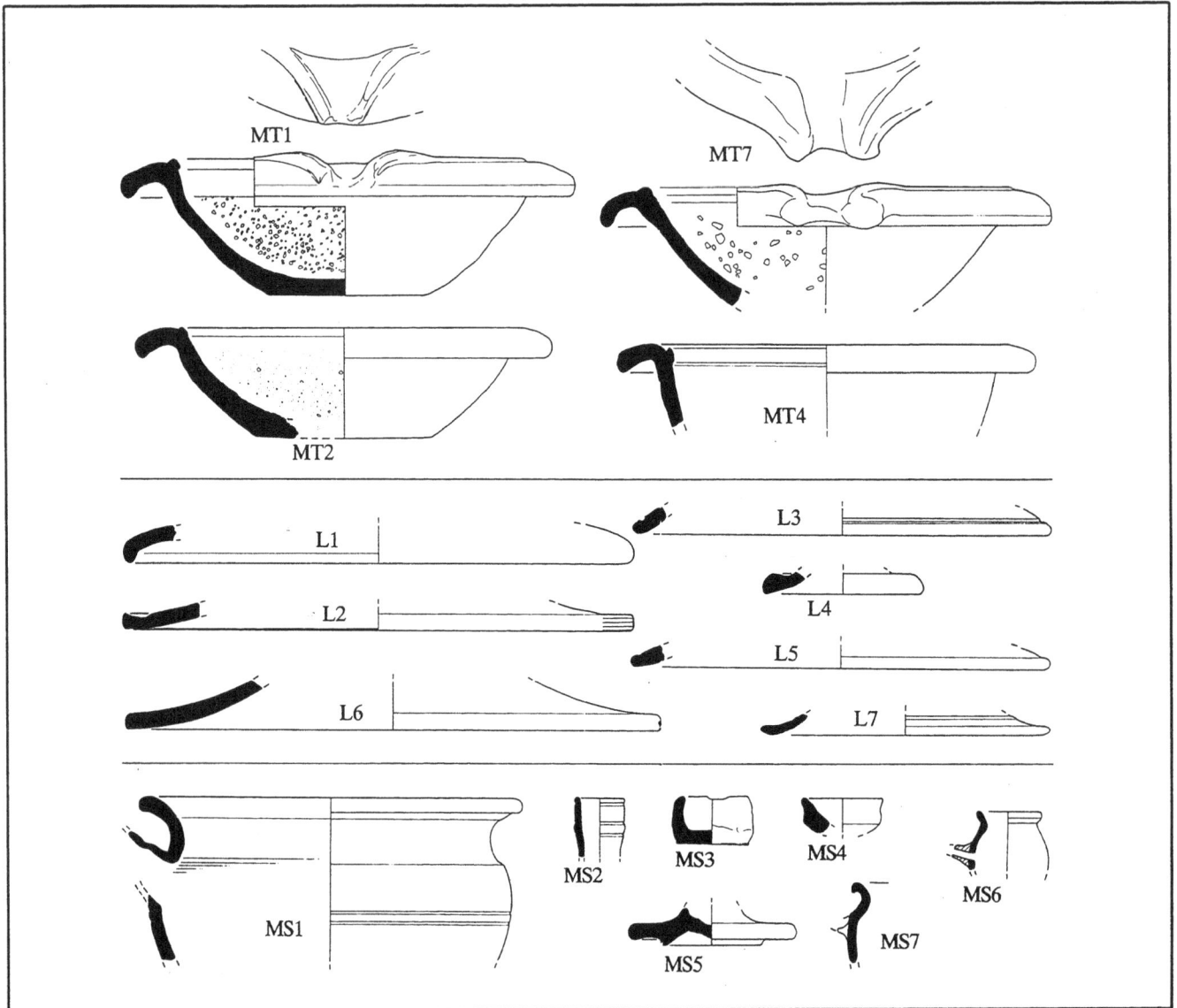

Figure 31: Severn Valley ware: mortaria, lids and miscellaneous forms; scale 1:4

Fig. 31

Mortaria
by Kay Hartley

MT1 Fourteen joining fragments making a nearly complete mortarium. The trituration grit (mainly brown material, ?sandstone, with some quartz and other material) appears never to have been used. The trituration surface in this mortarium is composed of a very thin layer. The deep embedding of the grit is unusual, but it does not appear to have been added in the same way as on MT2. The vessel had a thin, self-coloured slip and the lower half appears to have been trimmed and smoothed on the outside. Most mortaria show the marks of the wire used to cut them from the wheel but the underside of the base of this mortarium has also been trimmed and smoothed. It is also in pristine condition showing no wear at all. Diam 280mm; Fabric O4. Site 2, area B, group 7, F112, layer 7052

MT2 Six joining sherds making up about half of the vessel; one fragment is very slightly singed. This mortarium is similar to MT1, but is coarser to the touch; the exterior and the underside of the base have been treated in the same way as MT1. This is a different mortarium from the base fragment MT6 (not illustrated), but the trituration surface of the base has been treated in the same highly unusual way. The trituration material, however, differs (the extra clay is filled with mostly tiny quartz, some red-brown sandstone, and rarer opaque black and greenish material). On the

base this upper layer of clay is 4–5mm thick but it thins out upwards towards the rim. It provides an unusual, sandpaper-like surface. There are no obvious signs of wear either on the trituration or on the underside of the base. Diam 280mm; Fabric O1. Site 2, area B, group 7, F112, layer 7052

MT3 The fabric is identical to MT1, except for being soft and powdery. The trituration grit, however, differs completely, being composed almost entirely of clusters of quartz grains, some containing flecks of gold mica. The inside of the mortarium is mishapen which could mean that the vessel was warped. Alternatively it could result from applying trituration grit in the same way as on MT2 and MT6, though no layering is visible on this sherd which was broken above the base. In form, as in fabric, it is clearly related to MT1 and MT2, but has a slightly more rounded flange and a grooved head. There is no wear on this large fragment. Diam 240mm; Fabric O1. Site 2, area B, group 7, F118, layer 7031 (not illustrated)

MT4 A rim sherd, similar in fabric to MT3, but differing slightly in form, showing it to be from a different vessel. The trituration material on the small area surviving consists mostly of tiny to small quartz fragmemts with rare black ?iron-rich material. Diameter 250mm; Fabric O1. Site 2, area B, group 7, F118, layer 7031

MT5 Body and base sherd, with quartz and quartz clusters used for the trituration surface as on MT3, but the quartz is clearly embedded

42

in an extra layer of clay on the basal interior surface of what was up to the point of adding it, a bowl rather than a mortarium. If it were not for the hardness of the fabric, this sherd might be attributed to mortarium MT3, but it is probably from a different vessel. The inner surface is completely intact, showing no signs of use; Fabric O6. Site 2, area B, group 7, F118, layer 7031 (not illustrated)

MT6   A base fragment from a mortarium with the underside of the base as smooth as on MT1. The thin surface slip, probably intended to be self-coloured, is discoloured, as is part of the fabric, probably through slight misfiring in the kiln. Williams has drawn attention to the extra layer of clay on the inside of the base which provides what is essentially the trituration surface. Little of this is visible on the surface to the naked eye, but a x20 lens reveals fairly frequent tiny quartz fragments all over the surface. The underside of the base shows no indication of wear. This fragment is from a mortarium not otherwise represented; Fabric O8, thin section sample 10. Site 2, area B, group 7, F116, layer 7061 (not illustrated)

Nos MT1–6 all came from features F112, F116 and F118 associated with pottery production in area B (feature group 7). They almost certainly represent six different vessels, all in basically the same fine-textured, micaceous, orange-brown fabric, often with pale grey core. There are, however, at least three variations in the suite of materials used for the trituration surface. Although this can be paralleled, for example in the Mancetter-Hartshill potteries in the early second century, it is unusual for mortaria made at the same date and in the same workshop. Also, in at least three instances, the trituration surface has been created by adding a layer of what is essentially the same clay, packed with fragments of rock; this contrasts strongly with the rest of the fine-textured body. This is not just highly unusual; no other example is known of this practice and the only recorded examples of anything remotely reminiscent of it is at a kiln-site at Ellingham in Norfolk where some mortaria appeared to have a second layer of trituration grit added above the first (Hartley and Gurney 1997, 10). We do not know how this treatment would have stood up to use.

The four rim-profiles are clearly similar. No exact parallels are known, but in a general way they fit a source in the Severn valley. The closest parallels, and these are rather tenuous, are mortaria from Kingsholm, Gloucester. Without close parallels dating is difficult, but a date within the period AD 70–120 seems likely. MT1 was never stamped and it is most unlikely that any of the others were.

These mortaria have much in common and there is no evidence of use on any fragments. It seems very likely that they are waste pottery from a kiln and as such they are important because they represent the best evidence to date for mortarium production in the area of the Severn valley between Wroxeter and Gloucester. The lack of parallels suggests that production may have been short-lived and that they were serving only a local market.

MT7   Three joining sherds making up about half of the upper part of the vessel. The fabric indicates production in the same general area to MT1–6, but there are important points of difference. The fabric is finer and lacks the distinctive grey core present in all but MT6 above, not perhaps especially notable in itself. The rim-profile, however, is less distinctive, the spout is of a different type and the trituration treatment is dissimilar both in the general size of the fragments and probably in the way they were applied. It may be that MT1–6 were produced at one workshop and that MT7 was made nearby, perhaps at a different time.

This interpretation is supported by the fact that this vessel, unlike vessels MT1–6 which were all from group 7, came from one of the Area A ditches (group 3). The group 3 pottery assemblage was quite distinctive from the group 7 assemblage, and was also earlier, being earlier,being broadly dated Trajanic to Hadrianic or early Antonine. If MT7 appeared on a site without MT1–6 it would not be in any way distinctive and would merely be classed as made in the south-west. The only reason for it standing out in this group lies in its differences from MT1–6. It was, like them, never stamped and a date in the earry would fit the rim-profile; Fabric O3. Site 2, area A, group 3, F109, layer 7049

Lids
(Webster 1976, Group L)

Type 1:   Convex profile. Total rim EVE 0.10
L1   Fabric O1. Site 2, area B, group 7, F112, layer 7052

Type 2:   Concave profile. Total rim EVE 1.26
L2   Rim turned up at tip; Fabric O7. Site 2, area B, group 7, F108, layer 7059
L3   Beaded rim, with slight second groove; Fabric O5. Site 2, area A, group 3, F115, layer 7058
L4   Fabric O5. Site 2, area B, group 7, F143, layer 7134
L5   Small bead rim; Fabric O5. Site 1, trench 3, 1000
L6   Plain rim; Fabric O4. Site 2, area B, group 7, F108, layer 7034
L7   Plain rim; Fabric O4. EV1, layer 100

Miscellaneous

MS1   Spouted bowl. A similar vessel was found in a Flavian/Trajanic pit at Cirencester (Rigby 1982, 167, Fig. 51.71); Fabric O3. Site 2, area B, group 7, F108, layer 7059. Total rim EVE 0.25

MS2   Spout. Fabric O7. Site 2, area B, group 7, F112, layer 7052

MS3   Small, crudely made vessel with a plain rim and flat base; possibly a crucible or a spacer; Fabric O5. Site 2, area B, group 7, F116, layer 7061. Total rim EVE 0.73

MS4   Small, crudely made, carinated form with an out-turned rim, possibly from a candlestick; Fabric O5. Site 2, area B, F118, layer 7031. Total rim EVE 0.56

MS5   Kiln-stacker (Vivien Swan pers. comm.) or part of a candlestick; Fabric O3. Site 2, area B, group 7, F137, layer 7123. Total rim EVE 0.52

MS6   Spout and everted rim from a *tettina*. These spouted vessels were perhaps used as feeding-cups for infants or invalids, or perhaps as lamp-fillers. A similar vessel is known from Alcester (Lee *et al.* 1994, 49, fig. 38.439), and a Severn Valley ware *tettina* spout was found at Worcester, Deansway (Buteux and Evans forthcoming). A more complete example was noted from a late second to early third century context at Strensham (Jackson *et al.* 1996, fig. 6.6), in an assemblage that also included a number of Malvernian ware forms. Fabric O2. Site 2, area B, layer, 7085. Total rim EVE 0.15

MS7   *Tettina* with a hooked rim and handle scar; Fabric O5. Site 2, area B, layer, 7047

In addition to the vessels described above, a number of collander fragments were noted. None could be related to rim forms, however, and none is illustrated.

—◇—

THE MALVERNIAN-GRITTED WARE

Fabrics and forms

The Malvernian wares, which were probably also made on or near the site, were divided into three fabrics; two hand-made (R22, R24), and one wheel-made (R23), with the hand-made wares being far more common than the wheel-made variant (Table 2). Amongst the hand-made pottery the standard variant (R22) was used predominantly for the production of jars (Fig. 32a and b; Table 8). Tubby cooking pots (JC type 1) were the main form, although BB1 type cook-pots were also present (JC type 2). Large storage jars, which were produced in much smaller quantities, were mainly everted-rim types (JLS type 3). Bowls formed the second main vessel class, followed by dishes and lids. Most of the vessels produced date broadly to the second century, some perhaps lasting into the third (JC type 1, JC type 2.1, B type 1). The only exceptions to this were the large storage jars, the splay-rimmed jars (JC type 2.1), and some of the bowls (BC types 3 and 4), all of which are third- to fourth-century types.

The colour and finish of the other hand-made variant (R24), and the high proportion of BB1-type forms produced, suggests that this was primarily intended to imitate BB1. It was used predominantly for the production of bowls, and is perhaps similar to the fabric noted on some of the bowls described by Peacock (1967, fig. 4.70, 71). By far the most common individual form was a second- to third-century, BB1-type bowl (BC type 1). Jars were the second most common class; predominantly BB1-type cook pots. Second- to third-century BB1-type jars (JC type 2.1) were markedly less common than the third- to fourth-century types (JC type 2.2). The large storage jars were once again mainly the everted-rim type.

Jars were the main vessel produced in the wheel-made variant

(R23), and bowls the only other vessel class represented in any quantity. Like R24, this ware also seems to have been used mainly in the production of BB1 types, and is also a later variant. By far the most common individual form was the third- to fourth-century BB1-type cook pot (JC type 2.2), although earlier BB1 types were also present (JC type 2.1 and BC type 1). No large storage jars were made, presumably reflecting the technical problems of producing larger vessels on the wheel.

Considering the Malvernian coarse wares as a single group, it is possible to illustrate the relative frequency of individual form types within vessel classes (Fig. 33). When the fabric variants are considered separately, however, chronological trends are evident in the forms produced (Fig. 34). The potters producing coarse wares during the second century seem to have been primarily concerned with making jars derived from their traditional repertoire. They started producing hand-made copies of BB1 bowls and, to a lesser extent, jars. At some point they also started manufacturing wheel-made copies of BB1 forms. Unlike the hand-made copies, however, these tended to be jars rather than bowls.

By the third to fourth century the only cook pots produced are BB1 types, and these are predominantly wheel-made. The potters continue producing smaller quantities of BB1-type bowls and dishes, and these are still slightly more common in hand-made rather than wheel-made wares. Hand manufacture also continues to be used for large storage jars, which are the only other class produced in any quantity.

These trends are reflected in assemblages from consumption sites in the region. At Sidbury, Worcester, for example, BB1 types were noted to be increasingly common from around the mid-third century (Darlington and Evans 1992, 48), and by

Table 8: Malvernian gritted ware: rim diameters by form type

Form Type	Overall diameter range (cms.)	Most common range (cms.)	Mean Diameter (cms.)	Modal diameter (cms.)
JC type 1.1	5-20	15-18	16	17
JC type 1.2	11-21	11-15	14	11, 13
JC type 1.3	12-21	12-21	16	14
JC type 2.1	11-25	14-19	17	17
JC type 2.2	10-31	12-20	17	16
BC type 1	11-29	15-23	20	22
BC type 2	29			1 rim only
BC type 3	14	14	14	2 rims only
BC type 4	15-22	15-22	19	3 rims only
JLS type 1	39-57	39-57	47	5 sherds only
JLS type 2	50, 61		55.5	2 rims only
JLS type 3	19-31	19-22	23	20
L type 1	14-24	15-19	19	15
L type 2	31			1 rim only
L type 3	13-21	13-21	16	16
L type 4	uncertain			1 rim, very fragmentary

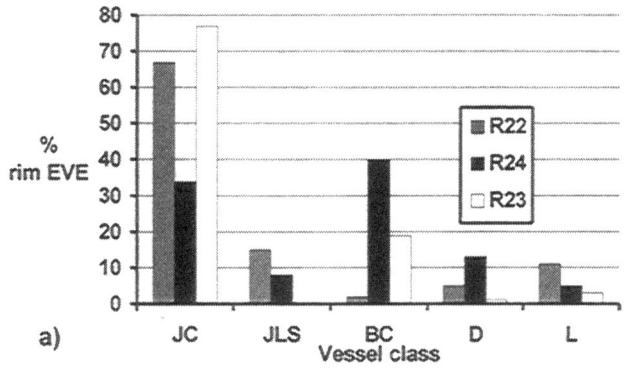

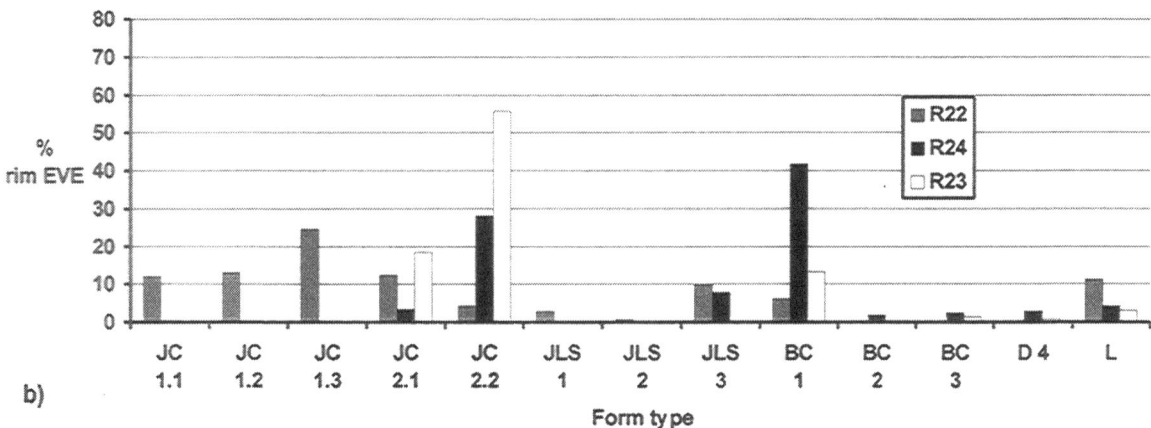

Figure 32: Malvernian gritted wares: a) vessel classes and b) form types by fabric (% rim EVE)

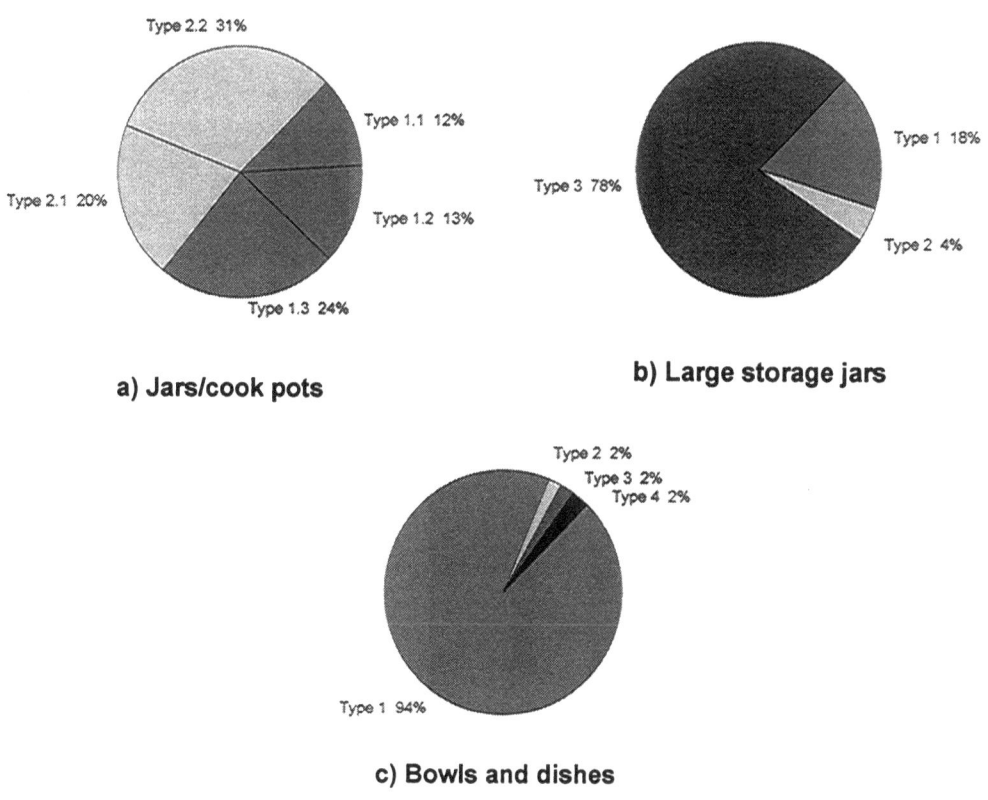

a) Jars/cook pots

b) Large storage jars

c) Bowls and dishes

Figure 33: Malvernian gritted wares: vessel classes by form type (% rim EVE)

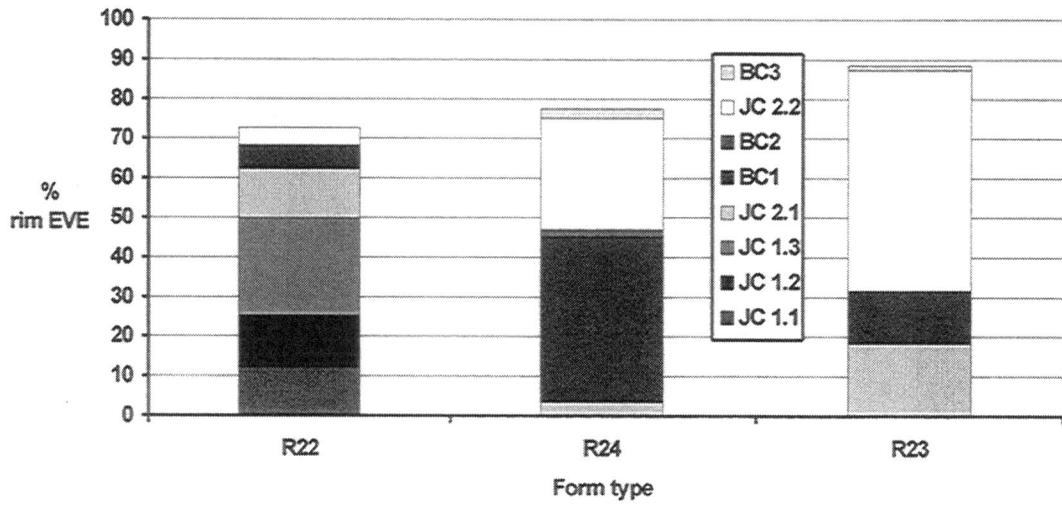

Figure 34: Malvernian gritted wares: seriation of fabrics by form type (% rim EVE)

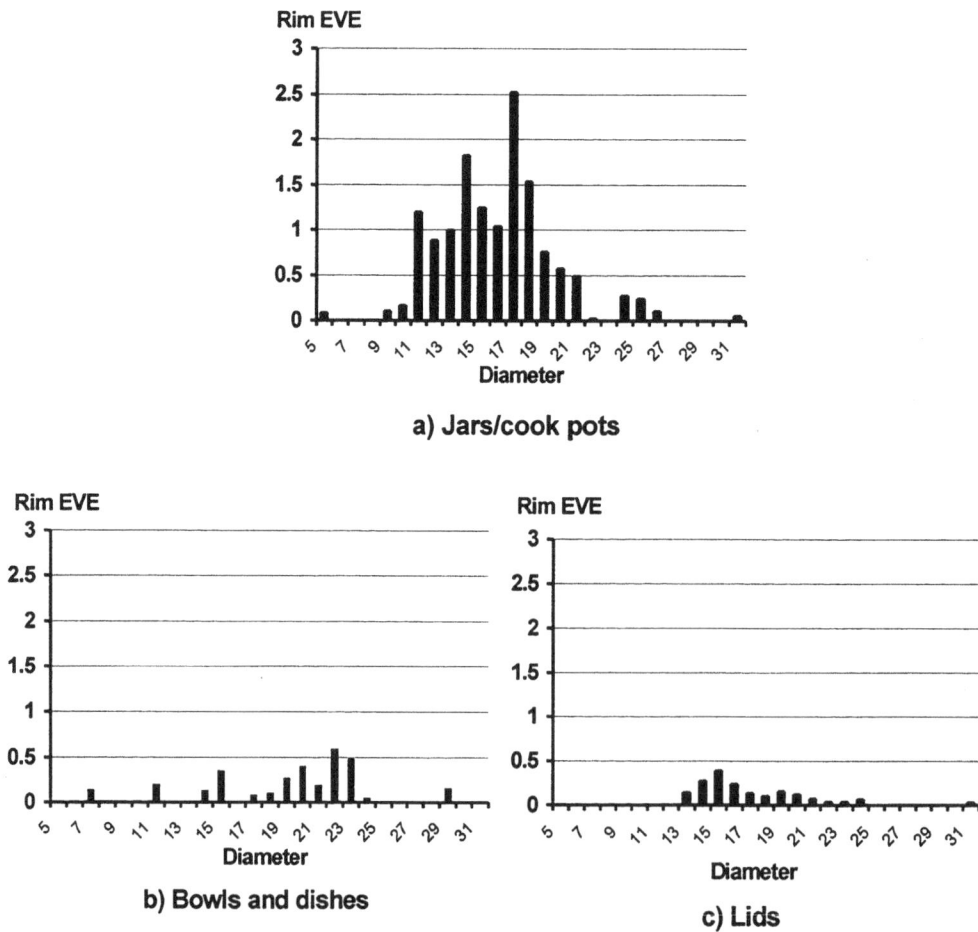

a) Jars/cook pots

b) Bowls and dishes

c) Lids

Figure 35: Malvernian gritted wares: rim diameters by vessel class

the late third to fourth century the wheel-made wares comprised 11% of the phase assemblage (ibid). Jars were produced in a range of sizes, with diameters centred around 17cms (Fig. 35a). The diameters of the lids seem to follow the same distribution, perhaps tending to be slightly smaller, so that they fit inside the rims of jars (Fig. 35c). The diameters of the bowls and dishes seem more-randomly distributed (Fig. 35b).

Description of fabrics

Fabric R22: Hand-made, Malvernian metamorphic ware
Soft to hard fired. Usually described as black or very dark grey throughout (2.5YR N3/0 or N2.5/0), less commonly with a red, oxidised, lens or patches (2.5YR 4/6). The assemblage also included sherds oxidised to yellowish-red or brown throughout (5YR 5/6 or 7.5YR), and reduced sherds, grey (7.5YR N5/0) with greyish-brown surfaces (2.5Y 5/2). The surface may be wiped or burnished, with either plain or pattern burnish, and may be slightly rough to the surface

where inclusions protrude through the surface. Inclusions of angular fragments of metamorphic rock, usually less than 1mm to 3mm in size, but larger fragments (up to 10mm) also found. The commonest inclusions are quartz, pink and white feldspar and hornblende.

Fabric R23: Wheel-thrown, Malvernian ware
Soft to hard. Characteristically, with a grey or light-grey, reduced core (7.5YR N6/0 or 10YR 6/1), and brown, oxidised, margins (7.5YR 5/4) and surfaces (7.5YR 6/4). May also be reduced throughout, with a light grey core (10YR 7/1), darker grey margins (10YR 4/1) and grey surfaces (10YR 5/1). Inclusions of moderate to abundant, angular, Malvernian rock fragments up to c. 30mm in size.

Fabric R24: Finer, Malvernian metamorphic ware, hand-made
Usually black throughout (7.5YR N2/0) with very dark grey surfaces (10YR 3/1), or less commonly with a brown core (10YR 5/3).

CATALOGUE OF ILLUSTRATED FORMS

Fig. 36

Jars/cooking pots

Defined as hand-made, coarsely tempered jars, often having evidence such as sooting to indicate use for cooking.

Type 1: Hand-made, tubby cooking pots (Peacock 1967, 16, fig. 1–12)
The tubby cooking pots are all types commonly found in regional assemblages, for example Worcester (Darlington and Evans 1992, fig. 24.1.2) and Droitwich (Rees 1992, fig. 26.3–8). They are also found further afield, for example at Wroxeter (Timby *et al.* 2000, fig. 144. JC1), and in Wales, particularly in the west and south-west (Peter Webster, pers. comm.). They may have been used as containers for another commodity

Type 1.1: With markedly in-turned rims
The only decoration surviving was plain burnish on the rim, although the type is often decorated with vertical burnished lines. The form is dated by Peacock to the late first or early second century (Peacock 1967, 18, fig. 1.9–11), and noted elsewhere in Flavian to Trajanix contexts, for example at Brompton (Evans forthcoming a). Total rim EVE 1.72

JC1   Bead rim; Fabric R22. Site 2, area B, group 7, F112, layer 7052
JC2   Rim flattened at tip; Fabric R22. Site 2 area A, group 3, F115, layer 7058

Type 1.2: With gently in-turned rims
The type is similar to Peacock nos 8 and 9 (1968, 16-18, fig. 17). Total rim EVE 1.86

JC3   With grooved, double-bead rim, decorated with horizontal burnish around the rim, and diagonal burnish around the body; Fabric R22. Site 2, area B, group 7, F116, layer 7061
JC4   With near-triangular rim; Fabric R22. Site 2, area A, group 3, F115, layer 7058
JC5   With slightly beaded rim; Fabric R22. Site 2, area A, group 3, F109, layer 7049

Type 1.3: With near-upright walls
Dated by Peacock predominantly to the Hadrianic and Antonine periods (Peacock 1967, 16–18, fig. 17.1-7), although he cites two examples of sherds coming from late first to early second-century contexts. There is increasing evidence for earlier production of this type. It is the most common variety of tubby cooking pot in the Flavian to Trajanic assemblage at Brompton fort and *vicus*, Shropshire (Evans forthcoming), and is represented at the broadly

contemporary site of Caersws (Webster 1989). At Metchley fort it was even noted in the phase 2 assemblage, dated c. AD 45 (Green *et al.* forthcoming). Total rim EVE 3.49

JC6   Beaded rim, projecting slightly internally; Fabric R22. Site 2, area A, group 3, F115, layer 7058
JC7   With groove under rim; Fabric R22. Site 2, area A, group 3, F115, layer 7058
JC8   Plain rim; Fabric R22. Site 2, area A, group 3, F109, layer 7049

Type 2: Everted-rim, BB1 types

Type 2.1: Moderately splayed rim
Peacock no. 14 (1967, fig. 1). The only decoration noted was plain burnish on the rim. Similar types are known from Worcester (Darlington and Evans 1992, fig. 24.6). Total rim EVE 2.97

JC9   Jar of wide girth, with a gently out-curving rim, decorated with acute cross-hatch burnish; Fabric R22. Site 1, trench 2000, layer 2021

Type 2.2: Increasingly splayed rims
Probably copying BB1 types; the only decoration comprised two sherds with right-angle cross-hatch burnish. Predominantly produced in the wheel-made Malvernian ware. Peacock publishes a similar hand-made type (Peacock 1967, fig. 1.13), and a number of wheel-made examples was produced at the Hygienic Laundry site (*ibid.* fig. 3.20–24). The form was also noted at Great Buckmans Farm and Grit Farm. It has been found, for example, in Worcester (Darlington and Evans 1992, fig. 24.9; Peacock 1967, fig. 5.92) and Droitwich (Rees 1992, fig. 26.12), the latter from a mid third to late fourth-century context. Total rim EVE 4.61

JC10   Splayed, cavetto rim. Predominantly a wheel-made form; Fabric R8. Site 1, area B, group 7, F141, layer 7132
JC11   Fabric R23. Site 2, area B, group 7, layer 7072

Large storage jars

The large storage jars often have heavy, thickened rims which appear to have been deliberately shaped, perhaps for seating lids. They are perhaps a continuation of a pre-Roman Malvernian class, the earliest examples of which date to the late Iron Age/Conquest period, for example from Aston Mill, Kemerton (Evans 1990, 31, fig. 17.2) and Beckford (Ford and Rees forthcoming). However, the examples from Newland Hopfields have parallels from third and fourth-century contexts.

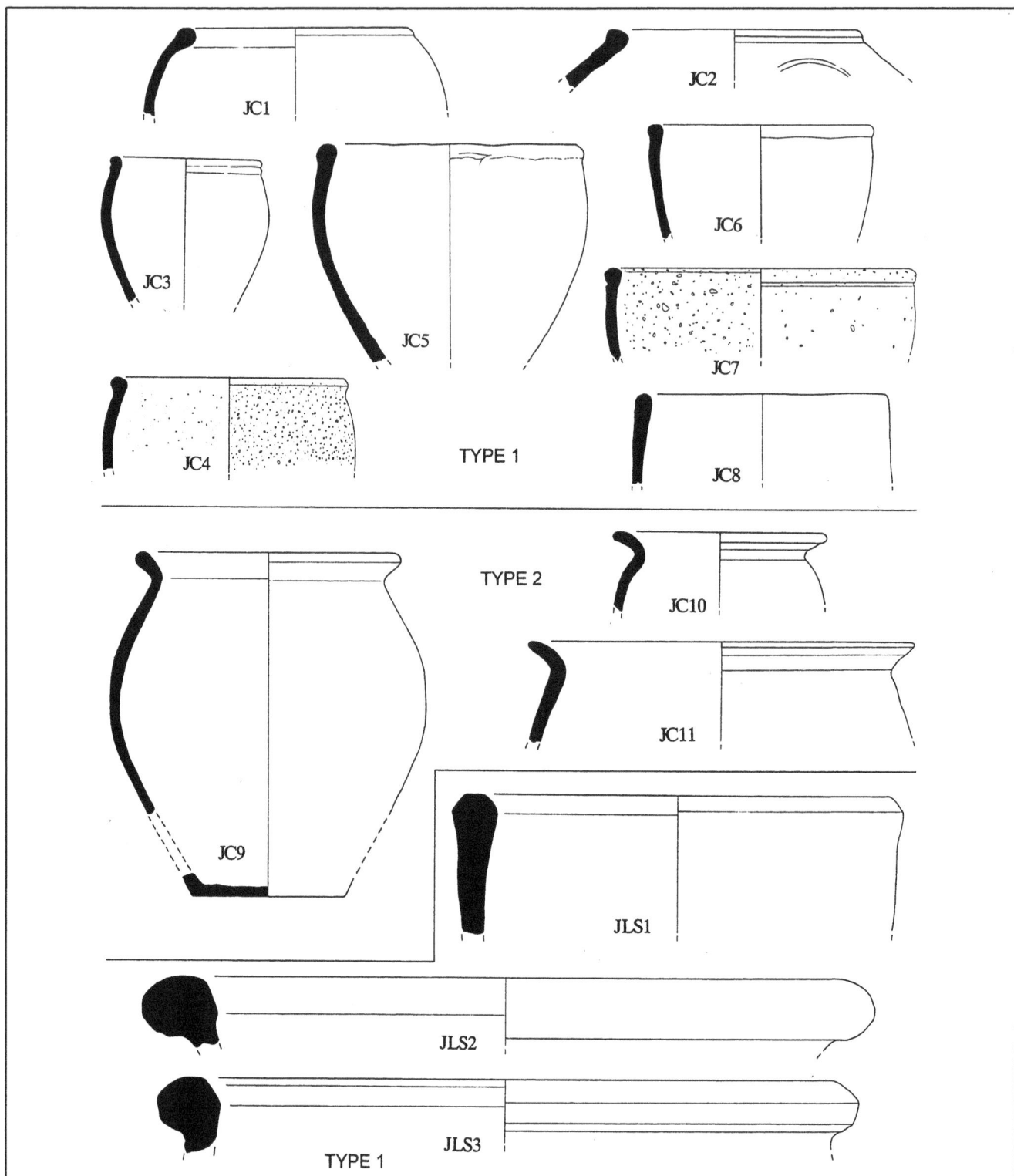

Figure 36: Malvernian gritted wares: cooking pots and large storage jars, type 1; scale 1:4

Type 1: With heavy, often angular, thickened rims. No decoration was noted. Total rim EVE 0.41

JLS1 In-turned, angular rim, from a very large tubby cooking pot type form; Fabric R22. Site 2, area A, group 3, F109, layer 7114

JLS2 Angular rim, similar to a wheel-made vessel published by Peacock (1967, fig. 1.12) and perhaps related to the angular forms produced at the Hygienic Laundry site (*ibid.* fig. 4.80–2). Similar forms are, however, also known from Beckford (Ford and Rees forthcoming, form 16.6); Fabric R22. Site 1, trench 1000, F1162, layer 1160

JLS3 Rounded rim, similar to types noted at Worcester (Darlington and Evans 1992, fig. 24.4,5); Fabric R22. Site 1, group 5, trench 2000, F2290, C2183

Fig. 37

Type 2: Heavy, flange-rimmed vessels
No decoration was noted. These have been included as large storage jars, but might be oven material. Parallels for these generally come from third and fourth-century contexts, for example from Beckford (pers. comm. James Dinn), Worcester (Darlington and Evans 1992, 68, fig. 35.4a; Buteux and Evans forthcoming), and Droitwich (Hurst and Woodiwiss 1992, 64, fig. 46.1). Total rim EVE 0.10

JLS4 Heavy, flat, angular, flange rim; Fabric R22. Site 2, area B, group 4, F113, layer 7051

Type 3: Jars with everted rims.

48

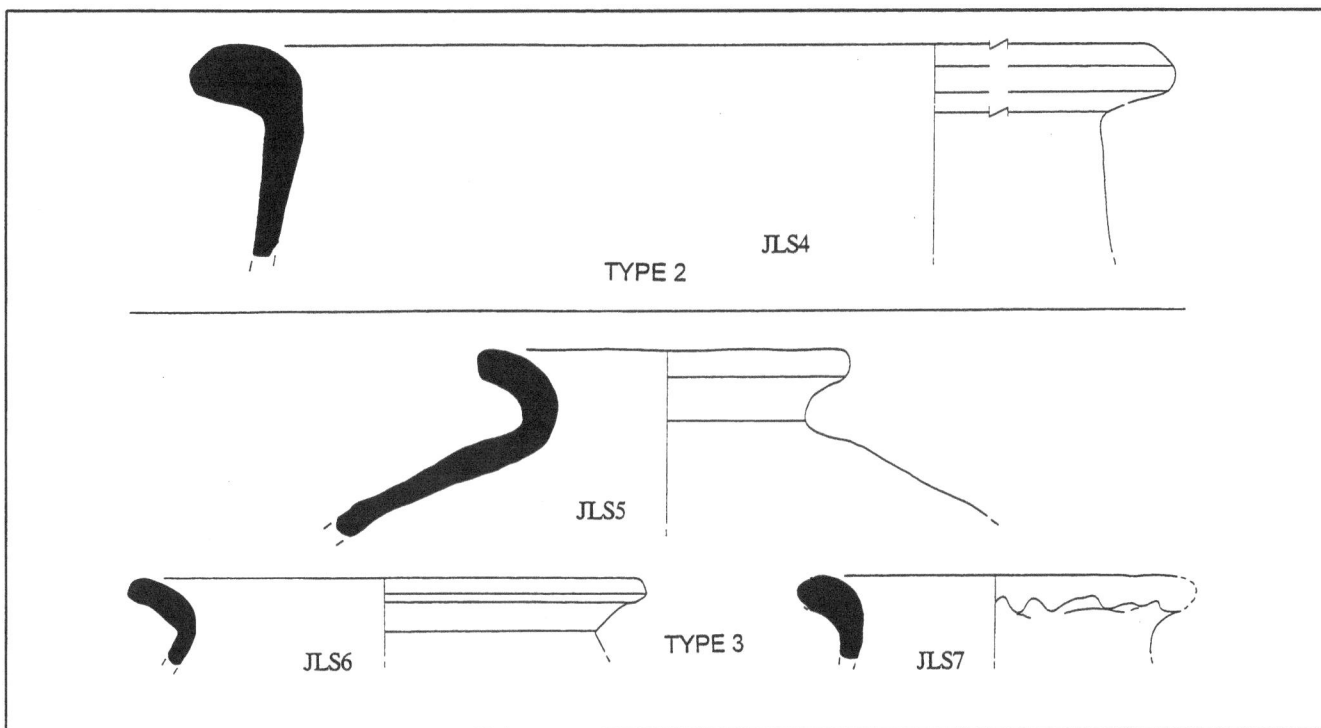

Figure 37: Malvernian gritted wares: large storage jars, types 2 and 3; scale 1:4

No decoration was noted. Total rim EVE 1.82. Similar to types produced at the Hygienic Laundry site (Peacock 1967, fig. 4. 88, 89), and found at Worcester (Darlington and Evans 1992, fig. 24. 3, 8) and Droitwich (Rees 1992, fig. 26.14).

JLS5 Crudely finished, with finger marks below the rim; Fabric R22. Site 2, area B, group 8, layer 7038

JLS6 Markedly everted, bead rim. The illustrated sherd has a blackened surface; Fabric R22. Site 2, area C, group 8, layer 7041

JLS7 The illustrated sherd is very abraded but appears to have frilled decoration on the tip; Fabric R22. Site 2, area B, layer 7124

Fig. 38

Bowls and dishes

These have been classified as cooking vessels because of the coarse temper and their similarity to BB1 types.

Type 1: Flat, flange-rimmed bowls and dishes
Copying mid second to mid third-century BB1 types. Similar forms were also produced at the Hygienic Laundry site (Peacock 1967, 24, fig. 4.72).

Type 1.1: Bowls. Total rim EVE 1.8
BC1 This is least like the BB1 types the others seem to copy, having curving walls and a crude flange rim. Decorated with plain, horizontal burnishing on the rim and body; Fabric R24. Site 2, area B, group 7, F112, layer 7052
BC2 Fabric R23. Site 2, area B, group 7, F112, layer 7052
BC3 Bowl with near-upright walls, rim has a slight internal projection, possibly unintentional but paralleled at Sidbury, Worcester (Darlington and Evans 1992, fig. 24.10); Fabric R22. Site 2, area B, group 7, F112, layer 7052
BC4 Straight-walled bowl, with splayed walls copying a later second-century type; Fabric R23. Site 2, area B, F112, unstratified

Type 1.2: Dishes. Total rim EVE 0.82
D1 Dish with splayed walls and gently everted rim; the illustrated sherd is very abraded and oxidised throughout; Fabric R22. Site 2, area B, group 7, F112, layer 7047
D2 Dish with thickened rim, and splayed walls; decorated with cross-hatch burnish both internally and externally; Fabric R24. Site 2, area B, group 7, F112, layer 7038

Type 2: Bowls with grooved, slightly dropped-flange rims
Copying third-century BB1 types. Total rim EVE 0.04
BC5 Flange slightly lower than the bead; Fabric R24. Site 2, trench7, layer 7027

Type 3: Bowls with dropped-flange rims
Copying a BB1 form (as BC6) post-dating c. AD 270 but not later than the early fourth century. Also produced at the Hygienic Laundry site (Peacock 1967, 24, fig. 4.73, 75). Total rim EVE 0.05

Type 4: Plain-rimmed dishes
Probably copying BB1 types. Total rim EVE 0.06
D3 Splayed, curving walls, surface of illustrated vessel blackened and burnished, imitating BB1; Fabric R24. Site 2, area C, group 9, layer 7125

Lids

Type 1: Lids with up-turned rims. Total rim EVE 1.13
L1 Bead rim; Fabric R22. Site 2, area B, group 4, F113, layer 7051
L2 Angular rim; Fabric R22. Site 2, area A, F124, layer 7092
L3 With incised, wavy line on rim; Fabric R22. Site 2, area B, group 7, F142, layer 7133
L4 Gently up-turned rim; Fabric R22. Site 1, trench 1000, layer 1191
L5 Plain rim; Fabric R22. Site 2, area B, group 7, layer 7072.
L6 Pulley rim, with internal groove; Fabric R22. EV1, layer 120
L7 Frilled rim; Fabric R22. EV1, F119, layer 118

Type 2: Tapered rims. Total rim EVE 0.03
L8 Fabric R24. EV1, layer 104

Type 3: Plain rims and concave profiles. Total rim EVE 0.39
L9 Fabric R22. Site 1, trench 1000, F1198/1204, layer 1191

Lid handles

L10 Fabric R23. Site 2, area B, group 7, F143, layer 7138.
L11 Fabric R23. Site 2, area B, group 7, layer 7072

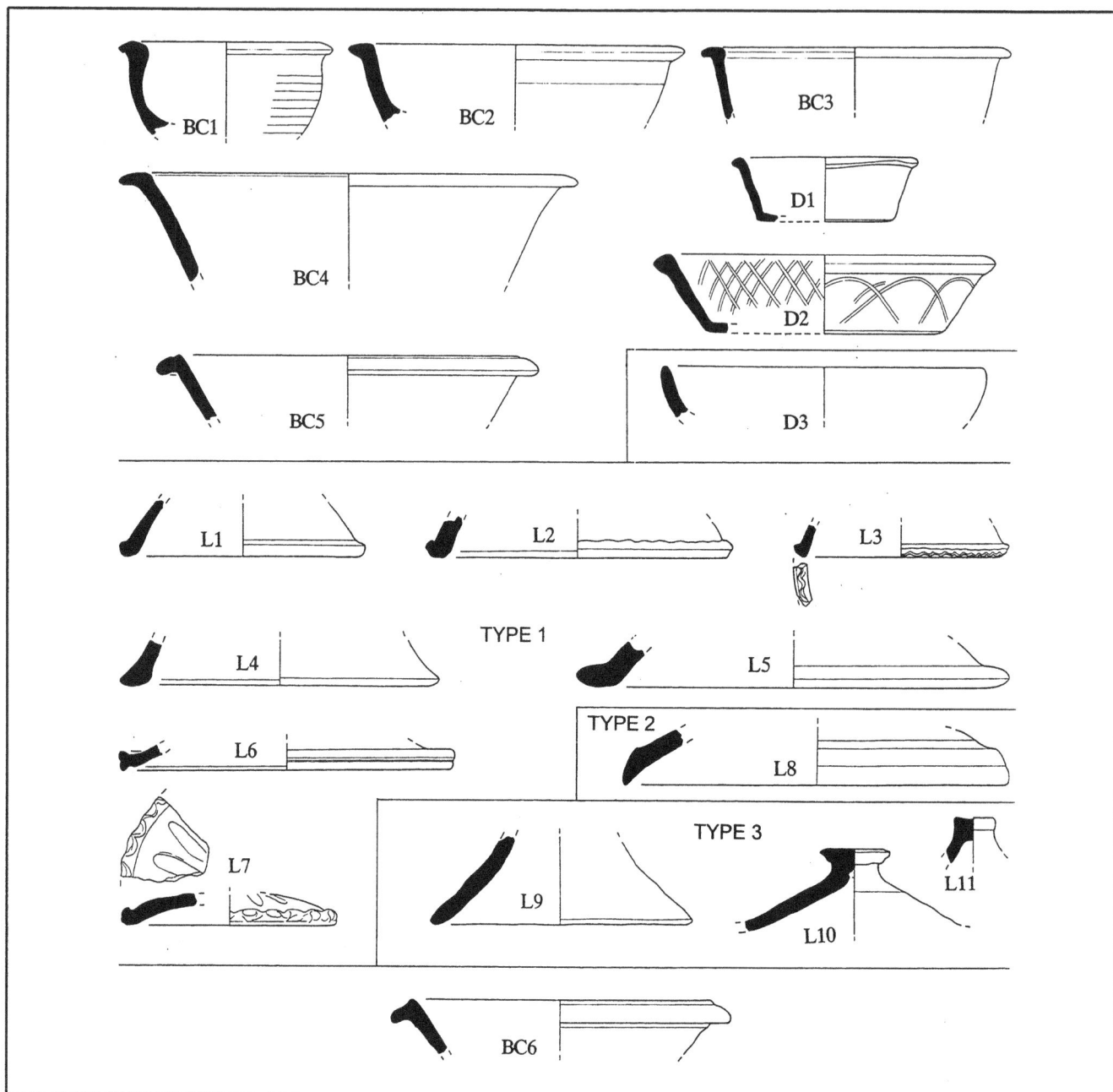

Figure 38: Malvernian gritted wares: bowls, dishes and lids; wares of uncertain source; scale 1:4

—◇—

WARES OF UNCERTAIN SOURCE

Fabrics and forms

Three other fabrics were identified, the precise sources of which are uncertain. Regional sources are, perhaps, most likely. The oxidised sandy ware (O25) was represented by only three sherds and no forms were identifiable. The reduced sandy ware (R25) was only slightly better represented (39 sherds). Forms were all third- to fourth-century types, similar to those produced in the Malvernian wares; everted-rim storage jars (JLS type 3), and BB1-type cook pots (JC type 2.2) and bowls (BC type 3). The grog-tempered ware was

represented by a single, large storage jar found in Area A. No rim sherds were recovered and the vessel is not illustrated.

Description of fabrics

Fabric O25: Oxidised sandy ware
Oxidised, reddish-yellow throughout (5YR 6/8 – 5/4).
Inclusions of moderate to abundant, sub-angular, quartz grains up to 1mm.

grains up to 1mm.

Fabric R25: Reduced sandy ware
Generally reduced, light to dark grey throughout (10YR 6/1 to 4/1). Illustrated sherd (Fig. 38) BC6, splayed walls; Fabric R25. Site 2, area C, group 8, layer 7041

Fabric R26: Coarse, grog-tempered ware
(described by David Williams)

A hand-made, soft, rough fabric. With a very dark grey (2.5Y 3/0) inner surface and core, and an oxidised, yellowish-brown, external surface (10YR 6/4 to 5/4) which has occasional dark grey patches (2.5Y N4/0). Inclusions of moderate, ill-sorted, angular fragments of fine-textured, highly fired grog up to 7mm, with occasional fine-grained sandstone also visible.

CATALOGUE OF ILLUSTRATED FORMS

Fig. 38

Bowls
BC   Splayed walls; Fabric R25. Site 2, area C, group 8, layer 7041. Total rim EVE 0.01

—◇—

TRADED WARES
with Brenda Dickinson, Kay Hartley and Joanna Mills

Fabrics and forms
As might be expected on a production site, only very small quantities of non-local pottery were deposited. The only fabric to be represented in any quantity was south-east Dorset Black-burnished ware (BB1), and even this represented less than 1% by count, weight and rim EVE (Table 2). This is much less than would be expected on other contemporary sites in the vicinity; for example, in Worcester BB1 represented 12% by count and 8% by weight (Darlington and Evans 1992, 35).

Bowls were the main BB1 vessel class reaching the site (Fig. 39a, d). These, combined with the dishes, accounted for over half of the assemblage. Again, this contrasts with nearby occupation sites such as Worcester where jars were the most common class (*ibid.* 54). Second- to third-century bowls (BC type 1) were most common (Fig. 39c), as they were in the Malvernian BB1 copies. The late third- to fourth-century form (BC type 3) was the next most common type, while the intermediate bowls (BC type 2) were relatively poorly represented.

The mid to late second-century bead-rim dishes (D type 5) were more common than the plain-rimmed types (D type 4), despite the latter having been produced throughout the period of BB1 production.

Amongst the jars (Fig. 39b), the late third- to fourth-century form (JC type 2) was more common than the second-century variety (JC type 1). This probably reflects the second-century preference for the locally produced tubby cooking pot form. Lids were very poorly represented in BB1, and were less common than in the Malvernian wares. A similar pattern was noted at Worcester; where lids were noted in Malvernian ware but entirely absent in BB1 (Darlington and Evans 1992, 50).

Only very small quantities of mortaria were brought onto the site: four vessels from the Oxfordshire kilns (fabric M2) and one from Mancetter-Hartshill (fabric M1). The Oxfordshire mortaria were dated late second to early third century (Young 1977, M10), and AD 240–300 (*ibid.* M18, WC5). The Mancetter-Hartshill mortarium was dated to after AD 230.

Small quantities of white ware were also recovered; all body sherds. Eight sherds probably came from Mancetter-Hartshill, and two from Oxfordshire. It is not possible to draw any meaningful conclusions from such small quantities, other than there was evidently little use for these wares on a production site. The only other traded fabric represented was first to early second-century, Savernake ware (R27), of which nine body sherds from a large storage jar were recovered from site 1, trench 2000.

Fabric R21 South-east Dorset Black-burnished ware 1 (BB1)

Fabric M1: Mancetter-Hartshill mortaria

Fabric M2: Oxfordshire white ware mortaria

Fabric M3: Oxfordshire white colour-coated mortaria

Fabric W1: Mancetter-Hartshill white ware

Fabric W2: Oxfordshire white ware

Fabric R27: Savernake ware

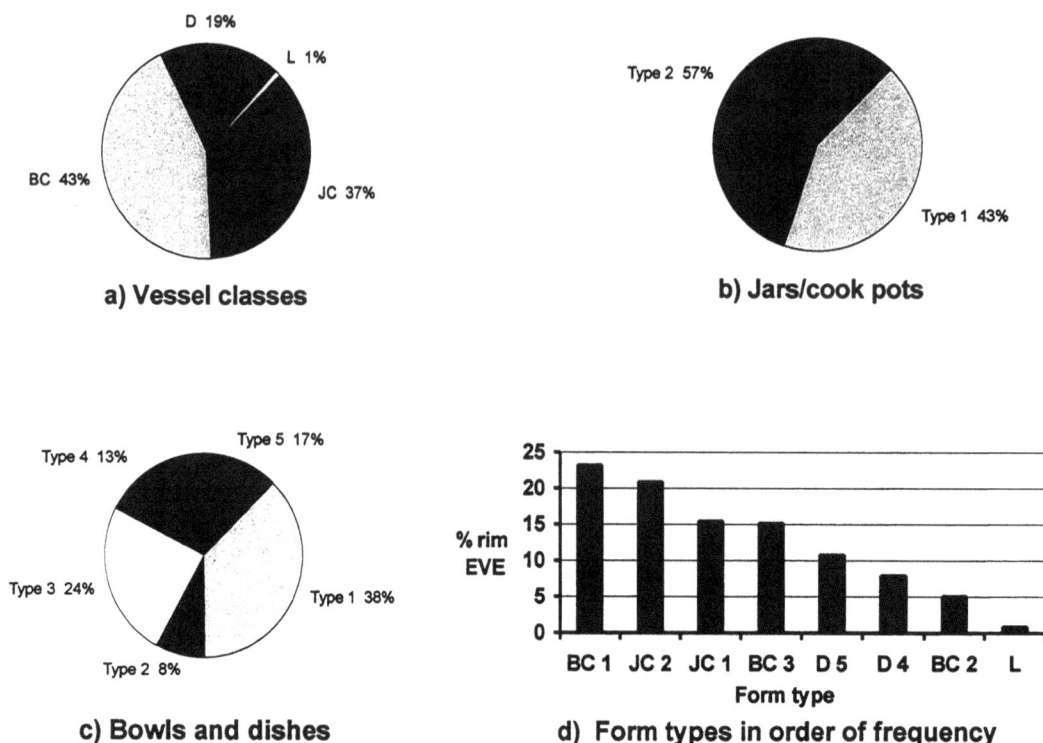

a) Vessel classes

b) Jars/cook pots

c) Bowls and dishes

d) Form types in order of frequency

Figure 39: Black-burnished ware vessel classes and form types (% Rim EVE)

CATALOGUE OF ILLUSTRATED FORMS

Fig. 40
BB1 (Black-burnished ware 1)

Jars/cook pots

Type 1: Jars of narrow girth with near-upright rims
Dorchester, Greyhound Yard, type 2. Usually decorated with acute, cross-hatch burnish and broadly dating to the second century (Seager Smith and Davies 1993, 231). Total rim EVE 0.49

JC1 Site 2, area B, group 7, F112, layer 7052
JC2 With burnished arcs on the neck. Site 2, area B, group 7, F118, layer 7031

Type 2: Everted-rim jars of narrow or near-equal girth, with splayed rims
Dorchester, Greyhound Yard, type 3. Usually decorated with obtuse, cross-hatch burnish and dating to the late third to fourth century (Seager Smith and Davies 1993, 231). Total rim EVE 0.66

JC3 Fabric R21. EV1, layer 102

Bowls and dishes

Type 1: Bowls or dishes with flat, flanged rims
Similar to Dorchester, Greyhound Yard, type 22, most common in contexts dated AD 150–300 (Seager Smith and Davies 1993, 233–5); and Exeter, South-East Dorset types 39 and 40, dated late Antonine to mid third century (Holbrook and Bidwell 1991b, 109, figs. 30 and 31). Total rim EVE 0.73

BC1 Site 1, trench 1000, layer 1191
BC2 Slightly splayed walls. Site 2, area A, layer 7035
BC3 With increasingly splayed walls. Site 1, area, trench 2000, F2061, layer 2162

Type 2: Bowls with grooved-flange rims
Dated from *c.* AD 180–210, to the mid to late third century (Gillam 1976, 67–70; Woodward 1987, 91, fig. 48.152). The form occurs in earlier contexts in the south, for example at Dorchester, Greyhound Yard (Seager Smith and Davies 1993, 235, type 24), but is not at Vindolanda in the north until the mid third century (Bidwell *et al.* 1985, 176). Total rim EVE 0.16

BC4 Flange higher than the bead. EV1, layer 118
BC5 Flange slightly lower than the bead, perhaps dating to the third, rather than the late second, century. Site 2, trench 7, layer 7027

Type 3: Bowls with dropped-flange rims
Dorchester, Greyhound Yard type 25 (Seager Smith and Davies 1993, 235). Gillam dated the first appearance of this form to *c.* AD 270, a date supported by subsequent evidence from Exeter (Holbrook and Bidwell 1991, 99) and Vindolanda (Bidwell *et al.* 1985, 177). Total rim EVE 0.48

BC6 Splayed walls. Site 2, area B, group 7, layer 7072

Type 4: Plain-rimmed dishes
Dorchester, Greyhound Yard type 20 (Seager Smith and Davies 1993, 233). The form is not closely datable, having been produced pretty much throughout the Roman period, although it does seem to be increasingly common from the late second century onwards. Total rim EVE 0.43

D1 Near upright walls. EV1, layer 120.

Type 5: Bead-rimmed dish
Also type 20 at Dorchester, Greyhound Yard (*ibid*). Probably mid to late second to early third century (Holbrook and Bidwell 1991, fig. 32 57.4). Total rim EVE 0.34

D2 Site 2, area B, group 7, layer 7072

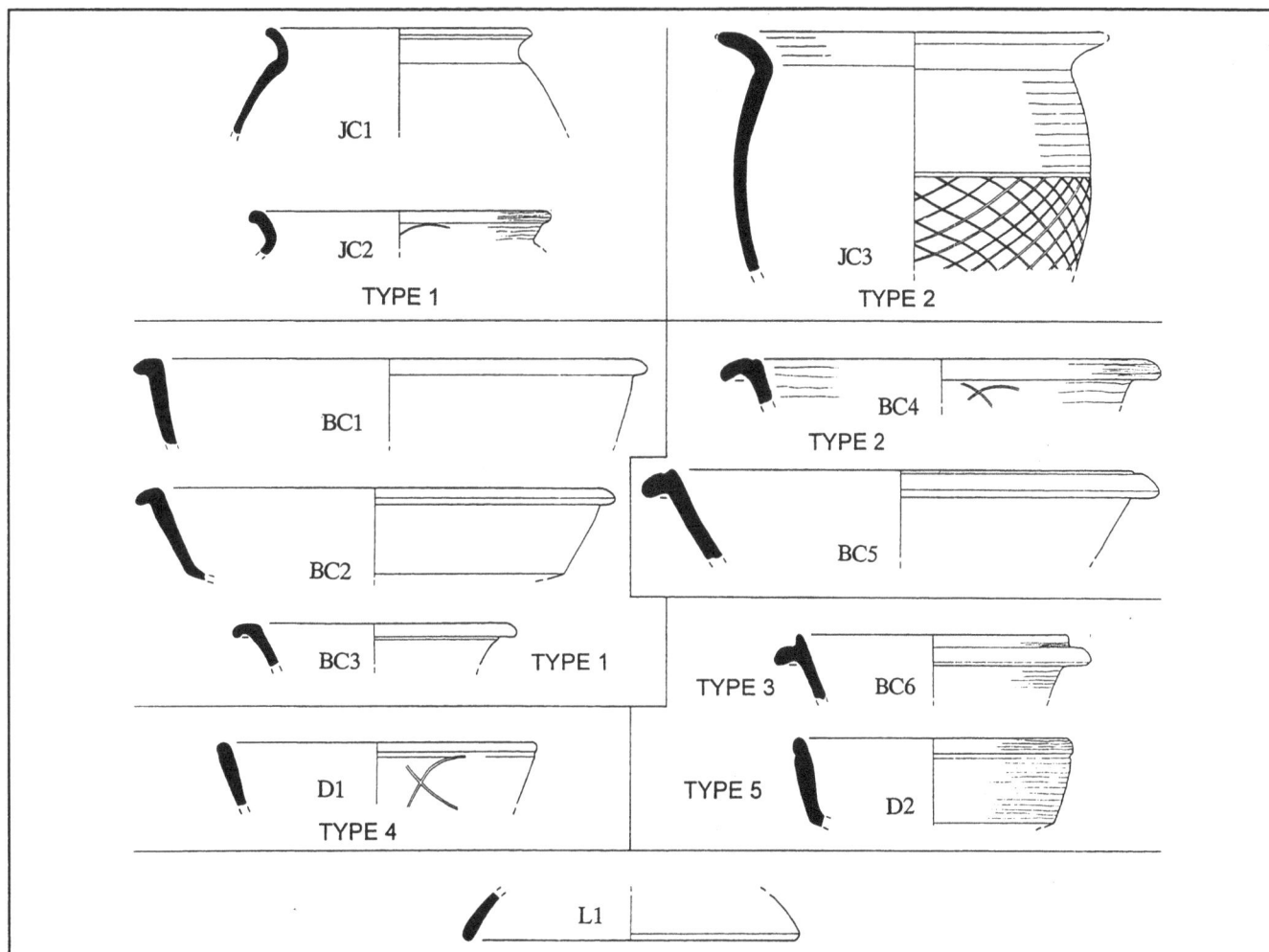

Figure 40: Black-burnished ware: jars, bowls, dishes and lids; scale 1:4

Lids

With plain rims and convex profiles. Total rim EVE 0.03

L1   R21. Site 1, trench 2000, F2061, layer 2165

The Mortaria
by Kay Hartley (not illustrated)

Mancetter-Hartshill

MT8   Multi-reeded hammerhead. Dated later than *c.* AD 230, with an optimum date in the second half of the third century to the early fourth century (Hartley 1973). Diameter 260mm; Fabric M1. Site 2, area B, group 7, F142, layer 7133. Total rim EVE 0.08

Oxfordshire

MT9   Incomplete rim section of form WC5 (Young 1977). A few specks of white slip survive underneath the flange; AD 240–300. Diameter 200mm; Fabric M3. Site 2, area B, group 7, F118, C7031. Total rim EVE 0.08

MT10   Young type M18 (Young 1977, 72–6, fig. 21) dated AD 240–300. Diam 330mm; Fabric M2. Site 2, area B, group 7, F118, layer 7031. Total rim EVE 0.27

MT11   Variant of Young form M10, with its bead broken and turned over the flange to make the spout. This type is probably dated too late by Young (1977). The best typological dating for Young M10–13 is AD 150–200+, judging from similar forms made in the Verulamium region. The earliest mortaria made in the Oxford potteries strongly indicate that at least some potters came from that area. Potters in the Verulamium region are likely to have been moving to other potteries throughout the second century, so the link may well have continued. This example could be early third century, but the basic form can be found in the mid second century. Diam 190mm; Fabric M2. Site 2, area B, group 7, F118, layer 7031

—◇—

IMPORTED WARES

The Samian
by Joanna Mills with a contribution by Brenda Dickinson

A total of 83 sherds (1005g) was recovered from the excavations (Tables 9 and 10). The majority of the samian is from Central Gaul (Lezoux) and is of Hadrianic or Antonine date. Of a possible maximum of 53 vessels, 49 were of main-export-period Lezoux fabrics. The usual range of the latter was observed including cups, bowls and dishes, although cups (seven vessels) may be slightly under represented and the absence of Dr 37 bowls is unusual. A single sherd from each of two closed vessels was found. With the exception of a possible Dr 30 base fragment no decorated wares were found.

In addition, a single South Gaulish vessel was recovered (D1, not illustrated); an East Gaulish bowl body sherd from Rheinzabern, dated late second or early third century, came from F142 at Site 2, Area B; and sherds from two Les-Martres-de-Veyre vessels were found (S2 and D2, not illustrated).

Judging from the samian, occupation appears to have started in the Trajanic or Hadrianic period, with the latter more likely. The form 29 bowl should probably be seen as pre-dating the occupation. The low percentage of Les Martres ware is not unusual (Marsh 1981). The last samian to reach the site seems to have done so towards the end of the second century, although it remains possible that the Eastern Gaulish vessel is early third century.

Some of the sherds are very abraded, suggesting either redeposition of the material or acidic soil conditions. Abrasion was particularly noticeable on sherds from the levigation ditches. Few sherds were burnt and none came from features associated with pottery production. It would seem likely that much of the samian was residual.

Samian tablewares are generally assumed to indicate a certain level of sophistication. However, a number of points suggest that the settlement was fairly impoverished, and of a relatively low status. Firstly, the decorated sherds are all of early dates within the assemblage, the Dr 29 almost certainly pre-dates the main occupation, and it is possible that the Dr 30 does as well. Secondly, there are no Dr 37 bowls from the site. Finally, despite the presence of mid to late Antonine forms such as Walters 79 and 80, there are no mortaria.

No definite examples of re-used vessels were noted, nor were there any examples of ungritted bowls with wear marks indicative of use, like mortaria, for grinding. A single vessel (S3, not illustrated) shows evidence of repair in the form of drilled rivet holes, in this example the rivets remain *in situ*.

The Potters' Stamps
by Brenda Dickinson (not illustrated)

S1   Form 18/31, Central Gaulish, stamped [BIGA.F]EC: Biga of Lezoux, Die 2a. This stamp occurs in Period IIB at Verulamium, *c.* AD 110–140 (Hartley 1972, S65), and is common in the Rhineland, which received little if any Central Gaulish samian in the second half of the second century. Evidence of Hadrianic and early Antonine activity is also indicated by the frequent use of the stamp on forms 18/31 and 27; *c.* AD 125/140. Site 2, Area B, group 7, F137, layer 7123

S2   Form 27, Central Gaulish, stamped [OV]IDI.M: Ovidius of Les Martres-de-Veyre, Die 1a (Terrisse 1968, pl LIII). This has been found in the London Second Fire groups, which include much Trajanic samian from Les Martres. However, some of the forms and fabrics associated with the stamp suggest that Ovidius may still have been at work under Hadrian; *c.* AD 110–130. Site 1, trench 2000, group 1, F2129, layer 2128

S3   AD\[on form 80 (riveted). Almost certainly a stamp of Advocisus of Lezoux, but it cannot be precisely paralleled because the glaze has flaked off the A and V; *c.* AD 160–190. Site 1, trench 2000, group 2, F2061, layer 2165

The decorated ware (not illustrated)

D1   SG, Dr 29. Approximately 50% of a form 29 bowl with flaring profile. The upper zone comprises a series of three panels separated by bead rows with rosettes at each end. The panels repeat around the bowl: a hare running right chased by two hounds; four rows of four horizontal leaf tips; hare and hounds repeated; wavy lines either side of a triangle of vertical leaf tips. The lower zone is a winding scroll with leaves in the upper compartments and a hare running to the right over three rows of vertical leaf tips in the lower. The use of horizontal leaf tips as in the upper zone is rare and is confined mainly to Muranus, although this is not his normal style. This device apart, the general layout is paralleled on a bowl from London with interior stamp of Celadus (Knorr 1952, taf 15B, where the upper zone has not been drawn). A bowl from Vindonissa, with interior stamp of Iucundus iii, has a similarly arranged lower zone but with leaf tip above the

Table 9: Samian: occurrence of sherds (nos of sherds/weight in grammes)

	South Gaulish	Les Martres	Lezoux	Rheinzabern	Total
Site 1					
Group 1		1/4			
Group 2			3/89		
Group 5			4/63	1/36	
other			20/108		
total		1/4	27/260	1/36	29/300
Site 2A	14/208	4/51	1/2		19/261
Site 2B					
Group 4			3/22		
Group 7			11/248		
Group 8			6/68		
other			15/106		
total			35/444		35/444
Total	14/208	5/55	63/706	1/36	83/1005

Table 10: Samian vessel forms by fabric (maximum no.)

Form	South Gaulish	Central Gaulish LesMartres	Lezoux	East Gaulish
18/31			7	
18/31R			3	
18/31 or 31			3	
27		1		
29	1			
30		1	1	
31			7	
31R			1	
33			4	
35			1	
36			3	?1
79			1	
79R or Lud Tg			1	
80			2	
Curle 15			1	
open			11	
closed			2	
unident			1	
Total	1	2	49	1

animals (Knorr 1919, taf 43A). This type of decoration occurs on bowls of the late 60s and early Flavian period; *c.* AD 65–80. Site 2, Area A, group 3, joining sherds from F109, layer 7043 and F115, layer 7058

D2   CG, Les Martres-de-Veyre, Dr 30. Body sherd of a Dr 30 bowl of potter X–2. The decoration is as follows: ovolo Rogers (1974) B28 and fine wavy line A23 below. The main decorated zone is a gladiatorial scene with large and small figures. On the far left is a small (unidentified) gladiator at the feet of figure O.14O (=D.86) which is minus the spear and O.166 (D.514) to the right (O = Oswald 1936). A shield (not in Rogers 1974, and possibly impressed from another gladiatorial stamp) is used as a space filler. Potter X–2 is not common in Britain and new figure types continue to be identified; *c.* AD 100–120. Site 2, Area A, group 3, F125, layer 7109

—◇—

DATING EVIDENCE

Introduction

The Newland Hopfields assemblage demonstrates the characteristic dating problems of kiln assemblages (Tyers 1996, 27). It is unfortunate that during the short period when the kiln was under excavation, arrangements could not be made for archaeomagnetic dating. Evaluation of the site prior to excavation indicated a settlement site, rather than a pottery production site, and the presence of a kiln had not therefore been anticipated. Only very small quantities of externally datable material were recovered, including some BB1 and samian, together with occasional sherds of Savernake ware, and white wares from Oxfordshire and Mancetter-Hartshill. The presence of BB1, albeit in very small quantities, was taken to indicate a *terminus post quem* of *c.* AD 120 for the features in which it occurred. This is the date when BB1 first appears in any quantity in the region. It should be noted, however, that Malvern is close to Wales and in south-east Wales at least BB1 is found in small quantities from the conquest period on (Peter Webster pers. comm.).

The Severn Valley ware forms generally had rather broad date ranges, based on the existing evidence, ranging from the late first to early second century, for example, or more broadly to the second to third century. Some were better chronological indicators than others, in particular the tankards (Fig. 21, T types 1–3), the carinated bowls (Fig. 26, BC type 1), and some of the jars (Fig. 21, JNM type 4; Fig. 24, JWM type 5). The proportion of the coarser, charcoal-tempered Severn Valley ware was a useful indicator of earlier activity. Some dating evidence was also provided by the presence of Malvernian tubby cooking pots (Fig. 36, type 1) and, more particularly, Malvernian vessels copying BB1 types (Fig. 36, JC type 2; Fig. 38, BC types 2–5, D types 1–3).

The more closely datable wares and forms could be used to suggest the duration of activity on the site overall, and indicate the *floruit* of activity, but they could not be relied on to exactly date the fills in which they had been deposited, or redeposited, since much of the pottery came from waster dumps which could have been moved and mixed many times during various phases of production. Despite these limitations, it is possible to propose three phases of activity based on the ceramic evidence. The earliest phase dates to the late first or early second century. This was hinted at by small quantities of Trajanic samian, and the typically late first- or early second-century coarse-ware fabrics and forms. The main phase of activity, associated with pottery production on the site, dated broadly from the second half of the second century to the early or mid third century. The bulk of the samian assemblage, for example, dated to the Hadrianic to late Antonine period, that is from c 120 AD to the late second century. A number of the Severn Valley ware forms produced were paralleled at the nearby Great Buckmans Farm kiln site, active some time between the middle and the end of the second century. The evidence for a third phase, with a low level of activity continuing to the late third century at least, came from some of the Severn Valley ware and BB1-type forms. This evidence, however, tended to come from the upper fills of features and surface spreads, and clearly post-dated the main period of deposition.

The dating evidence was assessed for each of the feature groups listed in Table 1, and for the individual features within them. The dating relied even more heavily on the coarse wares in these smaller assemblages. Where variations were noted between the composition of feature groups, however, these often reflected functional rather than chronological differences, which are discussed separately below.

Features associated with pottery production (Groups 5, 6, 7, and 8)

Group 7: individual features

About two thirds of all the pottery recovered, and much of the kiln debris, came from features in Area B associated with pottery production (Groups 7 and 8). Amongst these, F112, F116, F117 and F118 accounted for approximately half of the entire pottery assemblage and the great majority of the kiln debris.

The uppermost fill of F116 contained a characteristically third- or fourth-century Severn Valley ware type (Fig. 21, JNM type 4). The Severn Valley ware forms in the other fills, however, were broadly second to early third century in date, with tankard type 2, for example, very common. A residual sherd of Hadrianic or early Antonine samian was recovered from layer 7069. The gully also produced Severn Valley ware mortarium dated AD 70–120 (MT6, not illustrated).

Gully F112 produced a more mixed assemblage apparently deposited some time in the third to fourth century, but which contained mainly residual, second-century material. Characteristically later Severn Valley ware types included late second- or third-century tankards (Fig. 20, T type 3), and third- or fourth-century jars (Fig. 21, JNM type 4). A fragment from a mid to late second- to early third-century BB1 jar was also included (Fig. 40, JC type 1). Residual sherds of samian were present, one dated Hadrianic or early Antonine, and one mid to late Antonine. The assemblage also produced sherds from two Severn Valley ware mortaria dated AD 70–120 (Fig. 31, MT1, MT2). F117. The subsequent recut of the gully produced only second-century coarsewares.

Posthole F142 produced a Mancetter-Hartshill mortarium (MT8, not illustrated) dated to the second half of the third century to the early fourth century, and the only sherd of East-Gaulish samian recovered, dating to the late second to first half of the third century. Hearth F137 produced broadly second-century Severn Valley ware, and a stamped sherd of samian dated AD 125–40 (Samian catalogue S2, not illustrated). Pit F141 produced second- to early third-century tankards (Fig. 20, T type 2), and BB1 types dating from the late second or third century (Fig. 40, BC type 2, D type 5). A sherd of mid-to-late Antonine samian was also present, and need not be residual.

The layer of silty clay, 7031, overlying the features produced sherds of Oxfordshire mortaria dated to the early third century and AD 240–300 (MT9–11, not illustrated), and a BB1-type jar dating to the late third or fourth century (Fig. 40, JC type 2). The Severn Valley ware included late second- or third-century tankards (Fig. 20, T type 3), and a characteristically third- to fourth-century jar (Fig. 21, JNM type 4). Residual material included four sherds of second-century samian and fragments from three Severn Valley ware mortaria dated AD 70–120 (Fig. 31, MT4; MT3 and MT5, not illustrated)

Stone surface F151 and the overlying layer 7047 produced late third- or fourth-century types in addition to second- to third-century material. This included a fragment from an Oxfordshire mortarium, Young type M18 (Young 1977, fig 21) dated AD 240–300; BB1-type jars and bowls (Fig. 40, JC type 2, BC type 3). An upper fill of well F143 produced a late third- or fourth-century BB1 bowl (Fig. 40, BC type 6) as well as earlier material. Kiln F108 contained a number of third- to fourth-century types; the most common forms being characteristically later jars (Fig. 21, JNM type 4; Fig. 24, JWM type 5).

Group 7: summary
The bulk of the Group 7 assemblage indicates a main period of production dating to the Antonine period (c. 138-92 AD) or early third century, perhaps longer if the potters were conservative in the development of new forms. Late second- to third-century BB1 types were present in small numbers; a bead-rimmed dish (Fig. 40, D type 5; F112 and C7072) and a single groove-flanged bowl (Fig. 40, BC type 2; F141), perhaps dating to the early third century. Amongst the Severn Valley ware tankards, the second- to early third-century variety (Fig. 41, T type 2) was the most common type. BB1, and Malvernian BB1 copies, included characteristically second-century bowls (Fig. 38, BC type 1) and jars (Fig. 40, JC type 1), the latter sometimes having characteristically early, wavy-pattern burnish on the neck. Small numbers of earlier, Hadrianic-to-Antonine, Malvernian tubby cooking pots were also present (Fig. 36, JC3–JC8). The assemblage represents material used to infill the various features when they went out of use. The features produced fairly high proportions of wasters (Fig. 42) and the pottery had relatively high average sherd weights. The latter suggests that the pottery was either dumped directly into these features, perhaps from the kiln, or came from waster heaps that had not been greatly disturbed. If the latter is the case, some time may have elapsed before the pottery was redeposited.

Some third- or fourth-century forms were also present, including: Mancetter-Hartshill mortarium (MT8, not illustrated), Severn Valley ware and BB1 forms. This later material, particularly from the upper fills of features and surface spreads, shows that some level of activity continued in the area into the late third or fourth century. At this point the pits and gullies had been filled in, and there was presumably a change of activity on the site.

There was some evidence for residual material relating to Phase 1 activity. Characteristically late first- to early second-century Severn Valley ware forms were present. These included: locally produced mortaria dated AD 70–120, but only in very small quantities; carinated bowls (Fig. 26, BC type 1), upright-walled tankards (Fig. 20. T type 1), and platters (Fig. 30, DP type 8).

Group 8
The pottery from the Group 8 features was broadly similar to the pottery from Group 7 features, in both character and date. No kiln debris was found but four features produced wasters (Fig. 42b). There was a higher proportion of Malvernian ware in the assemblage as a whole (handmade 13%, wheel-made 2%), and a slightly lower proportion of Severn Valley ware (43% organic, 41% other), although all the Malvernian ware came from three features, F121, F127, and F133, and a layer of colluvium 7038.

A very narrow range of late second- to third-century BB1-type forms was included, with flat-flanged dishes (Fig. 38, D1, D2) and fragmentary rims from third-century or later splayed-rim jars (Fig. 36, JC10, JC11). The proportions of Severn Valley ware tankard types are very similar to those for Group 7 (Fig. 41); there were a few of the earlier upright-walled tankards (Fig. 20, T type 1) but the second to early third-century type dominated (T type 2). Six sherds of samian, also all from the colluvium, ranged in date from Hadrianic-Antonine to mid to late Antonine.

Groups 5 and 6
Elsewhere on the site, features thought to be associated with pottery manufacture produced smaller assemblages. The Group 5 features in Site 1 produced assemblages dominated

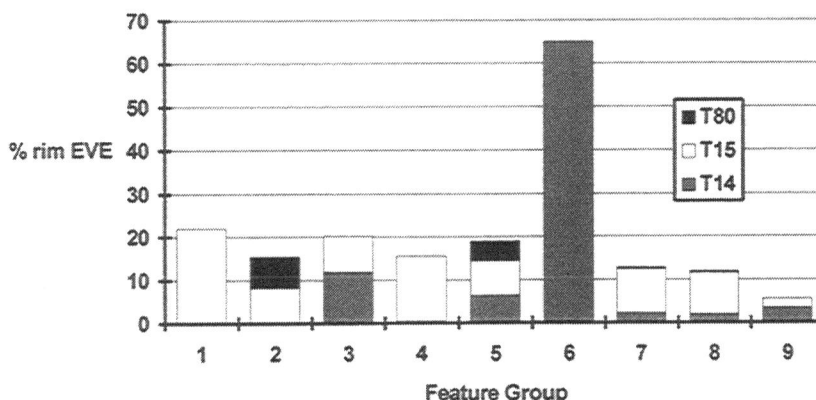

Figure 41: Ceramic dating evidence, Severn Valley ware tankards by feature Group (% rim EVE)

by Severn Valley ware, although Malvernian ware was noticeably more common than in the Site 2, Area B pottery production features. Ditch F1211 produced second- to early third-century tankard types (Fig. 20, T type 2, 21%), and characteristically later second- to third-century types were also fairly common (T type 3, 15%). Some possibly later material was included. Earlier tankard types were present in small quantities (T type 1, 3%), and a residual sherd of Hadrianic or Antonine samian was also noted.

The latest dating evidence from F2290 was provided by second- to early third-century tankards (Fig. 20, T type 2). The feature also produced four sherds of Antonine samian although much of the pottery appeared to be earlier than this, perhaps contemporary with the Group 3 assemblage discussed below. The coarser, and earlier, organic Severn Valley variant (Fabric O2) was common. First- or second-century upright-walled tankards (T type 1, 8.5%) were more common than the second to early third century type (T type 2, 2.5%). This feature also produced a fragment of first- to third-century glass. There was no diagnostic pottery in F1198, the only other feature in the group containing pottery.

The Group 5 assemblage as a whole included pottery dated from the first or second century through to the late second or third century. Comparing it with the assemblages from Groups 7 and 8, there is less late second- to early third-century pottery. This is evident from the more even split between diagnostic tankard types (Fig. 41), and the relatively higher proportion of the earlier organic-tempered Severn Valley variant.

Group 6, in area 1, produced only twelve sherds from four features F2161, F2164, F2205 and F2273. This seems to represent an earlier group. Seven sherds were in the early, organic-tempered Severn Valley variant (Fabric O2), and the remainder included hand-made Malvernian ware and one sherd of Savernake ware. The only Severn Valley ware tankard represented was of the earlier type (Fig. 41, T type 1).

Two-post structures (Group 1)

The Group 1 two-post structures from Site 1 produced a small assemblage. The latest pottery included a third-century BB1 groove-rimmed bowl (Fig. 40, BC type 2). Amongst the Severn Valley ware, only the second- to third-century tankards (Fig. 20, T type 2) were represented. A single stamped sherd of samian, dated AD 110–30 (Samian catalogue S3, not illustrated), was recovered from F2129.

Boundary ditches (Groups 2, 3 and 4)

Group 3

The Site 2, Area A, boundary features of Group 3 produced a small assemblage in which hand-made Malvernian ware was the most common fabric and Severn Valley ware was less dominant than in the pottery production groups. The assemblage appears to date between the Trajanic to the early Antonine period (late first to early second century), corresponding to the first phase of activity on the site. It produced a relatively high proportion of samian, in which mid to late Antonine samian was absent. The latest piece came from F109; a Central Gaulish sherd dated Hadrianic or early Antonine (c 161-180 AD). Ditch F125 produced four samian

fragments dated AD 100–120 (Samian catalogue D2, not illustrated). Joining sherds from a samian bowl, dated AD 65–80, came from F109 and F115 (Samian catalogue D1, not illustrated).

The evidence from the coarse wares suggests an earlier second-century date. The Malvernian tubby cooking pots (13%; Fig. 36, JC3–8) were mostly of the type predominantly associated with Hadrianic and Antonine contexts (broadly second century), but also found in Flavian to Trajanic assemblages (late first to early second century). Small numbers of the more typically late first- and early second-century types were also present (1%; Fig. 36, JC1, JC2). The earlier organic-tempered Severn Valley ware (Fabric O2) was almost as common as the other variants. Severn Valley ware forms included characteristically late first- to early second century types such as carinated bowls (2%; Fig. 26, BT type 1), and upright-walled tankards (13%; Fig. 20, T type 1), which were more common than the second-century tankards predominant elsewhere on the site (2%; T type 2). The assemblage also produced an early second-century mortarium in Severn Valley ware (Fig. 31, MT7). A range of other fabrics occurred in small quantities, including white ware, probably from Mancetter-Hartshill (F109, F115); BB1 (F109, F119); and a grog-tempered storage jar (Fabric R26; F115, F109).

Group 4

The Site 2, Area B boundary ditches of Group 4 (F113 and F107) produced pottery broadly similar in character and date to the rest of the Area B assemblage, although some variations were noted. The ditches contained a higher proportion of Malvernian ware than the features associated with pottery production, more similar to the proportions from the Area A boundary ditches, and no BB1. However, the presence of wasters in both features (Fig. 42b), and kiln debris in F107 suggests a similar source to the Group 7 material.

The latest forms were a third- to fourth-century Severn Valley ware jar (Fig. 21, JNM type 4), and BB1-copy jars with splayed rims dating to at least the third century, single examples of which were noted in both ditches. With the exception of these, the pottery was broadly late second to early third century, with tankards of this date (Fig. 20, T type 2) by far the most common variety. None of the later type (T type 3) was present, and proportionally fewer of the earlier type (T type 1) than were noted in Groups 7 and 8. Three sherds of second-century samian were present.

Group 2

The Site 1 ditch F2061 of Group 2 contained Severn Valley ware tankards dating to the late second to third century, and these were more common here than in most other features (Fig. 41. T type 3; 7%). The assemblage also produced three sherds of samian, one dated Hadrianic to early Antonine and another a stamped vessel dated AD 160–90 (Samian catalogue S1, not illustrated).

Site 2, Area C, features (Group 9)

The majority of the Group 9 pottery came from colluvium layer 7041, with much smaller quantities coming from layer

a) Wasters by Group

%
Count

Gp 7   Gp 2   Gp 5   Gp 4   Gp 6   Gp 8   Gp 3   Gp1   Gp 9

b) Area B: Wasters by feature/group

%
Count

F. No/Gp No of Sherds		
108/7	194	
112/7	1064	
116/7	1393	
117/7	246	
118/7	1490	
120/7	29	
122/7	79	
123/7	14	
128/7	30	
137/7	172	
141/7	78	
142/7	75	
143/7	81	
145/7	11	
121/8	51	
126/8	25	
127/8	101	
135/8	5	
107/4	209	
113/4	179	

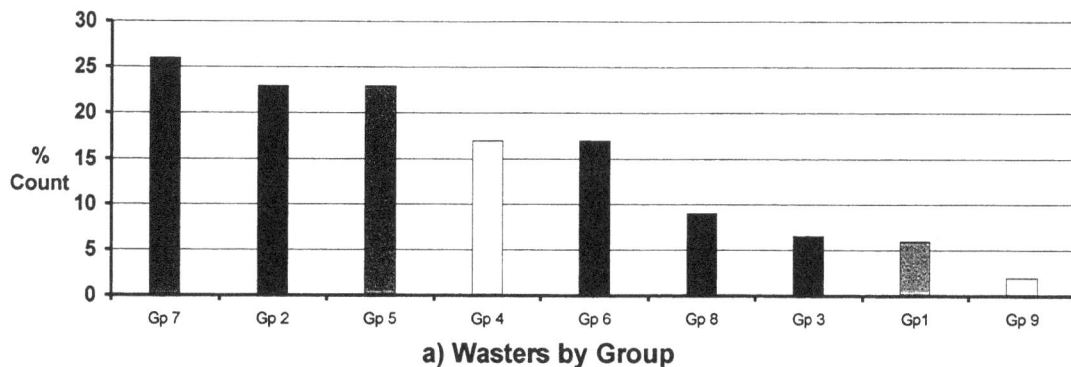

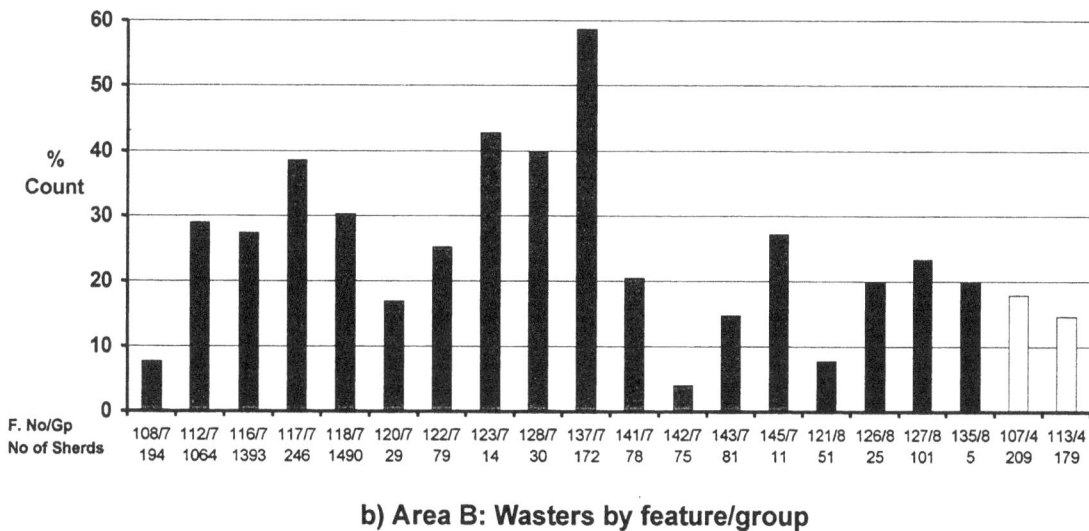

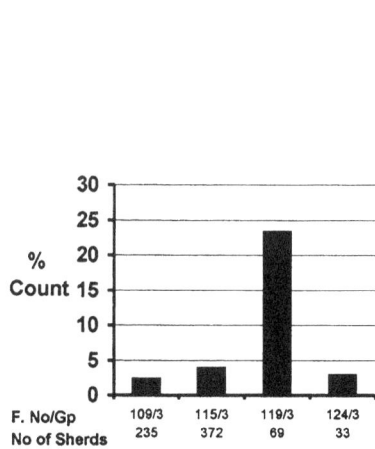

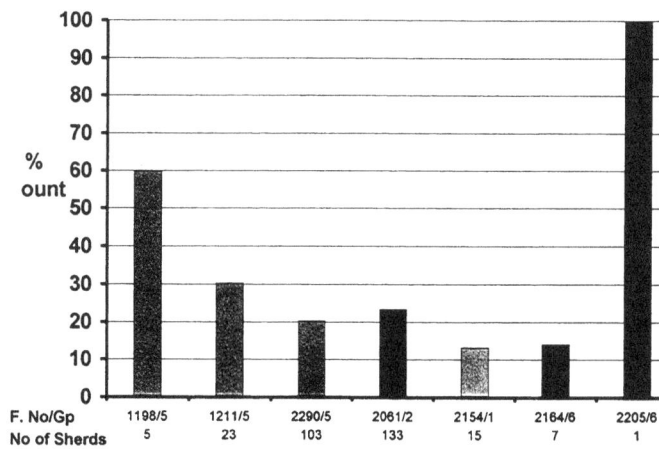

c) Area A:Wasters by feature/group

%
Count

F. No/Gp	No of Sherds
109/3	235
115/3	372
119/3	69
124/3	33

d) Site 1: Wasters by feature/group

%
ount

F. No/Gp	No of Sherds
1198/5	5
1211/5	23
2290/5	103
2061/2	133
2154/1	15
2164/6	7
2205/6	1

Figure 42: Ceramic functional evidence: occurrence of wasters (% count)

7125. This group produced the highest proportion of Malvernian pottery from the site and, in particular, the highest proportion of wheel-made Malvernian ware. Much of the pottery presumably derived from activity further up the hill. It reflects a long period of activity, starting perhaps in the earlier second century and continuing well into the third. A few third- to fourth-century Severn Valley ware jars were noted (Fig. 21, JNM type 4). The latest BB1 type represented was a bowl with a dropped-flange rim (Fig. 40, BC type 3), dating to at least the late third century. Amongst the

Malvernian ware most of the forms were BB1 copies, most commonly a splayed-rim cooking pot (Fig. 36, JC10, JC11). There were no tubby cooking pots. Other BB1 copies included second-century bowls (Fig. 38, BC type 1) and cook pots (Fig. 36, JC9), and plain-rimmed dishes of a type produced from the second century on (Fig. 38, D3). Amongst the Severn Valley wares, the earlier tankards (Fig. 20, T type 1) were slightly more common than the second- to early third-century type, T type 2 (Fig. 41).

—✧—

EVIDENCE FOR SITE FUNCTION

Some variations between the group assemblages relate to functional rather than chronological differences. All of the pottery appears to be rubbish dumped in features after they have gone out of use, and thus the evidence can only be used to determine the nature of nearby activity rather than the function of the features themselves.

Although the presence of wasters provides evidence that pottery was being produced in the vicinity, their absence need not imply that pottery production was not taking place, since underfired pots could also have been rejects. Wasters were present in varying proportions in all groups (Fig. 42), with the greatest numbers from the Site 2, Area B pottery production features (Group 7), reflecting the proximity of these features to the kiln. High numbers also came from the other Site 2, Area B groups.

In Area B the five features with the greatest number of wasters also produced much of the kiln debris. The evidence suggests systematic dumping, with the heavier kiln debris being thrown primarily into F116 and then F112 closest to the kiln, while the highest quantity of wasters came from F118 slightly further away. The kiln itself, F108, contained only a small number of wasters. This fact, the absence of kiln debris, and the fragmented nature of the pottery all indicate that the kiln was thoroughly dismantled and cleared after it had gone out of use.

There was a small number of Severn Valley ware wasters at Site 2, Area A, most commonly in F119. One kilogramme of fired clay, including flue arch material, was found and flecks of charcoal were noted in many fills. The area seems likely to have had some connection with an earlier phase of pottery production. In addition, there was a relatively high proportion of Malvernian ware, and this, with the range of other non-local fabrics represented, distinguishes this group from the pottery production groups in Area B. It is possible that a Malvernian ware kiln was located nearby. However, the presence of a high proportion of cooking pots, of the decorated samian vessels and of the animal bone also suggests waste from an occupation site nearby. Wasters were also present at Site 1 in small numbers, although no kiln debris was recovered.

Severn Valley ware wasters were rare at Site 2, Area C. However, Malvernian ware was very common here, with 119 sherds. Many of these were oxidised throughout, particularly in the hand-made fabric R22. These may well have been misfired, since the ware is usually black or very dark grey throughout, at most having an oxidised lens or patches. There was no evidence from sooting that these sherds had been used, although the evidence may have been lost through abrasion. This group of sherds may well represent the waste products of a potter working in the native tradition, the kiln lying outside the excavated area. Malvernian stone fragments are naturally abundant in the local clays, and would have been readily available for use as temper

—◇—

OTHER FINDS

KILN DEBRIS
by Sarah Watt

Introduction and method of analysis
About 4000 fragments of fired clay, weighing 153.45kg, were recovered from the Site 2 excavations. The material ranged from very small, worn fragments to more substantial, well-fired chunks. Both oxidised and reduced clay was represented, the oxidised pieces tending to be smaller and softer than the reduced pieces. Significantly, the assemblage contained no recognisable kiln furniture; all the pieces were identified as kiln-lining or as fragments of flue-arch. Most of the material came from Area B, mainly from F112 and F116. The bulk of the rest of the fired clay from Area B came from the other gullies close to the kiln and the pits associated with them. It has been assumed that the majority of this material originated from the kiln, F108, although other kilns may also have been located in the vicinity. The clay was sorted by type (either kiln lining or flue arch), fabric (only one uniform fabric was recognised), firing colour (oxidised or reduced), hardness, and whether or not it was imprinted, and was quantified by both weight and count. The data was analysed using Microsoft Access. Details of the recording system are available in the archive.

Sources of material on site
The bulk of the fired clay came from Area B, with less than a kilogram each coming from Areas A and C. Area A had five fired-clay producing features: F109, F115, F119, F124 and F146. Less than 1% of this material consisted of possible fragments of flue-arch, the rest of the material comprised mainly soft, oxidised fragments of kiln-lining. The main fired-clay producing features in Area B correspond to the features which produced the greatest amount of pottery, particularly F116, F112, F108, and F117. The main fired-clay-producing context was 7061 (in F116) — almost 40% of the total weight of kiln lining came from this context. F112, which was probably also part of the processing system, also produced a large amount of material. There was a lot less kiln material from the boundary ditches (F107 and F113) than from gullies more obviously associated with pottery production (F112 and F116). Only 23 pieces of kiln-lining came from F113, for example. However, the material probably arrived in the same process of abandonment and backfilling. The larger fragments of kiln lining (average fragment weight > 40g) came from the features nearest to the kiln (F112, F116, F118, F120, F122 and F137). Features beyond these latter had an average fragment weight of <40g. As the fragments from the kiln itself, F108, weighed only 17g on average, the kiln does not itself appear to have been used as a waste pit — instead, debris was cleared out of it. A total of 11.3% of the weight of material from the kiln was comprised of heavily fired fragments, probably from the flue arch, and 27.5% of the material had been imprinted by vegetation. F151, a cobbled surface on which raw clay may have been left to weather before being processed, produced some fragments of fired clay, which was mostly soft, oxidised material. Finally layer 7041 in Area C produced only 766g of fired clay, all of which was composed of small fragments with a mean fragment weight of 9.46g.

Description of the kiln debris
The majority of the assemblage by weight was reduced, while the majority by count was oxidised, reflecting the softer, more friable character of the latter. The reduced and often hard fragments would have been exposed to the greatest heat, and probably came from the vicinity of the flue.

Most of the fragments of kiln-lining can be placed into four broad groups. Those in Group 1 were small soft fragments. Those in Group 2 were harder, better fired fragments. Some were quite regular and rectangular in shape, possessing three smooth and one rough surface. Fragments from Group 3 were characterised by vegetation imprints, often recognisable as grass-blades, on one or both sides. They were generally flat, thin 'plates', measuring on average 10mm thick, and were usually oxidised. Finally, Group 4 comprised very highly fired fragments coloured dark-grey or black, sometimes vitrified with a green and glassy surface or pumice-like in appearance. This group also produced a large, prefabricated block (C7095) which was perhaps used to reinforce the flue arch.

Discussion
The Group 1 fragments of kiln-lining most likely either formed part of the temporary superstructure, away from the heat source and only used once before being replaced, or alternatively, could have been on the outside of the superstructure. The high level of fragmentation in this group reflects the softness of the clay.

The Group 2 kiln-lining probably represent the kiln's more permanent lining, and thus is more highly fired, and ranges in colour from orange and red through to grey, depending on how close it was to the source of heat. The blocks appear to have been preformed, and perhaps relate to repair or strengthening of the kiln structure at vulnerable points. The smooth sides were usually reduced, while the rough surfaces, which were attached to the kiln wall, remained oxidised.

The presence of the vegetation-imprinted fragments, Group 3, indicates a kiln roof made of turves, plastered over with a thin layer of clay. This would probably have been a temporary dome, renewed with each firing, the kiln having an open top above the permanent clay wall to facilitate loading and unloading of the firing-chamber. Some of the fragments also had imprints of the sticks or wattles used to support the turves. Fragments with imprints on both sides were perhaps used to bond turves together where they overlapped. The presence of some finger-shaped impressions implies that the plastering was done by hand rather than with a trowel.

The Group 4 pieces were thought to be from the flue arch, the hottest part of the kiln. The green glassy vitrification is presumably on the sides which faced inwards into the flue, and suggests that these pieces formed part of the more permanent lining of the kiln.

A few pottery wasters were also found fused to lumps of clay, suggesting that they were also used to reinforce the structure of the kiln, although wasters could also have been spread on the firing chamber floor on which the vessels were stacked, as there was no oven floor as such.

It is very difficult to estimate the amount of fired clay that would survive after a single kiln firing. F116 alone, however, produced a total of 21kg of heavily fired material (likely to be from around the flue), which seems very high. The debris may therefore represent more than one firing of the kiln or may, alternatively, have derived from more than one kiln.

The heavy truncation of the kiln means that there is a dearth of *in situ* evidence for the kiln's external and internal structure, and superficial kiln furniture could have been ploughed away. It is therefore impossible to say for certain whether or not it possessed any prefabricated kiln supports. However, given the complete absence of any evidence for permanent or portable kiln furniture anywhere on the site, it seems likely that the kiln required neither. The only good evidence for the superstructure of the kiln is the amount of grass-imprinted slabs of kiln-lining, making it likely to be the case that it was roofed temporarily with turves and overplastered with a layer of clay. Bryant (1973) has noted how easily this material can be dispersed and its retention in the channels at Newland Hopfields is a rare occurrence.

—◇—

BRICK AND TILE
by Kirsty Nichol

Only seven pieces of Romano-British tile were identified at Newland Hopfields. All appear to have been produced locally; five were in fabrics equivalent to Severn Valley ware variants O3, O6, and O8, and two were in Malvernian metamorphic ware. Tile production is known in the area; a specialised tile kiln dating to the latter half of the second century has been excavated at Upper Sandlin Farm, Leigh Sinton (Jack 1925; Waters 1963).

Four forms were present: the Severn Valley ware material included two joining pieces with combed keying (from 7085 and F127, 7102), making a significant part of a box flue tile. From context 4004 came a large *tegula* fragment with an abraded flange, in the coarser Severn Valley ware fabric O8. A fragment of *imbrex* in fabric O3 came from C4011 , and a piece of a bonding brick in fabric O6, was recovered during fieldwalking. The only form represented in the Malvernian

metamorphic fabric was a fragment of *tegula* from the Area B cobbled surface, C7072. Building materials in Malvernian fabrics have been noted on other sites, such as Sidbury, Worcester (Lentowicz 1992, 66).

There was no evidence to suggest that the tile was produced or used in the kiln. Only a single box flue fragment came from a gully associated with pottery production (F127, Group 8). Although this feature produced pottery wasters, no kiln debris was associated. The cut was shallow and may have been truncated, and the box flue fragment could have been intrusive from the overlying context (7085) which produced the joining fragment. The remaining material came from contexts interpreted as hillwash. The scarcity of ceramic building material also makes it improbable that any substantial structure was located in the vicinity of the area excavated.

—◇—

CERAMIC SPINDLE WHORLS
by Lynne Bevan

Two Roman ceramic spindle whorls were recovered, one of which was complete (Fig. 43.2 and 3). Both were in Severn Valley ware Fabric 04, and were deliberately formed, rather than being made from re-used pot sherds. They are most likely products of the kiln.

1   Spindle whorl, ceramic with flat surfaces and central perforation; Diam 40mm, Th 7–9mm. Site 2, Area B, layer 7052, fill of F112

2   Spindle whorl, ceramic, dome-shaped with double indentation around outer edge; Diam 40mm, Th 10mm. Site 2, Area B, layer 7031, fill of F112

—◇—

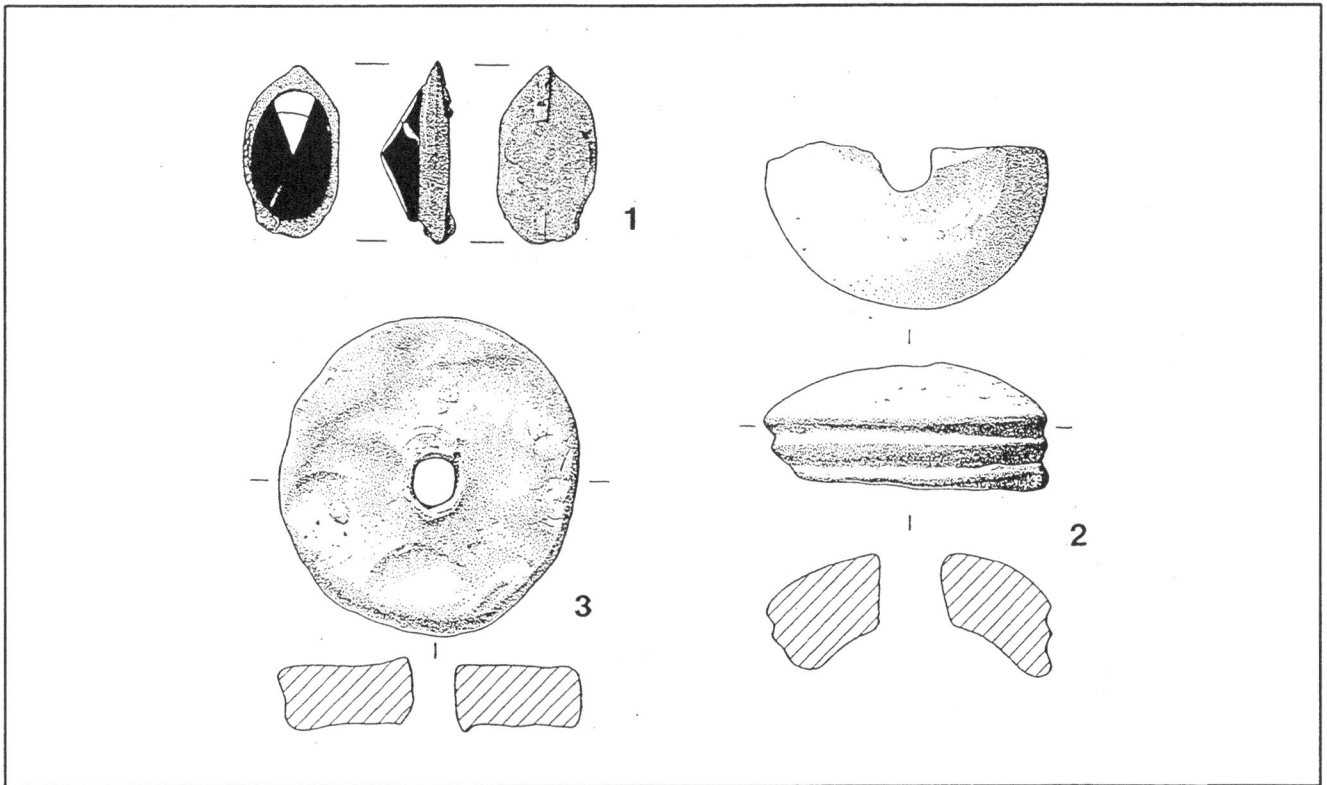

Figure 43: Brooch and spindle-whorls; scale 1:1

METAL OBJECTS
by Lynne Bevan and Donald Mackreth

Due to the generally poor and fragmentary condition of the metal objects, only one, brooch no 1, has been illustrated. (Fig. 43.1)

Romano-British Brooches
by Donald Mackreth

1   Plate; copper alloy. The bilateral spring had been mounted on a single pierced lug behind the plate. This had been oval, with one recessed zone bearing a series of circular stamps in the form of two concentric annuli. In the middle is a conical glass gem almost black in colour. Site 2, Area B, layer 7047, overlying F151. Fig. 43.1

The spring system and the myriad examples from Britain show that this is an exclusively British brooch. The earlier version of this brooch has enamel in the zones round the central area which may have either a repoussé plate over it or be fitted with a glass gem, usually in the form of an intaglio (eg Philp 1981, 150, fig. 32.73; Hattatt 1987, 252, fig. 79.1207). The gilded series almost invariably has stamps around the paste gem, although the latter may be replaced by a series of ribs radiating from a central spike (Pitt Rivers 1887, 41, pl 10.5). The plate may be round or oval and have one or two recessed zones, the most extreme examples having three zones, the middle one interrupted by four smaller settings for paste gems. The British dating is: Manchester, *c.*160 to early third century (Bryant *et al.* 1986, 65, fig. 5.5,3102); Hockwold Norfolk, shrine, late second century to ?late fourth century (Gurney 1986, 64, fig. 40.8); Dorchester-on-Thames, post-Antonine (Frere 1962, 137, fig. 27.8); Brancaster, with third-century pottery (Hinchliffe and Green 1985, 44, fig. 28.5); Inworth, Essex, AD 250/60–370 (Going 1987, 81, fig. 40.2); Fishbourne, AD 280/290 (Cunliffe 1971, 106, fig. 40.43: Cunliffe

1991, 162); Maxey, Cambridgeshire, late third century to fourth century (Crummy 1985, 164, fig. 111.6); Nettleton, shrine, AD 360–370 (Wedlake 1982, 148, fig. 63.5). For such a common type, the number of dated items is meagre, but does show that the family is not purely fourth century, a commonly held view. The gilded group began at least towards the end of the second century and ran through the third. The two brooches from shrines should perhaps be disregarded, as there is now good evidence that such items were retained as priestly equipment well into the fourth century. Examples found on the continent in datable contexts shed further light on the dating; Wierden, Netherlands, a pair with a cremation in a second half of the second century pot (van Es and Verlinde 1977, 80, fig. 28.28); Esch, Netherlands, two examples, AD 200–250, possibly 225–250 (van den Hurk 1977, 108, figs. 25 and 26); Saalburg and Zugmantel, three examples before AD 260 (Bohme 1972, taf 29.1132, 1134, and 1133 not illustrated); Augst, with third-century pottery (Riha 1979, 88, taf 13.309). These, in contrast to the British evidence, show that on the continent at least the type was in favour from the end of the second century until at least the middle of the third.

2   Colchester Derivative; copper alloy. The spring is held in the Polden Hill manner: the axis bar through the coils is seated in a pierced plate at the end of each wing, the chord being secured by a rearward-facing hook. Each wing is short and plain. The head of the plain bow is rounded and rises above the wings. The bow section is thin, giving the front a very shallow curve. The foot-knob is biconical, with a cross-moulding above, all under the base of the damaged catch-plate. Site 1, Area 1, layer 2168

Essentially a standard member of a large family centred on the western side of England, members of it can be found in all parts of Roman Britain. The chief difference here from the normal form is the lack of a curved moulding rising from each wing to clasp the sides of the head of the bow. Otherwise the proportions, shape and the foot-knob confirm that the brooch belongs to the family. Dating has recently been discussed and the conclusion was that the developed type was in being in the latter part of the first century and the family was passing both out of manufacture and use mainly between AD 150 and 175 (Mackreth 1998). There may be one strand which lasts a little longer, but this brooch does not belong to it.

3   Trumpet; copper alloy. The spring is mounted between two pierced plates behind the trumpet head. There are the remains of a cast-on loop on a pedestal which has a groove across it. The trumpet head is off-set from the head-plate by a groove and has a relieved cross-cut ridge down the front. On each side, and just above halfway, is a divided, elongated lenticular boss. The knop has a pair of cross-mouldings above and below and is of the usual 'petalled' form with a flat back. The lower bow has a ridge down the middle, with a groove along each border. The foot-knob has two divided lenticular bosses at the bottom of a pedestal under a cross-moulding. Site 2, Area B, layer 7061, fill of F116

The way in which the spring is held occurs most frequently in the western parts of Britain. There is a clutch of brooches which, at first sight, has features which mark a distinct group, but in detail its members differ too much for this to be the case. Dating is fairly well established, once all those which belong to varieties with applied white metal trim have been removed. The overall date-range runs from the latter part of the first century to the third quarter of the second century: by AD 175 practically all Trumpets have been consigned to the ground, very few running to AD 200, and those which are later should be seen as being residual in their contexts (Mackreth 1998).

Other jewellery and fittings of copper alloy
by Lynne Bevan

4   Head and partial shaft of small pin with a circular head; L 6mm, Diam of head 1.5mm. Site 2, Area B, layer 7124, beneath ploughsoil

5   Length of twisted wire with circular section, probably from a bracelet; L *c*.100mm, Diam 1mm. Site 2, Area B, layer 7031, fill of F112

6   Three lengths of wire, probably from a bracelet, one with ferrous encrustations. They have a circular section and one has a deliberately bent end suggestive of a fastening; L 75mm, 47mm and 42mm, Diam 1mm. Site 2, Area B, layer 7060, fill of F117

7   Two lengths of wire with 'D'-shaped section, possibly joining pieces of a bracelet, perhaps a child's. Both fragments have retained original tapered ends; L 100mm, 40mm, Th 2mm. Site 1, Area 1, layer 2126, fill of F2127

8   Tack with domed head, probably used for furniture or small boxes. L 14mm, of head 4mm, Th (max) 3mm. Site 1, Area 1, layer 1191

9   Dome-headed disc rivetted on to piece of iron plate which has since corroded, destroying any original edges. Diam (of disc) 14mm, Th (of disc) 3mm. Site 2, Area B, layer 7124, under ploughsoil

Iron objects
by Lynne Bevan

The condition of the iron objects was generally very poor with a high incidence of corrosion. Identifiable in this small collection were: a hook of post-Roman date (Site 1, Area 1, layer 2134), three lengths of wire (Site 1, Area 1, layer 2257 and unstratified), and two possible sections of implement shafts (Site 2, Area B, layers 7138, 7140, both fills of F143), one of which might have been part of a chisel. There were also 13 nails, two of which could be related to Type 1b in Manning's nail typology (Manning 1985, 134–7). Both of these broad, flat-headed nails might have been used for general building purposes. They came from Site 2, Area B, layer 7047, overlying F151. A further three nail fragments came from the same layer and two from F151 itself. Of the remainder, four came from overall Site 1 layers, and two from Site 2, Area B, from layer 7031 a fill of F112, and from the ploughsoil.

—◇—

ROMAN GLASS
by Lynne Bevan

Six small fragments of Roman glass were recovered, three from each of the two phases of excavation. None was worthy of illustration. The fragments, all of which are 4–5mm in thickness, were from blue-green bottles. Three were flat base fragments from square or hexagonal bottles, and the remainder were small, body fragments from square, hexagonal or cylindrical bottles. This general type of vessel was most common during the late first and second centuries, falling out of use at some time during the third century (Cool and Price 1995, 184–5). Two of the square or hexagonal bottle fragments came from Site 1, Area 1, layer 2183 in F2290, while the third came from layer 7047 overlying the stone spread F151 at Site 2, Area B. The other bottle fragments came from layer 2225 at Site 1, Area 1, and from F112, layer 7031, and F118, layer 7079, at Site 2, Area B.

—◇—

THE WORKED STONE
by Fiona Roe

The worked stone divides between materials imported for specific uses, such as quartz conglomerate, Millstone Grit and Coal Measures sandstone, and local materials, which appear to have been used in a more casual manner.

The imported materials were all needed for grinding purposes, and some had been brought to the site over considerable distances. Two rotary quern fragments are made from Upper Old Red Sandstone quartz conglomerate from a relatively local source in the Forest of Dean/Welsh Border area, some 53km away. Although an almost entirely riverine route, down the Wye and up the Severn, could have been used for these querns, the site itself lying only 3km from the Severn, another quern fragment (from Site 1, Area 1, layer 2166) made from Millstone Grit, is likely to have been transported by road from the Sheffield area, over a distance of *c.*150km. A whetstone and a point sharpener (from Site 2, Area B, F151) both appear, on macroscopic examination, to be made from Coal Measures sandstone from the same Yorkshire or Derbyshire area.

These materials have been recorded from other Roman sites in the area. Objects made from the quartz conglomerate from the Forest of Dean/South Wales source area were widely distributed in Worcestershire, Warwickshire, Gloucestershire and Oxfordshire. They occur in local Roman contexts in Worcester at Sidbury (Roe 1992a, 85), Deansway (Roe forthcoming a) and Farrier Street (Dalwood *et al.* 1994, 102), and also in Droitwich (Roe 1992b, 72; Roe forthcoming b) and Alcester (Evans and Crossling 1994, 247).

Millstone Grit objects occur in smaller quantities in the area, no doubt because of the ready availability of the Old Red Sandstone, but are still known from a number of sites, including Sidbury in Worcester (Roe 1992a, 86), sites in Droitwich (Roe forthcoming b and c), and again in Alcester (Evans and Crossling 1994, 247). Newland Hopfields is, however, well within the limits for the distribution of Millstone Grit at Roman sites, since it is known as far from the source area as Kent and Wiltshire.

Whetstones made from Coal Measures sandstone are less readily identified than the Millstone Grit querns, but they also appear to have been widely distributed during the Roman period. As with the ubiquitous whetstones of Kentish Rag, it seems possible that they may come from a single source area,

in this case in the Pennines, which was to continue to be important for the provision of grindstone and whetstone materials (Farey 1811). It should, however, be noted that there are smaller exposures of Coal Measures Sandstone nearer to Newland Hopfields, in both Shropshire and Staffordshire. Similar whetstones are known from Alcester (Webb and Crossling 1996, 119), while ones which have been attested by thin sectioning have come from West Hill, Uley (Roe 1993, 197) and the Chessalls, Kingscote (Roe 1998), both sites in Gloucestershire.

The artefacts made from local stone are less well defined than those of imported stone. There was a variety of local stone available for use at this site, situated just to the east of the Malvern Hills, though the granites, diorites, tonalites and ultramafics that form the Malverns Complex (Barclay *et al.* 1997, 4) would on the whole have been too hard for practical use. Mainly sedimentary rocks were chosen for utilisation, and amongst these the Silurian Wyche Beds, which break naturally into small slabs (*ibid.* 25), were used for three implements, a polisher with a glossy surface, but with a side also used for whetting (Site 2, Area B, layer 7084, fill of F112), an apparently unsuccessful attempt at a whetstone (Site 2, Area B, F151) and a whetstone or smoother (also F151). The coarser-grained Silurian Cowleigh Park Beds (*ibid.* 25) were used for a possible rubber (Site 1, Area 1, layer 999). A point-sharpener was made from local Triassic sandstone, probably the Bromsgrove sandstone (*ibid.* 49).

Only two fragmentary artefacts were made from igneous rock; Malvernian diorite was used for a possible rubber (Site 2, Area B, layer 7061, fill of F116), and for a possible small weight (Site 2, Area B, layer 7048, fill of F113). Another fragmentary weight (Site 2, Area B, 7067, fill of F118) was made from quartzitic sandstone obtained from local Quaternary deposits.

There was also a quantity of unworked local stone from these excavations, consisting of mainly angular fragments of Malvernian rocks, including in particular granite, diorite and ultramafic rock, with further fragments from the Cowleigh Park Beds. These, when smashed into fine-grained pieces, would have been suitable for inclusion as temper in the coarser, handmade Malvernian ware of Peacock's type A (Peacock 1967; pers. comm. Jane Evans).

CATALOGUE (not illustrated)

1   Fragment with a possibly worn surface, possibly a rubber; Cowleigh Park sandstone; Site 1, u/s

2   Fragment of rotary quern, Roman disc type, diam *c.* 410mm, max thickness, 59mm; Upper Old Red Sandstone: Quartz Conglomerate; Site 1, layer 1191

3   Fragment of point sharpener with one narrow groove; fine-grained, grey pink, slightly micaceous sandstone: Triassic; Site 1, layer 2166, fill of F2167

4   Fragment of rotary quern, weathered, max thickness 54mm; Millstone grit; Site 1, layer 2166, fill of F2167

5   Fragment of an upper stone from a rotary quern, Roman disc type, diam *c.* 430mm, max thickness 57mm, secondary wear on upper surface; Upper Old Red Sandstone: Quartz Conglomerate; Site 2, Area B, group 7, layer 7031, fill of F118

6   Weathered and burnt fragment, with one flattened surface, 59x54x43.5mm, possibly part of a weight; Malvernian: diorite with biotite; Site 2, Area B, layer 7048, fill of F113

7   Fragment, with a possibly worn surface, possibly a rubber; Malvernian: diorite; Site 2, Area B, layer 7061, fill of F116

8   Broken slab whetstone. Now 86x55x14mm, wear on one flat surface, burnt; micaceous sandstone: probably Coal Measure sandstone; Site 2, Area B, layer 7062, fill of F117

9 Fragment, possibly small weight, burnt, now 50x45.5x30mm; quartzitic sandstone, probably from Drift; Site 2, Area B, layer 7067, fill of F118

10 Small fragment of whetstone or smoother, with one worn, flat surface, 40x30x7.5mm; fine-grained slightly micaceous sandstone: probably from Wyche Beds; Site 2, Area B, layer 7072, fill of F151

11 Small fragment of point sharpener with a single narrow groove, 45x43.5x18mm; micaceous sandstone: probably Coal Measure sandstone; Site 2, Area B, layer 7072, fill of F151

12 Apparent trial whetstone, a rod with a square section, 111.5x29.5x27.5mm, a little wear on one side; fine-grained slightly micaceous sandstone: probably from Wyche Beds; Site 2, Area B, layer 7072, fill of F151

13 Large slab used as polisher/whetstone, with gloss on worn flat side and worn edge, 165x58.5x28mm; fine-grained slightly micaceous sandstone: probably from Wyche Beds; Site 2, Area B, layer 7084, fill of F112

—◇—

PREHISTORIC LITHICS
by Lynne Bevan with stone identifications by Rob Ixer

A Neolithic ground stone axe was recovered (Fig. 44). This was petrographically identified as being of an altered non-ophitic alkali basalt comprising dominant plagioclase laths, equant crystals of clinopyroxene and a euhedral FeTi oxide mineral. The axe does not match any of the known groups such as the Scottish Midland Valley Basalt Group XVIII or the Windsill Group 13. Small outcrops of alkali basalts have been identified in the Midlands Group and it is possible that the axe had a local, perhaps Welsh, origin, or that it may have originated from a glacial erratic. Wear traces were visible along the working end but there were no signs that the object had been used as a burnisher in pottery production.

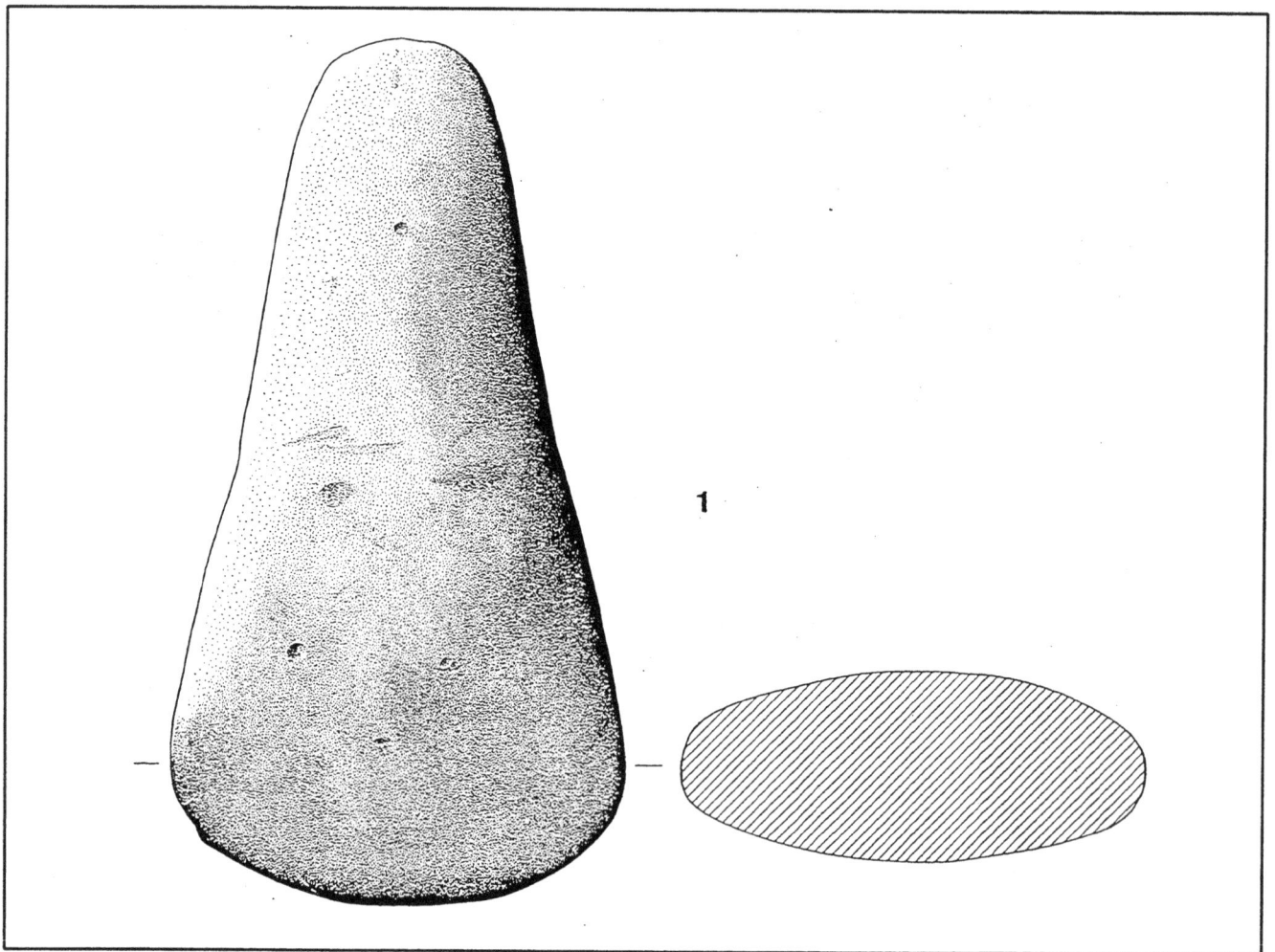

Figure 44: Stone Axe; scale 1:1

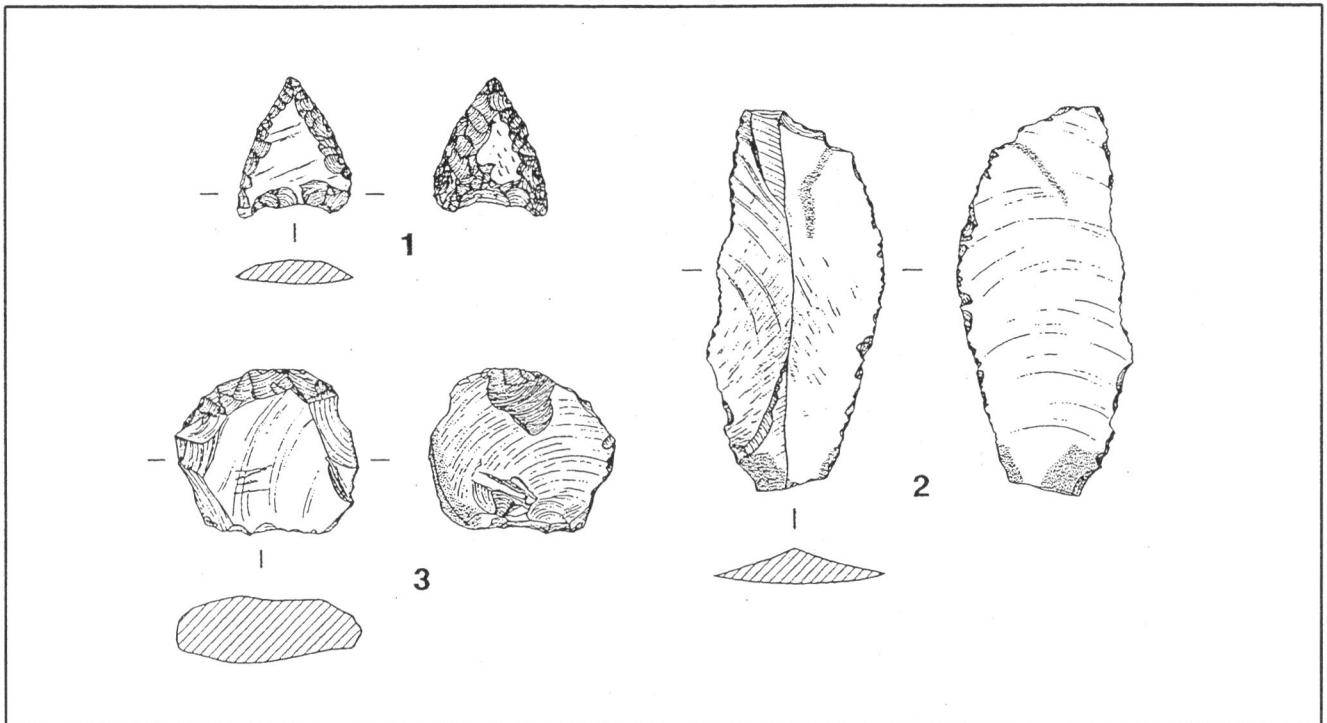

Figure 45: Flint objects; scale 1:1

Chronologically diagnostic flint finds consisted of one arrowhead of translucent light brown flint (Fig. 45.1), a knife (Fig. 45.2), and a small thumbnail scraper (Fig. 45.3). Although damaged, the arrowhead was originally barbed and tanged, conforming to Green's Sutton B type, dated to the Beaker/Early Bronze Age period (Green 1980, 122, fig. 45).

It might be contemporary with the scraper, a common Beaker type (Healy 1984, 15). The broad knife, which came from the same context as the stone axe, is probably of Neolithic origin. Non-diagnostic finds consisted of three broken flint flakes (descriptions in archive).

CATALOGUE OF ILLUSTRATED ITEMS

Fig. 44

Stone axe; L 118mm, W (max) 66mm, Th 27mm; SF 12. Site 2, Area B, layer 7047, over F151

Fig. 45

45.1 Barbed and tanged arrowhead; L 20mm, Th 3mm; SF 10. Site 2, Area B, layer 7124, below ploughsoil

45.2 Knife with retouched edge; light grey-brown opaque flint; L 52mm, W (max) 22mm, Th 5mm. Site 2, Area B, layer 7047, over F151

45.3 Scraper, thumbnail type; grey-brown translucent flint, some cortical survival on right-hand side; L 23mm, W 23mm, Th 7mm. Site 1, Area 1

—◇—

THE ANIMAL BONE
by Stephanie Pinter-Bellows

The animal bone assemblage from Site 2 was briefly examined for the assessment report (Evans and Jones 1995, 19–20). A full report was not thought worthwhile and the following is an edited version of the assessment report.

Site 1 produced 78 bones (Dalwood 1992, 17) and Site 2 844, making an overall site assemblage of 922 bones and bone fragments. The bones were in a very fragmentary condition and generally under 40mm in greatest dimension, though the structure of the bone itself was usually in good condition. For the most part, bones were not abraded or eroded, although bones from F119, Site 2, Area A, and F117, Site 2, Area B,

were in poor condition and very fragile. One bone from F118, Site 2, Area B, showed signs of having been gnawed by a rodent. Site 2, Area B also had a great deal of fragmented maxillary and mandibular teeth of cow and sheep/goat, and a few horse. The only articulated bone group, a group of five caudal (tail) vertebrae from a sheep/goat, was found in F109, Site 2, Area A. More burnt and calcined bones were recovered from Site 2, Area A (31%) than Site 2, Area B (5%).

The brief examination of the bone showed that the assemblage is dominated by the usual domesticates: cattle, sheep/goat, and pig were found in roughly equal numbers, with horse scarcer in Site 2, Area A, while the majority of domesticate bones from Site 2, Area B were cattle.

From both areas, the number of bones in general and of informative bones in particular is few. The fragment size is small; the number of loose teeth is large compared to jaws. The bone structure is good, and gnawed bones are almost non-existent. The impression is that these are not fragments which were above ground for a long period of time being walked over and broken. They could, perhaps, represent the smaller fragments left behind when larger pieces of bone were removed to be used or dumped elsewhere. The bone left behind includes a high proportion of bones which were not directly food related, in particular the large number of fragmented teeth from Site 2, Area B, which were mostly too fragmented to be considered informative.

—◇—

THE ENVIRONMENTAL REMAINS
by Simon Butler and Rowena Gale

Introduction
by Simon Butler

Features and contexts from the Site 2 excavations were extensively sampled for environmental remains. The following report is an edited version of the assessment of the potential of these samples (Evans and Jones 1995, 21–4). At Site 2, the collection of samples was intended to illuminate the local environments surrounding the site and the economic activities taking place on the site. For charred plant remains, bulk 20 litre samples were taken routinely from the majority of excavated contexts. Pollen samples were taken from ditches F109, F115, F141, F116 and well F143.

A number of samples contained large quantities of wood charcoal, and the results of analysis by Rowena Gale are described separately. Seeds were sparsely represented; a sample identified by Lisa Moffett showed few samples with many varieties. The highest number was 29 species from F144 (Site 2, Area B) and the group included seeds of cereals with *Hordeum vulgare* (hulled) and *Triticum* species represented. However, many of the charred plant remains occurrences were modern contaminants and none of the samples contained sufficient quantities of material for meaningful analysis. At Site 1, too, only very small quantities of charred plant remains were recovered (de Rouffignac 1992). The pollen samples were largely negative, with only two samples, from ditch F141 and well F143, containing sufficient numbers for individual analysis, too small a number of samples to make a broader synthesis. The absence of charred seed remains tends to support the hypothesis that the site functioned primarily in an industrial capacity.

The charcoal
by Rowena Gale

Five samples of charcoal from Site 2, Area B, were examined and identified to establish the use of fuel woods. Two came from layers 7034 and 7059, fills of the pottery kiln F108, and five from F116 (layers 7071, 7073 and 7100), F136 (layer 7122) and the hillwash layer 7041. In general the charcoal was rather friable and poorly preserved; some pieces were heavily contaminated with sediments. In contrast, the larger fragment of maple (*Acer*) from layer 7034 in the kiln were firm and clean. Some samples included large aggregates composed of small pieces of charoal and soil.

Fragments measuring 2mm square in cross section were isolated from each sample. These were fractured to expose fresh transverse surfaces and sorted into groups based on the anatomical features observed using a x20 hand lens. Representative fragments were selected and fractured to expose tangential and radial longitudinal surfaces. These were supported in sand and examined using a Nikon Labophot incident-light microscope at magnifications of up to x400. The anatomical structure was matched to reference material.

The taxa identified (Table 11) included:
Acer sp., maple
Fraxinus sp., ash
Pomoideae, sub-family of the Rosaceae, which includes *Crateagus* sp., hawthorn; *Malus* sp., apple; *Pyrus* sp., pear; *sorbus* spp., rowan, whitebeam and service tree. These genera are anatomically similar.
Prunus sp., blackthorn, cherry and bird cherry
Quercus sp., oak
Slicaceae which includes *Salix* sp., willow and *Poplulus* sp., poplar, also anatomically similar.

The sample from layer 7034 from the kiln included some large chunks of charcoal. The largest piece was a portion of maple (*Acer*) roundwood which measured some 35mm in length, c.40mm in diameter (when charred) and included 12 growth rings. Layer 7059 from the kiln included a piece of material tentatively identified as coal. Also a cylindrical fragment of poplar/willow measuring c.7.5mm in diameter. This was of particular interest, since the anatomical structure indicated that it was not roundwood; ie the three growth rings were not concentric but aligned across the diameter. The size and shape conformed to those of some treenails and, by inference, this would suggest the reuse of timber as fuel.

Direct evidence of coppicing was inconclusive, since most of the identified fragments were fairly small and it was not possible to assess whether they arose from roundwood. The sample from F116 included oak heartwood and samples from the kiln, F136 and layer 7041 included some young growth (stem/branch) of oak. The maple fragment in kiln layer 7034 retained a small piece of bark still *in situ,* thus confirming its origin as roundwood; it was 12 years old and probably measured some 50mm+ in diameter when living.

Table 11: Charcoal: occurrence in the analysed samples (nos of fragments)

Features/contexts	Acer	Fraxinus	Pomoideae	Prunus	Quercus	Salicaceae
F108 (7034)	13	-	-	7	5	21
F108 (7059)	2	3	-	4	6	11
F116 (7071)	-	-	1	-	11	-
F116 (7073)	8	-	-	-	1	-
F116 (7100)	1	-	2	-	15	6
F136 (7122)	3	-	-	-	9	-
7041	-	-	-	-	22	2

—◇—

DISCUSSION
by C Jane Evans

The preliminary reconnaissance work, prior to the selection of the areas to excavate, established that much of the archaeology of the Newland Hopfields site had been destroyed. This destruction seems likely to have been the result of recent ploughing, as witnessed by the surface scatters of pottery observed over recent years. Why the archaeology of Site 1, Area 1 and of Site 2, Areas A and B, survived is not clear. The areas may have been protected by plough headlands or activities associated with hop growing, or have lain slightly below surrounding levels.

What is clear is that these areas do not represent the main focus of Roman activity and a more widespread Romano-British landscape should be envisaged. Kilns were often located on the periphery of occupation sites, sometimes just within their outer boundaries (Swan 1984, 6). This appears to be the case at Newland Hopfields. If a Romano-British settlement lay nearby, as would have been likely, it may have been sited to the west, beneath the present day built up area of Malvern Link. At Site 1, Area 1, pit F2290 may have been sited in the corner of a field, if the east–west ditch in Area B is projected west to join with F2061. At Site 2, Area B, the pottery production features are apparently in the angle of the field boundary. The first layout of the field boundaries at Site 1 and Site 2, Area B is undated, but would seem likely to predate pottery production.

A detailed discussion of the dating evidence has been presented in the pottery report. On the basis of fieldwalking in the 1950s, Walker proposed a second- to third-century date for the site (Walker 1960), with some activity continuing to the fourth century. Analysis of the excavated assemblage supports this dating. The main period of production has been defined by the most common forms represented, which date from the mid to late second century to the third century (Fig. 20, T type 2, Fig. 21, JNM type 3, Fig. 22, JM type 2.1, Fig. 23, JWM type 2, Fig. 25, JLS type 2, Figs. 27–29, BT type 3). The broader chronological span is reflected in the range of Severn Valley ware forms represented. The earliest evidence of pottery production at Newland Hopfields is provided by the characteristically first to early second century forms, in particular the mortaria dated AD 70–120 from Area 2, Site B. At Site 2, Area A pottery from ditch fills was of first or early second-century date, perhaps suggesting that the layout there had gone out of use by the mid second century. These ditch fills were the only excavated deposits to contain quantities of animal bone which, together with the pottery evidence, indicated some domestic occupation associated with the boundaries.

The ceramic dating evidence does not allow the real duration of activity to be defined more closely; whether, for example, it was continuous over this period, or whether there were intermittent periods of activity. The stratigraphic evidence, however, suggested a succession of activities with layouts superseding each other. At Site 1, Area 1, there was a clear sequence of F1211, followed by a pit-like feature F1204 which was in turn cut by F1198. The two-post structures, perhaps representing pottery drying racks, clearly supersede each other, while one pair cuts ditch F1164. At Site 2, Area

B, the levigation channel beneath F108 showed that pottery production was underway before the kiln was constructed. The life of the kiln itself may have been extended by repositioning its flue. It was not clear whether the kiln and the levigation channels at Area 2, Site B were associated. It would seem best to assume that F108 was one of a succession of kilns around which increasing mounds of potsherds were sited, parts of these mounds being eventually levelled out into open levigation ditches. While the latter were infilled with pottery the kiln was not, and the dating evidence from the kiln infill suggested a later date. A similar backfilling of open features, although in this case including the kiln itself, was seen at Alkington, Lower Wick (Fowler and Bennett 1973).

The other Malvern kiln sites reflect an overlapping sequence of production, from the late first or early second century at Half Key Lane, through to the third or more probably fourth century at the Hygienic Laundry site (Table 12). The assemblages from these other sites have not been fully quantified, but the forms represented have been summarised and it is possible to compare them with Newland Hopfields in terms of the presence or absence of certain forms (Table 13). Rusticated jars, the diagnostic form in the small Half Key Lane assemblage, were absent at Newland Hopfields. There are parallels between Newland Hopfields and both the Swan Inn and Hygienic Laundry sites. The best parallels, however, are with assemblages from Great Buckmans Farm and Grit Farm, in the Malvern Link complex, and Marley Hall, situated well away from the complex, to the west of the Malvern hills.

These sites, with Newland Hopfields, are all broadly in the area now known as Malvern Link. Malvern Link was, until fairly recently, common land, like Malvern Chase, the focus of the medieval pottery industry. It is located on Mercian Mudstone (formerly Keuper Marl), in an area of glacial drift, with clays incorporating Malvernian rock fragments, ideal for the prehistoric and Romano-British coarse-ware industries discussed by Peacock (1967, 1968, 1982). The origin and extent of these Pleistocene fan gravels are discussed elsewhere (Hurst 1994, 116–8). It seems likely that this land was always marginal land, unsuitable for agriculture but suitable for grazing. Judging from the long history of pottery production in the area, it is clear that the location was ideally suited to providing both the necessary raw materials for pottery production, and access to viable distribution routes for the kiln products.

The exact source or sources of the clay used at Newland Hopfields are not known, although it is obviously local. It is likely that the Roman potters were digging clay on or near the site, and two large pits, F2290 at Site 1 and F118 at Site 2, Area B, probably result from clay extraction. The potters may well have used a number of slightly different sources of clay. This might explain some of the minor variations between fabrics. The distinctive colour of fabric O5, for example, was thought to indicate a slightly more iron-rich source for the clay, rather than just a variation in its firing (pers. comm. Vivien Swan). Other raw materials would also have been available close by. In addition to the well (F143),

Table 12: Romano-British pottery: kiln sites from the Malvern area (based on Tomber 1980; Swan 1984).

Site Name	HWCM no.	Evidence	Webster 1976	Swan 1984	Tomber 1980	Other refs	Products	Date
Half Key Lane	7061	Concentration of pottery, including wasters		674	39-40	Waters 1976, 66; Peacock 1967, 18, fig. 5.93	Rustic jar	Late first or early second century
Swan Inn	4073	2 pottery scatters, including a high proportion of wasters	Malvern Kiln IV, 38		38-39	Waters 1976, 66	Oxidised; mainly carinated bowls and narrow-mouthed jars; some storage jars and double-lipped jars	Second (Webster 1976), or early second century (Tomber 1980, 39)
Great Buckmans Farm	1315	Pottery and kiln debris	Malvern Kiln II, 37	676	34-36	Waters 1976	Oxidised; mainly plain tankards, wide-mouthed jars (mainly long-necked, some short), narrow-mouthed jars, large storage jars and bowls; some double-lipped jars, a mortarium. Some coarse grey ware	Mid-to-late second century
Little Buckmans Farm	3700	Dense scatter of pottery				Sawle 1980		Second and third century
Newland Common, Lower Howsell	1510	Kiln cut by gas pipeline				SMR Report 1978		Second and third century
Newland Hopfield	4072	2 pottery scatters, including wasters		764	36-37	Walker 1960; Waters 1976, 66;	Oxidised; mainly wide-mouthed jars (predominantly long necked but some with short necks), narrow-mouthed jars and large storage jars; some double-lipped jars, bowls, tankards and dishes. Some coarse grey ware	Second and third century, with some fourth century material
Marley Hall	1596			352	42-44	Watkins 1932, 110-12; Ward-Perkins 1938	Oxidised; mainly double-lipped jars, narrow-mouthed jars, storage jars, tankards, and wide-mouthed jars; some handled beakers, bowls (some with red colour coating), dishes, flagons	Possibly second, but mainly third-to-fourth century
Grit Farm	4585 and 4584/11392	Pottery, including many wasters, and kiln debris, evidence of a kiln?	Malvern Kiln III, 38	675	37-38	Waters 1969; Waters 1970; Waters 1976, 66; Waters 1979	Oxidised; mainly narrow-mouthed jars (including double-lipped jars), then wide-mouthed jars (both long and short necked), tankards; some storage jars and bowls. Some coarse grey wares.	Late third or possibly fourth century
Hygienic Laundry	6004	Pottery, including a small number of wasters, and a fragment of kiln lining	Malvern Kiln I, 37	673	32-34	Haverfield 1901, 219; Peacock 1967	Oxidised; mainly wide-mouthed jars (mainly short necked), narrow-mouthed jars, dishes. Some coarse-grey-ware jars and native wares?	Third or more probably fourth century
Upper Sandlin Farm, Tile kiln	3758	Tiles, some pottery				Jack 1925; Waters 1963, 3		
Chase Secondary School	15577	Surface finds.		673	40	Waters 1976, 66		
Leigh	26398	Large group of pottery noted by metal detectorist				SMR Report 1997		

Table 13: Romano-British pottery: seriation of chronologically diagnostic forms from Newland Hopfields and other Malvern kilns

Form type noted at Newland Hopfields	Newland Hopfields (% rim EVE)	Swan Inn	Great Buckmans Farm	Marley Hall	Grit Farm	Hygienic Laundry
BT type 1	0.4	X				
T type 1	**3.1**					
JWM type 7	0.2	X				
F type 1	1.6		X			
F type 2	0.9		X	X		
T type 2	**10.5**	X	X	X		
JNM type 2	**2.5**		X			
JNM type 3	**3.2**			X	X	
JM type 2.1	**4.4**		X			
JLS type 2	**4.2**	X	X	X	X	
JWM type 2	**4.5**	X	X			
BT type 2	**2.3**		X		X	
BT type 3	**6.1**		X	X	X	
BT type 4	**2.9**	X	X	X	X	
T type 3	0.5				X	
JWM type 3	0.2			X	X	
JNM type 4	1.5		X	X	X	X
JM 2.2	1.9		X		X	X
JWM type 5	**2.5**			X	X	X
JWM type 6	0.8					X

X denotes presence, forms representing more than 2% at Newland Hopfields in bold

a common feature on Roman pottery production sites (Peacock 1982, 54), the site is located between two sources of water; Sandy's Spring to the south and Madresfield Brook to the north. Fuel would also have been an important consideration. Vince notes (1977, 290) that the medieval industries at Hanley Castle would have used large amounts of wood from Malvern Chase. The Link area may also have provided easy access to fuel. The five samples of charcoal analysed by Rowena Gale, however, do not provide evidence of coppicing. As on other Romano-British kiln sites (pers. comm. Vivien Swan) a variety of fuels seems to have been used, reflecting current availability, including maple, reused timber and perhaps even coal.

Before being formed into pots the clay would have been prepared. It would first have been dried out and allowed to weather, perhaps on stone surfaces similar to F151 at Site 2, Area B. Impurities in the clay would then have been removed in levigation ditches or pits. This involved mixing the clay with water and allowing the coarser material to settle out. Some of these features may also have been used to moisten the clay. Stone surfaces, and again F151 is a possibility, could also have been used for mixing the clay, as has been suggested for the paved areas at Cowley, Dorchester (Young 1977, 18). Buildings, interpreted as workshops, have been noted on other production sites (Peacock 1982, 73–4) and in these the pots might have been thrown and perhaps stored prior to distribution. F151, once more, with its nearby postholes is the only candidate at Newland Hopfields.

The Newland Hopfields site provided little evidence for the potters' tools noted on production sites elsewhere, including wheels and socket stones (Peacock 1982, 55–7). The stone assemblage included quern fragments, which have been found on other production sites (ibid., 57), but there was no evidence to suggest that these had been used as wheels. There was also a polisher and a possible smoother, both in local stone, which could perhaps have been used for burnishing. Several flat stones with polished surfaces were recovered from the Perry Barr site, for example, which have been interpreted as potters' tools (Hughes 1959, 35). Neolithic handaxes have been found on other kiln sites, and are thought to have been reused as polishers (pers. comm. Vivien Swan), but there was no evidence for reuse on the example from F151. Metal knives are also a common find on kiln sites, but none was recovered from this site.

Before firing, the pots would have had to be thoroughly dried. No drying ovens or other specialised drying facilities were identified at the Newland Hopfields site. However, a number of two-post structures was noted which may well have been pottery drying racks. Peacock suggests that the absence of specialised drying facilities is a feature of seasonal potteries (1967, 66–7). The soils on the site were not very permeable and must have been subject to seasonal waterlogging, which would have restricted the period of production. There was no evidence, however, to indicate the precise season in which pottery production might have taken place; none of the kiln lining, for example, had impressions of bracken or other seasonally diagnostic vegetation.

The kiln appears to have been a simple, single-chambered, single-flued, updraught kiln. As such it is an outlier in the distribution described by Swan, redefining the western edge (1984, 113, fig. 11) which previously had outliers only in Warwickshire. Swan notes that this type is not found in areas with a strong pre-Conquest, La Tène III tradition, and postulates that they represent the Romanisation of a much older technology (*ibid.*, 113–4). There was no evidence for portable kiln furniture or an inbuilt floor, placing the kiln in the third and most basic of Swan's three categories. Some of the complete wasters may have formed part of an expendable supportive layer of vessels, but could also have been used to deflect the main blast of heat from the flue (pers. comm. Vivien Swan). The kiln is similar to the Severn Valley ware kiln excavated at Alkington in Gloucestershire (Fowler and Bennett 1973, 58–9). These kilns, however, both situated at the heart of the main Severn Valley ware production area, are simpler than those noted at peripheral production sites such as Shepton Mallet, Somerset (Scarth 1866; Swan 1984, microfiche 594), Perry Barr, Warwickshire, (Hughes 1959; Swan 1984, microfiche 635) or the Colchester-type kiln at Sherifoot Lane, Sutton Coldfield. The level of control that the potters had over firing conditions may be indicated by the fact that the great majority of the misfired vessels achieved the desired oxidised colour, with a tendency towards under-, rather than over-, firing. It is impossible, however, to know what proportion of the total kiln output is represented by the pottery sample excavated.

The potters producing Severn Valley ware at Newland Hopfields, and at the other Malvern kiln sites, were producing a very utilitarian range of forms. In this respect the workshop is similar to the many small-scale, grey-ware industries that supplied local demand across Roman Britain. The full range of forms produced can be summarised as follows. Jars were by far the most common form, representing more than 60% by rim EVE, followed by tankards and bowls. The vast majority of forms, the jars and flagons, are containers (Fig. 46), most probably for foods or liquids. Most of the flagons produced have open mouths and are, arguably, better suited to storing commodities such as milk rather than wine. The remainder can be divided into four further categories: food preparation vessels (medium to large bowls and mortaria),

Figure 47: Ceramic functional evidence: function of forms from assemblage by feature Group (% rim EVE)

serving vessels (tankards, which could have been used as drinking vessels or perhaps measures), and a small number of tablewares and miscellaneous forms. These have been represented diagramatically by Feature Group (Fig. 47).

More specialised wares are very poorly represented in the Newland Hopfields assemblage. There are no colour-coated wares and few samian copies, although the latter are produced in Severn Valley ware elsewhere, for example bowls copying samian form 38 (Webster 1976, fig. 9.62, 63, 64). There are no segmental bowls (*ibid.*, type J, fig.10.65), another type noted by Webster and a common second-century form in other fabrics. Apart from the small to medium bowls, there are few forms that could be defined as tablewares. There are no beakers and, as noted above, very few flagons suitable for wine. Finally, only a very few mortaria were produced on the site. These had a very local distribution, and none was stamped. Although well made, they were mostly quite unusual in their form and, in particular, the method by which the trituration grits were applied. Once again, this reflects a pattern evident in other Malvern kiln assemblages. Only the Marley Hall kiln, located away from the Malvern Link group on the other side of the hills, provided evidence for the production of beakers. This assemblage also produced a red colour-coated bowl, probably copying samian form 31 (Tomber 1980, fig. 16.235). No mortaria has previously been found at the Malvern kiln sites (Tomber 1980), and no mortaria attributable to the Malvern kilns have as yet been identified at Worcester, although a Malvern mortarium is recorded from Gloucester (Ireland 1983, 109 fabric TF9H).

This near absence of specialist wares in the Malvern kiln assemblages provides a marked contrast to the peripheral

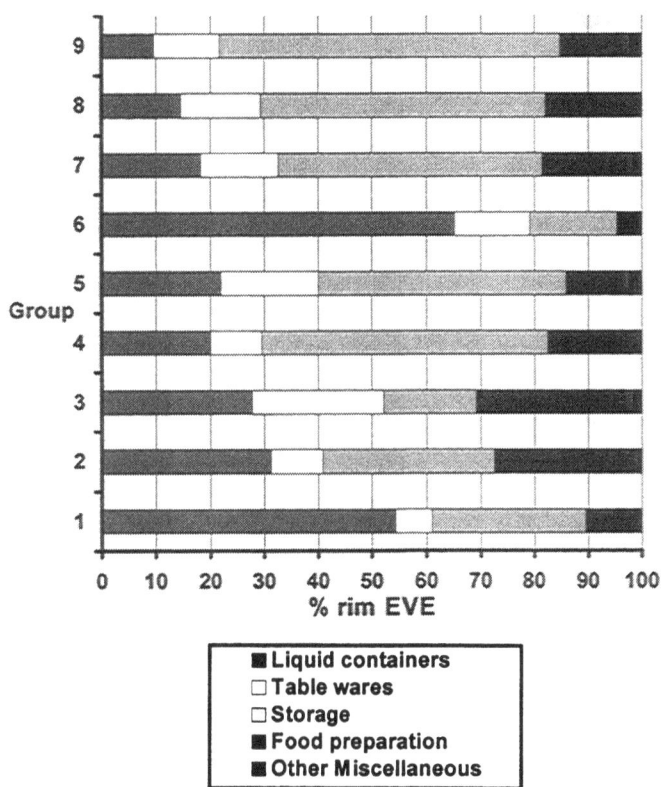

Figure 46: Ceramic functional evidence: function of Severn Valley ware forms (% rim EVE)

Severn Valley ware production sites at Shepton Mallet, Somerset (Evans in press) and Wroxeter (Houghton 1963; Swan 1984, microfiche 579). At both of these sites specialist potters were producing mortaria and a range of other fine ware forms. This highlights the complex nature of the industry currently defined by fabric within the very broad term 'Severn Valley ware'. There seems to be a division between the producers of the utilitarian wares, and potters producing the more specialised types that would originally have been imported. This is not surprising, but is a distinction that has been more immediately obvious beyond the Severn Valley area, where reduced wares were used for the utilitarian wares, and oxidised or white wares were generally used for the specialist wares. More specialised forms in Severn Valley ware are found in small quantities on sites not far from Malvern, presumably supplied by specialist potters who, on existing evidence, were not based at the Malvern Link kilns. The assemblage from Sidbury, Worcester, for example, included butt and roughcast beakers (Darlington and Evans 1992, fig. 17) and flagons with more restricted mouths (*ibid.,* fig. 16.1–7). Local mortaria fabrics have also been noted at the Worcester Sidbury and Deansway sites (Darlington and Evans 1992, 39; Buteux and Evans forthcoming, fabric 37). One of the latter, dated AD 65–120, was stamped by a specialist potter who is known from Wroxeter and Caersws (pers. comm. Kay Hartley).

It is particularly interesting that at Newland Hopfields coarsely tempered, hand-made Malvernian wares seem to have been produced in close proximity to the wheel-made Severn Valley wares. There are even examples of forms traditionally made in the hand-made ware occurring in Severn Valley ware (Fig. 22, type JM1). This raises important questions about the relationship between these two seemingly distinct technologies in the Romano-British period. Hand-made pottery need not reflect household production nor wheel manufacture more specialisation (Peacock 1967, 26). There is no reason why an industry producing predominantly wheel-made wares could not also have produced pots by hand, when the size or function of the vessel demanded a coarser temper. The kiln excavated at Newland Hopfields is, technologically, closely related to a bonfire kiln (Swan 1984, 114) and could perhaps have been used to fire both types of pottery. It is tempting to try and draw wider conclusions on the structure of the industry. Ethnographic evidence, for example, suggests that where two such technologies are used side by side, the hand production is undertaken by women and the wheel production by men. While an interesting possibility, however, this must remain pure speculation.

The Newland Hopfields kiln represents a potential source for many assemblages excavated in the region, and full publication defines the products for future comparative studies. The problems of distinguishing Severn Valley ware fabrics from different sources have been discussed elsewhere (Tomber 1980, 119). Malvern fabrics have been identified macroscopically in assemblages from Alcester, in particular fabrics O1 and O4 (pers. comm. Jeremy Evans), and some of these identifications have been confirmed using neutron activation analysis (Evans forthcoming c). The presence of charcoal in some of the Malvern fabrics could also be an important indicator of their source. Certain diagnostic forms

have been used to suggest marketing models (Hodder 1974, 346, fig. 6), although Severn Valley ware forms are generally very standardised. Some of the flagons (Fig. 19, types F1 and F2) and bowls (Fig. 29, type BT4) found at Newland Hopfields appear to be characteristically Malvern types. The flagons have been noted in Alcester, supporting the identification of Malvern products by fabric. These more diagnostic forms might perhaps be used to suggest the source of the less diagnostic forms and fabrics with which they are associated.

As more quantified data become available it may be possible to assess the distribution of Malvern Severn Valley wares by studying the distribution of the more diagnostic Malvernian wares. Severn Valley ware in general is found on sites running primarily north–south along the length of the Severn Valley (Allen and Fulford 1996, 262, fig. 14a, b). The location of the Malvern Severn Valley ware kilns to the east of the hills is ideal for distribution by this eastern route. The coarser Malvernian ware has been noted on sites both to the east and the west of the hills, prompting Hodder to suggest two distribution routes: one through Worcester to the east, and one through Kenchester to the west (Hodder 1974, 346, fig. 5). The Marley Hall kiln was, perhaps, specifically established to the west of the hills to service a western trade route. A distribution relationship may have existed between the Malvern pottery industry and the Droitwich salt industry, as has been proposed for the prehistoric period (Morris 1981, 1985). The location of Malvern on the periphery of the Dobunnic *civitas* may also give some indication of its distribution pattern, as well as being a factor in its success (Millett 1990, 167). The evidence from the small, worked stone assemblage hints at wide trade contacts, ranging from the Forest of Dean/Welsh Border area, some 53km away, to the Yorkshire or Derbyshire area, roughly 150km away.

The regional distribution pattern for Malvernian wares, and Severn Valley wares, contrasts with that of Dorset Black-burnished ware (BB1). Relatively low proportions of BB1 are noted on sites along the River Severn. Based on this, the western route, using the road from Kenchester, has been proposed as a more likely route for transporting commodities to sites such as Wroxeter (Allen and Fulford 1996, 259–260, fig. 13). The low proportions of BB1 on sites along the River Severn may, however, reflect other factors, such as the dominance of local industries supplying this area. The Malvernian coarse wares, for example, have similar properties to BB1, and are used for vessels with similar functions. These two wares could have been in direct competition.

One area of debate regarding the Severn Valley ware industry has been its origin in relation to the military. Webster (1976, 41) proposed that the early potters were civilians catering for a mainly military market. More recently, Timby (1990) has argued against any military connection, demonstrating that the military brought with them their own potters, who produced vessels in a continental tradition. The two views can perhaps be reconciled if the function of the vessels is taken into account, and the earliest origins of the industry are considered separately from the reasons for its early growth and subsequent success. The quantified data from Newland Hopfields focuses attention on the very limited range of forms being produced, predominantly storage and food preparation vessels. It is not possible to say whether these were intended primarily for domestic use, or were supplying a more organised food processing industry. However, the use of storage vessels to market more valuable commodities has been used to explain the distribution of other wares (Lyne and Jeffries 1979, 57; Peacock 1982, 111–3), and might explain the long distance marketing of Severn Valley ware jars and associated forms to the northern frontier in the Hadrianic, and more particularly Antonine, period (Webster 1977). Bowls, which could not have been used for storage are not widely distributed. Like the Alice Holt jars, many of the Severn Valley forms seem ideally suited for liquid or semi-liquid commodities. Foods preserved in brine, valuable commodities such as honey, and less valuable commodities such as alcoholic beverages are all possibilities. Both Webster and Timby agree that the clearly native origin of the Severn Valley ware forms indicates civilian production, and Hodder (1974) has argued that supplies to the army would have been largely a matter of civilian enterprise. Other wares with clearly native origins can be related to military supply; most famously BB1, and more locally the coarse Malvernian wares which are often found on military sites in Wales and along the Welsh border (Hodder 1974). If Severn Valley ware vessels were reaching military sites as containers for some more important commodity, then the military would, presumably, have had little interest in the stylistic origins of the forms. In contrast, the form of vessels required for particular everyday activities would have been of concern to the army, and it is these more specialised forms such as mortaria, flagons and table wares that were generally made by the military potters.

Thus pottery production, in varying levels of intensity, may have continued at Newland Hopfields over a period of a century and a half, perhaps longer. The main floruit of activity can only be broadly dated from the second half of the second century to the early or mid third century. The kiln excavated would not have been in use throughout this period and it is likely that other, as yet unlocated, kilns would have been constructed. There is no evidence for significant changes in production methods over this period, both hand-made wares and wheel-made wares being produced throughout. The potters continued to make established forms which changed very gradually through time, in line with Severn Valley ware generally. This suggests a production system aimed at a conservative and stable market, which was not heavily influenced by changing fashions or fluctuating economic circumstances. The excavation evidence indicates that this was a major activity on this site rather than one peripheral to agriculture. The two-post structures, for example, were repeatedly sited in the same place and no breaks in activity are apparent at Site 1 or Site 2, Area B. Two of the three main areas excavated had pottery production features, while early production is possible at Site 2, Area A, and contemporary or later production at a Malvernian ware kiln off Site 2 Area C. The pottery fills of the levigation channels can be interpreted as representing an overall clearance of the site after cessation of pottery production. This took place only at Site 2, Area B, but nevertheless represents a decisive closure, within the Romano-British period, of a long-standing activity of which this report is the archaeological record. Later pottery in the upper fills of features and from surface spreads seems likely to derive from activity of a different nature, although this could be material from unlocated pottery production nearby.

—✧—

CONCLUSIONS AND SUGGESTIONS FOR FUTURE STUDY
by C. Jane Evans

The Newland Hopfields excavations make a significant contribution to Romano-British studies at a local, regional and national level. The evidence they provide for the layout of a pottery production site demonstrates the importance of excavating an area around a kiln, rather than excavating the kiln in isolation, as has so often been done in the past (Swan 1984, 128). This is not only the first Severn Valley ware production site to be studied in such detail, but is also one of the few Romano-British pottery production sites generally for which this level of information has been gathered. A more complex picture of the Severn Valley ware industry seems to be emerging as more information becomes available, with variations between production areas in the range of forms produced and the kiln structures used. Detailed analysis and quantification of the assemblage from Newland Hopfields provides a major body of data, which can be compared in the future with assemblages from both production and use sites.

Both the fieldwork and post-excavation analysis have been facilitated by previous research in the area. Prior to these excavations, the Malvern Link area had already been identified as the largest and best-studied group of Severn Valley ware kilns (Webster 1976, 38). This owed much to the work of local archaeology groups, in particular P. Waters and the Malvern Research Group, who identified a number of the sites, and I. Walker and the Kidderminster Archaeological and Historical Society, who fieldwalked the Newland Hopfields site. The published pottery assemblages, and Roberta Tomber's unpublished Msc. thesis on the pottery from the kilns have provided a major source of reference for the Newland Hopfields assemblage. However, most of the work referred to was undertaken twenty to thirty years ago, and analysis of this new assemblage highlights a number of areas which might benefit from additional research.

The Malvern kilns have potential to address a number of the research questions identified by the Study Group For Roman Pottery (Willis 1997). Further study would therefore not only enhance our understanding of the Malvern pottery industry, but also make an important contribution to Romano-British pottery studies generally. The Malvern kiln complex can be studied in its wider geographical context, for example by exploring the relationship between this rural area and nearby towns, in particular Worcester.

The concentration of kilns at Malvern provides an opportunity to study the structure of a Romano-British pottery industry. Webster (1976, 38) felt that the identification of a large pottery producing complex at Malvern was premature. Other possibilities, for example a smaller-scale but long-lived industry, need to be explored. However, we still do not know the full extent of the pottery production area at Malvern Link, and there may well be further kilns to be discovered. A further programme of fieldwalking and geophysical survey could build on existing work and fill in many gaps in our knowledge. We need to understand how the pottery industry fitted in with other agricultural or industrial activities taking place in the landscape. We still do not know how many kilns were in production at any one time, or for how long. It is regrettable that there is no thermoremanent dating for this kiln, or for others in the complex. However, new developments in archaeomagnetic dating, relying on variations in the intensity of the magnetic field rather than its direction, may mean that one day it will be possible to date samples no longer *in situ*. This could open up the possibility of retrospective dating for the kilns, perhaps as part of a broader study of Severn Valley ware kilns.

The archaeology at the Newland Hopfields site was very truncated and the evidence for the kiln structure was therefore very fragmentary. Excavation of a kiln on a site with better preservation, if this exists, would allow the structure of the Malvern kilns to be defined with more certainty. Further excavation could also better define the assemblages relating to the known kilns. The evidence provided by the fieldwalking assemblage from Newland Hopfields was in most respects confirmed by the evidence from the excavated assemblage. There were some discrepancies however. The fieldwalking assemblage had a bias towards the later material; so, for example, the later short-necked, wide-mouthed jars (Fig. 24. types JWM5 and JWM6) were proportionly very common in this group but not so common in the excavated assemblage. Also, the characteristic charcoal-tempered wares were not identified in the fieldwalking assemblage.

Analysis of the Malvern kiln assemblages has shown that useful distinctions can be made between the products of individual kilns (Tomber 1980). However, none of the Malvern kiln groups, or assemblages from Severn Valley ware production sites elsewhere, are quantified to modern standards. It is not currently possible, therefore, to undertake any statistical analysis of the forms produced. A reassessment of these groups could provide this data. Nor can we, on existing evidence, assume the function of the forms produced with any confidence. A programme of residue analysis, focusing on the more widely distributed forms, might be useful in this respect.

Some progress has been made over the last decade in sourcing Severn Valley ware by fabric. Recent programmes of neutron activation analysis on Severn Valley wares from Wroxeter, Malvern, Worcester and Alcester (Faiers 1990; Evans 1991) have suggested that useful groups can be determined by this method, and that these can be related to visible characteristics of fabric and form. A further programme could analyse samples from the Newland Hopfields kiln, selected on the basis of form, and these could be compared with additional samples from sites along the possible distribution routes. This might clarify the marketing pattern of the Malvern products, which could be supported by an updated distribution of the hand-made, coarsely tempered wares.

BIBLIOGRAPHY

Allason-Jones, L, and Miket, R L, 1984 — *The Catalogue of Small Finds from South Shields Roman Fort, Newcastle upon Tyne*, Society of Antiquaries of Newcastle-upon-Tyne Monograph Series 2

Allen, J R L, and Fulford, M G, 1996 — 'The distribution of South-East Dorset Black Burnished category 1 pottery in South-West Britain', *Britannia*, 27, 223–281

Barclay, W J, Ambrose, K, Chadwick, R A, and Pharoah, R, 1997 — *Geology of the Country around Worcester*, Memoir British Geological Survey, Sheet 199 (England and Wales)

Barfield, L, forthcoming — *Bays Meadow Roman Villa, Droitwich*

Barker, P, White, R, Pretty, K, Bird, H, and Corbishley, M, 1997 — *The Baths Basilica, Wroxeter. Excavations 1966–90*, English Heritage Archaeological Report 8

Bidwell, P T, Evans, J, Hartley K F and Williams, D,1985 — 'The coarse pottery', *in* Bidwell, P, *The Roman Fort of Vindolanda at Chesterholm, Northumberland*, English Heritage Archaeological Report 1, 172–205

Bohme, A, 1972 — *Die Fibeln der Kastelle Saalburg und Zugmantel*, Saalburg Jahrbuch, Bericht des Saalburg Museums, 29

Bryant, C, 1973 — Experimental Romano-British kiln firings, *in* Detsicas, A, 1973, 149–60

Bryant, S, Morris, M, and Walker, J S F, 1986 — *Roman Manchester, a Frontier Settlement*, The Archaeology of Greater Manchester Vol 3, Manchester

Buteux, V 1992 — 'The finds', *in* Dalwood, H, 1992

Buteux, V, and Evans, J, forthcoming — 'The Iron Age and Romano-British pottery', *in* Dalwood, C H (ed.), unpublished

Carrington, P, 1977 — 'Severn Valley ware and its place in the Roman pottery supply at Chester: a preliminary assessment', *in* Dore, J and Greene, K, 1977, 147–62

Cool, H, and Price, J, 1995 — *Roman Vessel Glass from Colchester, 1971–85*, Colchester Archaeological Report 8

Cracknell, S (ed.), 1996 — *Roman Alcester: Defences and Defended Area, Gateway Supermarket and Gas House Lane*, CBA Research Report 106

Cracknell, S, and Mahany, C, 1994 — *Roman Alcester: Southern Extramural Area, 1964–1966 Excavations, Part 2: Finds and Discussion*, CBA Research Report 97

Crummy, N, 1985 — 'The brooches', *in* Pryor, F, French, C, Crowther, D, Gurney, D, Simpson, D, and Taylor, M, *Archaeology and Environment in the Lower Welland Valley, The Fenland Project, No 1*, East Anglian Archaeology, 27, 164–6

Cunliffe, B, 1971 — *Excavations at Fishbourne, 1961–1969, Vol II, The Finds*, Report Research Committee Society of Antiquaries 27, Leeds

Cunliffe, B, 1991 — 'Fishbourne revisited: the site in its context', *Journal of Roman Archaeology*, 4, 160–9

Dalwood, H, 1992 — *Interim report on an excavation (Phase 1) at North End Farm, Madresfield*, Hereford and Worcester Archaeological Service Report 121

Dalwood, C H (ed.), unpublished — *Excavations at Deansway, Worcester 1988–89*, Unpublished typescript, on file at Worcestershire County Council Archaeological Service

Dalwood, H, Buteux, V A, and Darlington, J, 1994 — 'Excavations at Farrier Street and other sites north of the city wall, Worcester 1988–1992', *Transactions of the Worcestershire Archaeological Society*, 14, 75–114

Darlington, J, and Evans, Jane, 1992 — Roman Sidbury, Worcester: excavations 1959–1989, *Transactions of the Worcestershire Archaeological Society*, 13, 5–104

de Rouffignac, C, 1991 — 'The plant remains from North End Farm, Madresfield', *in* Jackson, R, 1991, 14–18

Dore, J, and Greene, K, 1977 — *Roman Pottery Studies in Britain and Beyond*, BAR International Series 30

Evans, C Jane, and Jones, L R, 1995 — *North End Farm, Madresfield, Hereford and Worcester. Phase 2: Interim report and post-excavation assessment (Phases 1 and 2)*, BUFAU Report 351

Evans, C Jane, 1995 — 'Assessment of the Romano-British Pottery and fired clay', *in* Evans, C J and Jones, L R 1995, 7–16

Evans, C Jane, in press — 'The Roman pottery', *in* Leach, P J and Evans, C J, in press

Evans, C Jane, forthcoming — 'The pottery', *in* Excavations at Pentrehyling Fort, Brompton, Shropshire

Evans, Jane, 1990 — 'The finds', *in* Dinn, J and Evans, J, 'Aston Mill Farm, Kemerton: excavation of a ring-ditch, Middle Iron Age enclosures, and a Grubenhaus', *Transactions of the Worcestershire Archaeological Society*, 12, 5–66

Evans, Jeremy 1991 — *Neutron activation analysis of Severn Valley wares: analytical assessment programme*. Unpublished typescript, on file at Worcestershire County Council Archaeological Service

Evans, Jeremy, and Crossling, J, 1994 — 'Worked stone and quernstones', *in* Cracknell, S and Mahany, C, 1994, 231–43

Faiers, J E, 1990 — *The socio-economic aspects of the Roman pottery industry in Britain at Viroconium*, unpub M.Phil thesis, London

Farey, J, 1811 — *General View of the Agriculture and Minerals of Derbyshire, vol 1*, London

Farrar, R A H, 1973 — 'The techniques and sources of Romano-British Black-burnished ware', *in* Detsicas, A, 1973, 67–103

Fennell, D, 1964 — 'The excavation of a Romano-British enclosure at Hawford, Worcestershire', *Transactions of the Worcestershire Archaeological Society*, 40, 6–9

Ford, D A, and Rees, H, forthcoming — 'The pottery', *in* Wills, J (ed.), *Excavations at Beckford*

Fowler, P J, and Bennett, J, 1973 — 'Archaeology and the M5 motorway', *Transactions of the Bristol and Gloucestershire Archaeological Society*, 92, 21–81

Frere, S S, 1962 — 'Excavations at Dorchester on Thames', *Archaeological Journal*, 114–149

Gillam, J P, 1976 — 'Coarse fumed ware in North Britain and beyond', *Glasgow Archaeological Journal*, 4, 57–80

Going, C J, 1987 — *The Mansio and other sites in the south-eastern sector of Caesaromagus: The Roman Pottery*, CBA Research Report 62, London

Green, H S, 1980 — *The Flint Arrowheads of the British Isles*, BAR British Series 75, Oxford

Green, S, Dickinson, B, Evans, J, Hancocks, A, Hartley, B, Hartley K, Pengelly, H and Williams, D, forthcoming — 'Pottery (areas 1–6)', in Jones, A, 'Roman Birmingham 1. Metchley Roman forts, excavations 1963–4, 1967–9 and 1997', *Transactions of the Birmingham and Warwickshire Archaeological Society*

Greene, K, 1993 — 'The fortress coarseware', in Manning, W (ed.), 1993, *Report on the Excavations at Usk 1965–1976. The Roman Pottery*, Cardiff, 3–121

Gurney, D, 1986 — *Settlement, Religion and Industry on the Roman Fen-edge, Norfolk*, East Anglian Archaeology 31

Hartley, B R, 1972 — 'The samian ware', in Frere, S S 1972, *Verulamium Excavations, Vol I*, Report of the Research Committee of the Society of Antiquaries, 28, 216–62

Hartley, K F, 1973 — 'The kilns at Mancetter and Hartshill, Warwickshire', in Detsicas, A, 1973, 143–7

Hartley, K, and Gurney, D, 1997 — *A mortarium kiln at Ellingham, Norfolk*, East Anglian Archaeology Occasional Paper, 2

Hattatt, R, 1987 — *Brooches of Antiquity, a third selection of brooches from the author's collection*, Oxford

Haverfield, F, 1901 — Romano-British Worcestershire, *VCH Worcestershire, 1*, 199–221

Healy, F, 1984 — 'Lithic assemblage variation in the late third and early second millennia BC in Eastern England', *Lithics*, 5, 10–18

HWCAS, 1992 — *Research design and proposal for an excavation at Madresfield*, Hereford and Worcester County Archaeological Service

Hinchliffe, J, and Green, C S, 1985 — *Excavations at Brancaster, 1974 and 1977*, East Anglian Archaeology, 23

Hodder, I, 1974 — 'Some marketing models for Romano-British coarse pottery', *Britannia*, 5, 340–59

Holbrook, N, and Bidwell, P, 1991a — *Finds from Exeter*, Exeter Archaeological Report 4

Holbrook, N, and Bidwell, P, 1991b — 'The coarse pottery' in Holbrook, N and Bidwell, P, 1991a, 88–185

Houghton, A W J, 1963 — 'A Roman Pottery Factory near Wroxeter, Salop', *Transactions of the Shropshire Archaeological Society*, 57, 101–11

Hughes, H V, 1959 — 'A Romano-British kiln site at Perry Barr', *Transactions of the Birmingham and Warwickshire Archaeological Society*, 77, 33–9

Hughes, J and Lentowicz, I J forthcoming — *Excavations at Hanbury Street, Droitwich*

Hurst, D and Rees H 1992 — 'Pottery fabrics; a multi-period series for the County of Hereford and Worcester', *in* Woodiwiss, S (ed.), 1992, 200–9

Hurst, D and Woodiwiss, S 1992 — 'Other ceramic objects' in Woodiwiss, S (ed.), 1992, 158

Hurst, H R, 1985 — *Kingsholm: excavations at Kingsholm Close and other sites with a discussion of the archaeology of the area*, Gloucester Archaeological Report 1

Hurst, J D, 1994 — 'A medieval ceramic production site and other medieval sites in the parish of Hanley Castle; results of fieldwork in 1987–1992', *Transactions of the Worcestershire Archaeological Society*, 14, 115–128

Ireland, C, 1983 — 'The Roman pottery', in Heighway, C, 1993 *The East and North Gates of Gloucester*, Western Archaeological Trust excavation Monograph, 4, 96–124

Jack, G H, 1925 — 'A supposed Roman pottery at Sandlin Farm, Leigh Sinton, Worcestershire', *Antiquaries Journal, 5*, 285–6

Jackson, R, 1991 — *Evaluation at North End Farm, Madresfield*, Hereford and Worcester Archaeology Section Report 89

Jackson, R, Hurst, D, Pearson, E and Ratkai, S, 1996 — 'Archaeology on the Strensham to Worcester Aqueduct', *Transactions of the Worcestershire Archaeological Society*, 15, 1–62

Knorr, R, 1919 — *Töpfer und Fabriken verzierter Terra-Sigillata des ersten Jahrhunderts*, Stuttgart

Knorr, R, 1952 — *Terra-Sigillata-Gefässe des ersten Jahrhunderts mit Töpfernamen*, Stuttgart

Leach, P J, and Evans, C J, in press — *Fosse Lane: Excavations of a Romano-British Roadside Settlement at Shepton Mallet, Somerset, 1990*, Britannia Monograph Series 18

Lee, F, Lindquist, G, and Evans, J, 1994 — 'Romano-British coarse pottery', *in* Cracknell, S and Mahany, C, 1994, 3–92

Lentowicz, I, 1992 — 'Ceramic building material', in Darlington, J and Evans, J, 1992, 66–7

Lyne, M A B, and Jefferies, R S, 1979 — *The Alice Holt/Farnham Roman Pottery Industry*, London

Mackreth, D 1998 — 'The brooches' in Timby, J, *1998*

Manning, W H, 1985 — *Catalogue of the Romano-British Iron Tools, Fittings and Weapons in the British Museum*, London

Marsh, G, 1981 — 'London's samian supply and its relationship to the Gallic samian industry', *in* Anderson, A and Anderson, A (eds), *Roman Pottery Research in Britain and North-West Europe*, BAR, International Series 123, 173–328

Millett, M, 1990 — *The Romanization of Britain: an essay in archaeological interpretation*, Cambridge

Morris, E L, 1981 — 'Ceramic exchange in Western Britain: a preliminary view', *in* Howard, H and Morris, E (eds), *Production and Distribution: a Ceramic Viewpoint*, BAR British Series, 120, 67–81

Morris, E L 1983 — *Salt and ceramic exchange in western Britain during the first millenium BC*, unpublished PhD thesis, University of Southampton

Morris, E L, 1985 — 'Prehistoric salt distributions: two case studies from western Britain', *Bulletin of the Board of Celtic Studies*, 32, 336–79

Orton, C, Tyers, P and Vince, A, 1993 — *Pottery in Archaeology*, Cambridge

Oswald, F, 1936–7 — *Index of Figure types on Terra Sigillata, samian ware*, Liverpool

Peacock, D P S, 1967 — 'Romano-British pottery production in the Malvern District of Worcestershire', *Transactions of the Worcestershire Archaeological Society*, 1, 15–28

Peacock, D P S, 1968 — A petrological study of certain Iron Age pottery from Western England, *Proceedings of the Prehistoric Society*, 34, 414–27

Peacock, D P S, 1982 — *Pottery in the Roman world: an ethnoarchaeological approach*, London

Peacock, D P S, and Williams, D F, 1986 — *Amphorae and the Roman Economy: an Introductory Guide*, London

Philp, B, 1981 — *The excavation of the Roman forts of the Classis Britannica at Dover, 1970–1977*, Kent Monograph Series, 3, Dover

Pitt Rivers, A H L F, 1887 — *Excavations in Cranborne Chase, I*, privately printed

Rawes, B, 1982 — 'Gloucester Severn Valley ware', *Transactions of the Bristol and Gloucestershire Archaeological Society*, 100, 33–46

Rees, H 1992 — 'Pottery', *in* Woodiwiss, S, 1992, 35–57

Renow, S, 1985 — *Vertical Archaeological Photography*, IFA Technical Paper, 2

Rigby, V 1982 — 'The coarse pottery' *in* Wacher, J and McWhirr, A, 1982, *Early Roman Occupation at Cirencester*, Cirencester Excavations 1, 153–200

Riha, E, 1979 — *Die Römischen Fibeln aus Augst und Kaiseraugst, Forschungen in Augst*, Band 3, Augst

Roe, F, 1992a — 'The worked stone', *in* Darlington, J and Evans, J 1992, 85–88

Roe, F, 1992b — 'Querns' *in* Woodiwiss, S (ed.), 1992, 72

Roe, F, 1993 — 'Worked stone', *in* Woodward, A and Leach, P J, *The Uley Shrines: Excavation of a ritual complex on West Hill, Uley, Gloucestershire: 1977–9*, English Heritage Archaeological Report 17, London, 197–201

Roe, F, 1998 — 'The worked stone' *in* Timby, J, 1998

Roe, F, forthcoming a — 'The worked stone', *in* Dalwood, C H (ed.), unpublished

Roe, F, forthcoming b — 'The worked stone', *in* Barfield L, forthcoming

Roe, F, forthcoming c — 'The worked stone', *in* Hughes, J and Lentowicz, I J, forthcoming

Rogers, G B, 1974 — *Poteries Sigillées de la Gaule Centrale, I, Les Motifs Non-figurés*, Paris

Sawle, J, 1980 — 'Little Buckman's Farm, Malvern, Hereford and Worcester', *West Midlands Archaeological News Sheet*, 23, 99

Scarth, H M, 1866 — 'Roman potters' kiln, discovered at Shepton Mallet, November 1864, on the site of a large brewery belonging to Messrs. Morris, Cox and Clarke', *Proceedings of the Somerset Archaeological and Natural History Society*, 13, 1–5

Seager Smith, R, and Davies, S M, 1993 — 'Black Burnished ware and other southern British coarsewares', *in* Woodward, P *et al*, *Excavations at Greyhound Yard, Dorchester 1981–4*, Dorset Natural History and Archaeological Society Monograph 12, 229–84

Swan, V G, 1984 — *The Pottery Kilns of Roman Britain*, RCHME, Supplementary Series 5

Tarrant N and Sandford A 1972 — 'A Romano-British kiln at Fulmer'. *Records of Buckinghamshire* 19, 174–88

Terrisse, J, 1968 — *Les céramiques sigillées gallo-romaines des Martres-de-Veyre (Puy-de-Dome)*, Gallia supplement 19, Paris

Timby, J, 1990 — 'Severn Valley wares: a reassessment', *Britannia*, 21, 243–51

Timby, J, 1998 — *Excavations at Kingscote and Wycomb, Gloucestershire, A Roman Estate Centre and Small Town in the Cotswolds, with Notes on Related Settlements*

Timby, J, Darling, M, Evans, J, and Faiers, J, 2000 — 'The Roman pottery', *in* Ellis, P, 2000, *The baths and macellum at Wroxeter*, English Heritage Archaeological Report 9

Tomber, R S, 1980 — *A petrological assessment of Severn Valley ware: kilns and selected distribution*, Unpublished MSc Dissertation, University of Southampton

Tomber, R and Dore, J, 1998 — *The National Roman Fabric Reference Collection. A Handbook*, Museum of London Archaeology Service Monograph 2

Tyers, P, 1996 — *Roman Pottery in Britain*, London

van Es, W A, and Verlinde, A D, 1977 — 'Overijssel in Roman and early medieval times', *Berichten van de Rijksdienst voor het Oudheidkundig Bodemonderzoek*, 27, 7–89

van den Hurk, L J A M, 1977 — 'The Tumuli from the Roman period of Esch, Province of North Brabant', *Berichten van de Rijkdienst voor het Oudheidkundig Bodemonderzoek*, 27, 91–138

Vince, A G 1977 — 'The medieval and post-medieval ceramic industry of the Malvern region: the study of a ware and its distribution', *in* Peacock, D (ed.), *Pottery and early commerce*, 257–305

Walker, I, 1959 — 'Excavations on a Romano-British site at Astley, 1956–58', *Transactions of the Worcestershire Archaeological Society*, 35, 29–57

Walker, I, 1960 — 'Romano-British kiln waste from a hopfield at Newland', *West Midlands Archaeological News Sheet*, 3, 6

Ward-Perkins, J B, 1938 — 'A report on the Roman pottery found at Marley Hall, Ledbury', *Transactions of the Woolhope Nature Field Club*, 21–3

Waters, P L, 1963 — 'A Romano-British tile kiln at Upper Sandlin Farm, Leigh Sinton, Worcestershire', *Transactions of the Worcestershire Archaeological Society*, 40, 1–5

Waters, P L, 1969 — 'Grit Farm, Malvern Link', *Worcester Archaeological Newsletter*, 4, 4

Waters, P L, 1970a — 'Grit Farm, Malvern Link', *Worcester Archaeological Newsletter*, 6, 6

Waters, P L, 1970b — 'Grit Farm, Malvern Link, Worcs', *West Midlands Archaeology News Sheet*, 13, 39

Waters, P L, 1976 — 'Romano-British Pottery Site at Great Buckhams Farm', *Transactions of the Worcestershire Archaeological Society*, 5, 63–72

Waters, P L, 1979 — CBA Annual Report, 63

Watkins, A, 1932 — 'A Romano-British pottery kiln in Herefordshire', *Transactions of the Woolhope Nature Field Club*, 27, 110–12

Webb, L, and Crossling, J, 1996 — 'Stone objects', *in* Cracknell, S, 1996, 119

Webster, G 1976 — *Romano-British Coarse Pottery: a student's guide*, CBA Research Report 6, 3rd edn

Webster, P V, 1971 — *Severn Valley ware: a study of the forms, fabric, chronology, distribution and manufacture of a distinctive form of Romano-British coarse pottery*, Unpublished M Phil dissertation, University of London

Webster, P V, 1976 — Severn Valley ware: a preliminary study, *Transactions of the Bristol and Gloucs Archaeological Society*, 94, 18–46

Webster, P V, 1977 — Severn Valley ware on the Antonine frontier, in Dore and Greene 1977, 163–176

Webster, P V 1989 — The Pottery, in Britnell, J, *Caersws Vicus, Powys: Excavations at the Old Primary School, 1985–86*, BAR British Series 205

Webster, P V 1989   The post-fortress coarsewares, in W Manning (ed.), *Report on the Excavations at Usk 1965–1976. The Roman Pottery*, Cardiff, 227-361

Wedlake, W J, 1982   *The Excavation of the Shrine of Apollo at Nettleton, Wiltshire, 1956–1971*, Report Research Com Soc Antiquaries, 40, Dorking

Williams, D F 1977   The Romano-British black-burnished industry: an essay on characterization by heavy-mineral analysis, in D P S Peacock, *Pottery and early commerce: characterization and trade in Roman and later ceramics*, 163–220

Willis, S (ed.) 1997   *Research frameworks for the study of Roman pottery*, Study group for Roman Pottery

Woodiwiss, S (ed.), 1992   *Iron Age and Roman Salt Production and the Medieval Town of Droitwich*, CBA Research Report 81, Worcester

Woods, P, J, 1974   Types of Late Belgic and Early Romano-British Pottery Kilns in the Nene Valley, *Britannia*, 5, 262–81

Woodward, P J 1987   The excavation of a Late Iron-Age trading settlement and Romano-British pottery production site at Ower, Dorset, in *Romano-British industries in Purbeck*, Dorset Natural History and Archaeological Society Monograph Series 6, 44–123

Young, C J, 1977   *The Roman Pottery Industry of the Oxford Region*, BAR British Series, 43

Plate 1   Site 2, Area A, following excavation; view north (photo L Jones)

Plate 2 Site 2, Area B, following excavation; view north (photo L Jones)

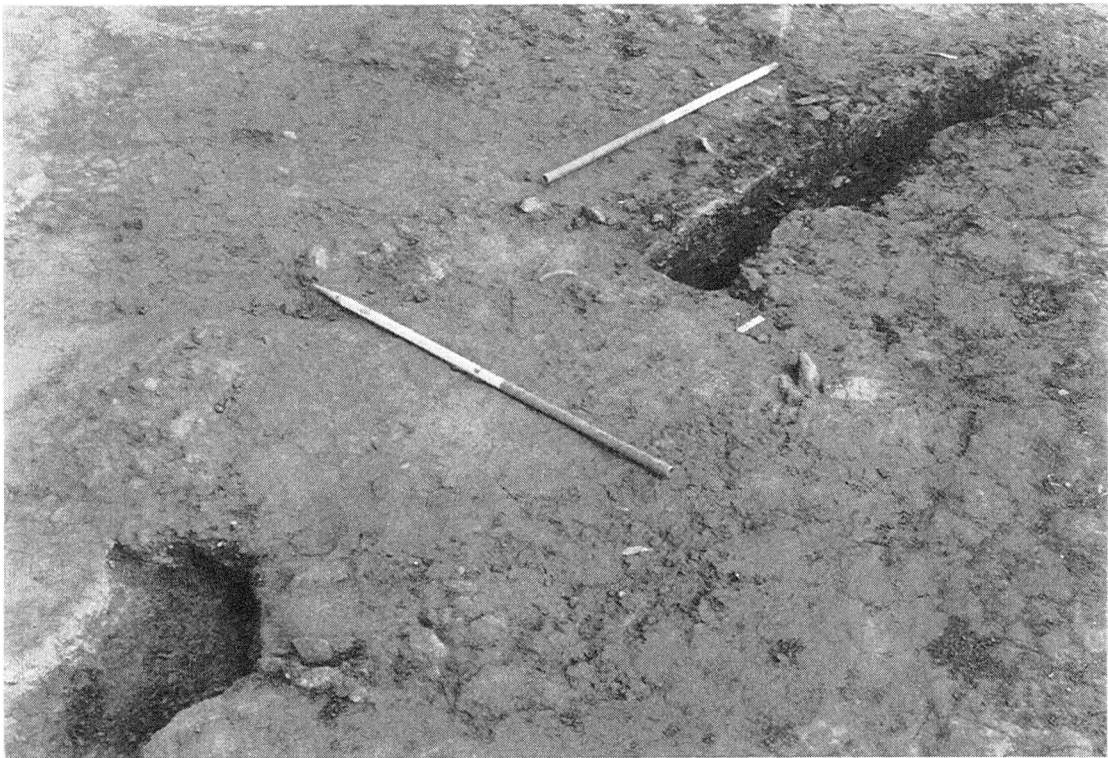

Plate 3 Site 2, Area B, kiln F108 with flues excavated; view east (photo L Jones)

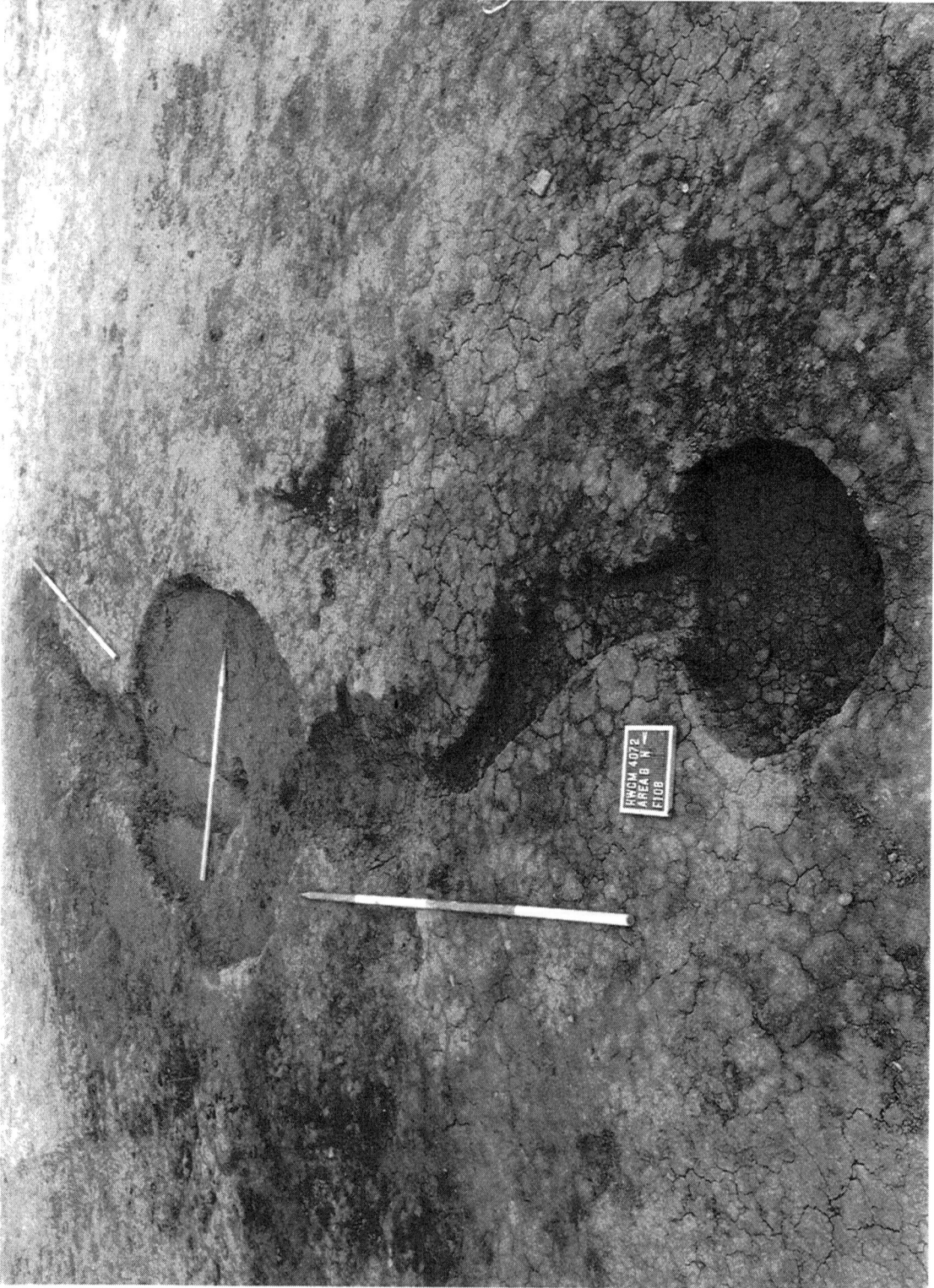

Plate 4   Site 2, Area B, hearth F150 with kiln F108 beyond; view east (photo L Jones)

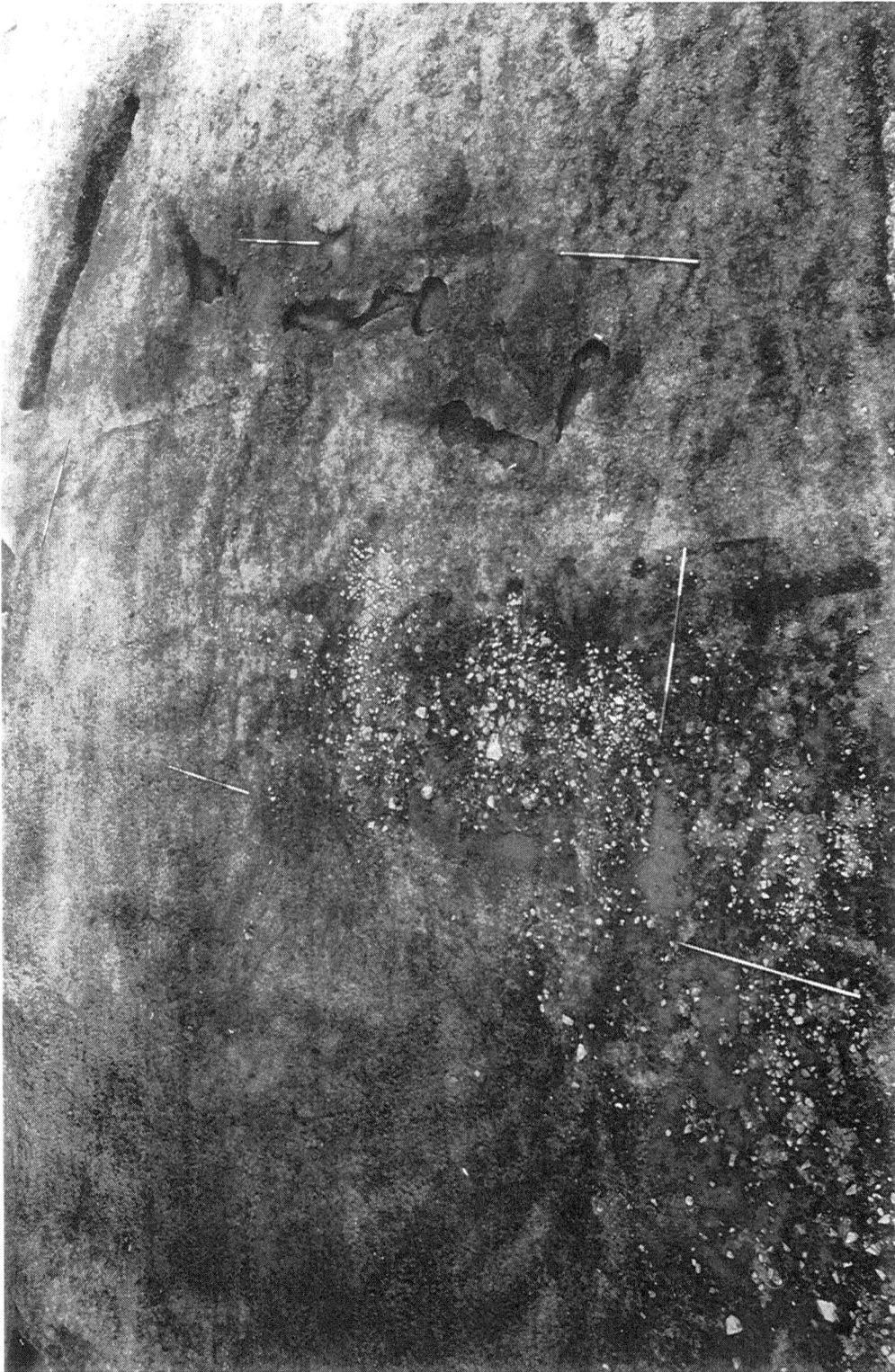

Plate 5 Site 2, Area B, stone surface F151 with kiln F108 and hearths to right; view east (photo L Jones)

Plate 6   Site 2, Area B, well F143; view north (photo L Jones)

Plate 7   Site 2, Area B, levigation channel F116 and backfilled wasters; view east (photo L Jones

Plate 8   Site 2, Area B, levigation channel F116 under excavation; view north (photo L Jones)